Samuel T. Hallman

History of the Evangelical Lutheran Synod of South Carolina,

1824-1924

Samuel T. Hallman

History of the Evangelical Lutheran Synod of South Carolina, 1824-1924

ISBN/EAN: 9783337036041

Printed in Europe, USA, Canada, Australia, Japan

Cover: Foto ©ninafisch / pixelio.de

More available books at **www.hansebooks.com**

HISTORY

of the

Evangelical Lutheran Synod of South Carolina

1824-1924

Prepared by a Committee of the Synod
Rev. S. T. HALLMAN, D.D., Editor

Published by Authority of the Synod

Printed for the Synod

Press of Farrell Printing Company, Inc.
Columbia, South Carolina

TABLE OF CONTENTS

ILLUSTRATIONS

ILLUSTRATIONS—*Continued*

PREFACE

AT the convention of the South Carolina Synod held November 1-4, 1917, it was *"Resolved, That the chairman appoint a committee to compile a history of this synod, the same to be bound and presented to this synod on its one hundredth anniversary"*. The chairman appointed Rev. Drs. S. T. Hallman, M. O. J. Kreps, J. H. Wilson, and Mr. A. H. Kohn. In 1918 Rev. H. A. McCullough was appointed in place of Rev. S. T. Hallman, D.D., resigned. In 1919 the committee was reconstituted as follows: Rev. Drs. M. O. J. Kreps, H. A. McCullough, J. W. Horine, and Messrs. A. H. Kohn and W. P. Houseal. Rev. Dr. S. T. Hallman was added to the committee in 1920 and C. M. Efird, Esq., in 1922. At the meeting of synod in 1921 Rev. Dr. S. T. Hallman was requested to serve as editor of the proposed history and this request was heartily endorsed by the committee charged with the duty of preparing and publishing the book. This endorsement was readily given by reason of the fact that Dr. Hallman had been an active member of the synod for upwards of fifty years and was able to supplement the written records from the stores of memory. Dr. Hallman has well performed his laborious task and there are due to him the thanks of the synod and of the historical committee for his service in the production of this centennial history. It is herewith submitted to the synod with the earnest hope of those concerned in its preparation and publication that it will fulfil the synod's instruction to the committee and be a suitable memorial of the centennial anniversary of the Evangelical Lutheran Synod of South Carolina.

THE COMMITTEE.

FOREWORD

THE writer has lived as a participant through what he is firmly persuaded has been the most important period in the formative life of our Southern Lutheran Church.

The time was when our Church in the South drifted away from her rich liturgical heritage and lost in large measure the power which comes from a proper adherence to the time-honored customs and practices of the Church of the Reformation.

This was the result of the peculiar conditions surrounding our people in the South. The congregations were widely scattered; preachers were few; literature, along the line indicated, was scarce; and the rising generation was therefore denied the training necessary to the appreciation of liturgical usage and of our glorious history.

With the introduction of the "Book of Worship" of the General Synod in the South, in 1868, the tide began to turn. Discussions in *The Lutheran Visitor*, in synods and conferences, and among our preachers and people, soon convinced the membership of the Southern Lutheran Church that a veritable mine of devotional and doctrinal wealth had been opened up to us, and that we were coming again into the possession of our own glorious heritage.

The final outcome is the unification of our forces, settled doctrinal positions, and a pleasing conformity to the principles and practices of our great Church.

And now, if this history shall serve further to build up our people in "the faith once delivered to the saints", and encourage us to greater devotion to God and loyalty to His Church, it will not have been written in vain.

S. T. HALLMAN.

Spartanburg, S. C.,
May 19, 1924.

ACKNOWLEDGMENT

IN the preparation of the manuscript of this History of the Evangelical Lutheran Synod of South Carolina, I hereby acknowledge my indebtedness to the pastors who gave valuable information, together with laymen who also contributed some material facts as to pastoral charges; to C. M. Efird, Esq., who furnished sketches of churches formerly belonging to the Tennessee Synod; to Ruth Efird Carroll for article on Young People's Federation; to Mrs. M. O. J. Kreps for the history and work of the Woman's Missionary Society of the South Carolina Synod, and for valuable matter furnished for the sketches of women especially prominent in our mission work; to A. H. Kohn for his valuable help in the development and execution of this somewhat difficult task; to Wm. P. Houseal for his invaluable help in handling copy and seeing the book through the press; to Rev. J. W. Horine, D.D., secretary of the history committee, who has not only given the benefit of expert knowledge, but has carefully handled all copy and is giving general supervision to its publication; to Rev. P. E. Monroe, D.D., for sketch of Summerland College; and special thanks to Hon. Geo. B. Cromer, LL.D., and Miss Carolyn Cromer, librarian, for a well prepared roster of the Faculty of Newberry College from 1868 to 1924. While the committee could not well incorporate the list in this volume, it has been of great value in tracing facts essential to the completion of this history of the life and activities of the synod.

My earnest hope and prayer is that God will use our combined labors to the good of the Church and the glory of His Name.

S. T. HALLMAN.

INTRODUCTION

NO history of any Lutheran synod in this country can be properly written without reference to the early Lutheran settlers, the causes which led to their coming to the shores of this American land, and the principles for which they stood.

Every movement and enterprise involving great issues must rest on tenable grounds and be actuated by high and worthy motives. Otherwise such procedure would not be worthy of our acceptance and support. Nothing worthy of a great soul can be tolerated that does not bear the test of reason, sound judgment and the principles of Christianity. Starting from these premises, it will be easy to show that our fathers were influenced and guided by the purest motives and the highest reasons when their faces were turned towards this country as an asylum from the persecutions of the Fatherland. The oppressions of the old world were bitter and prolonged. Rome was not disposed to yield to the wishes of her Protestant subjects, especially since the Catholics were greatly in the majority; they therefore barely tolerated Protestant Christians.

Catholic rulers were generally oppressive in their treatment of all Protestants and frequently made their lives sorrowful indeed. Then sects came into being; dissensions and disputes followed; some loved their creeds more than they loved God; it sometimes happened that rulers changed their creeds and then demanded that their subjects adopt the form of confession which such rulers had espoused.

And so, as one authority affirms, "A vast quantity of human blood was shed, countries were laid waste, cities destroyed and the inhabitants reduced to poverty and want."

Under these most trying circumstances many devout Lutherans in several of the European kingdoms turned towards this "new world" to escape persecution and to find a home where they could worship God, unmolested by relentless foes.

Much has been written and said about William Penn and the Pilgrim Fathers; but the Lutherans were here more than forty-four years before William Penn made his treaty with the Indians. One of the last things recommended by Gustavus Adolphus, King of Sweden, only a few days before he fell in the battle of Lutzen, in defense of Protestant Christianity, was the colonizing project so dear to his great soul.

Accordingly, in due time two ships laden with people, provisions and merchandise for traffic with the Indians, landed near Cape Henlopen in 1638, in the vicinity of what is now the State of Delaware. They did not neglect to bring books of devotion and manuals for instruction in their holy faith. Immediately upon landing, they purchased lands from the Indians.

The first buildings erected were a fort for protection and a church for worship. The first Lutheran church in this country was built at Wilmington, Delaware, in 1638, and the first Protestant missionary to the Indians was a Lutheran preacher, Rev. John Campanius, and the first book translated into the Indian language was Luther's Catechism, by this same missionary, which was printed in 1646.

In a series of sermons preached by Rev. Prof. S. S. Schmucker, D.D., in 1851, we have the positive statement, supported by a quotation from the distinguished patriarch Henry Melchior Muhlenberg, that Lutherans from Holland were in New York as early as August, 1619. Muhlenberg says, "This small congregation took its rise almost at the first settlement of this country."

Rev. J. C. Kunzmann, D.D., is authority for the statement that Admiral Coligny founded a colony in Florida in 1564, many of whom were Lutherans. These, however, were slain by the Spanish General, Menendez, in 1665, as he said, "Not because they were Frenchmen, but as Lutherans." Thus the first martyr blood shed on American soil was Lutheran.

Subsequently Lutheran people came from Germany to Pennsylvania, Maryland, Virginia, New York, and to the southern and western states. In 1711 about three thousand Germans, mostly Lutherans, who had been sorely oppressed by Romish intolerance, settled in New York; in 1713, one hundred and fifty families settled in Schoharie, New York. In 1717 a Provincial Council in Pennsylvania called attention to the fact, "That great numbers of foreigners from Germany, strangers to our language and constitution, had lately been brought into the province."

The tide of immigration which had thus set in, continued, and our Lutheran people found their way into Virginia, North and South Carolina, Georgia, and into many other parts of the South. However, in no record by historians in their chronicles of that period is to be found any account of a body of Germans (all Lutherans) who came direct from Pennsylvania and chose the Dutch Fork section of Newberry County as their permanent abode. In this respect they were distinguished from many of the other German settlers of the Dutch Fork who landed at Charleston and proceeded by varying stages through Orangeburg and Lexington Counties to the Dutch Fork. These German settlers coming directly to Newberry County from Pennsylvania were attracted by the inviting landscape of the valley of Broad and Saluda Rivers. As they reached that vicinity on their long journey, being reminded so much of the Fatherland as they stood on the eastern bank of Broad River, in Fairfield County, they almost involuntarily determined to cast their lot in such a favored land. Carrying out this desire, they crossed the river to Newberry County at Cohoes Falls, the present site of the hydro-electric Parr Shoals Power Company.

In 1674 Lutherans were located on the Ashley River, South Carolina; at an early period they made their appearance in Wilmington, N. C.; in Beaufort County, South Carolina, in 1732; in Charleston, South Carolina, in 1734; the same year in Ebenezer, Ga.; in Orangeburg County, South Carolina, in 1735; on Congaree River, South Carolina, in 1737; and in the County of Abbeville, South Carolina, in 1763; and in various other sections of the state.

The religious conditions existing in Europe in the early part of the Seventeenth century constitute a sufficient reason for the emigration of Lutheran Christians. Escape from oppression and persecution, combined with an ardent desire to serve and worship God without molestation, brought them to these friendly shores; and we thank God that we are the descendants of a people who stood for high principles and put the Triune God and His cause above the things of this temporal and material world.

Chapter I

EARLY HISTORY

IN a careful study of the sources at our command we thus find that Lutheran congregations existed in South Carolina as early as the middle of the Eighteenth century.

There was a small congregation in Charleston in 1750, and their first house of worship was built in 1756.

In 1740 there was a congregation in Amelia township, Orangeburg County, and the churches called in history St. Bartholomew and Shiloh existed in Barnwell County in 1750, and in the town of Orangeburg there was a congregation at an even earlier date. The early settlers of the former county were mostly German and Swiss Lutherans who came here in 1735 and 1737. Their first pastor, who organized a Lutheran congregation, was Rev. John Ulrich Geissendanner. His labors ended in death in the fall of 1738. The second pastor was the nephew of the first, bearing the same name. He labored there ten years as a Lutheran minister, and then, in 1749, went to London and received ordination at the hands of an Episcopal Bishop; and so, finally, a Lutheran congregation with over one hundred members was taken over by the Episcopal Church, under an unjust law which did not allow them to hold property without the so-called "apostolic ordination".

There were Lutherans in Saxe-Gotha township, Orangeburg County, now Lexington County, in 1737, forty years before American Independence.

In that early period we read of a church at Sandy Run in 1765, and a little later of churches called Zion, near Saluda River; St. Peter's, about four miles from Lexington Court House; Piney Woods; St. Jacob's; St. John's in the northwestern part of Lexington County, and of others in Edgefield and Laurens Counties.

Rev. Ernest L. Hazelius, D.D., is authority for the statement that seven ministers were serving these congregations in 1787. These were Frederick Daser, Christian Theis. J. C.

Bamberg. M. Carl Dinninger, Frederick Augustus Wallburg, Frederick Joseph Wallern, and Carl Frederick Froelich.

The Legislature of South Carolina incorporated, during its session in February, 1788, fifteen congregations; and these, with the ministers already named, formed what is known in history as "The Corpus Evangelicum". This organization, however, seems not to have lived beyond the year 1794. Nine of the churches included in this organization were Lutheran, but the others were German Reformed, or "German Protestants", whatever that meant.

When and by whom these churches were first organized will never be known; for the learned Dr. E. L. Hazelius, in his day, failed to find any satisfactory record of their early history.

At an earlier period the Salzburgers were in Georgia, having planted a colony about Springfield in 1733. These had also left their Fatherland to find relief from the persecutions of Rome, whose leaders sought the extermination of all who favored the cause of the Lutheran Reformation.

The history of the Salzburgers forms one of the most interesting stories of the American Lutheran Church—how they crossed the sea on the same ship that brought the famous John Wesley; their strong faith and joyous hope amid a storm at sea; the effect on Mr. Wesley, his subsequent realization of this hope through Lutheran influence, and his candid acknowledgment that they had a faith which he did not possess.

There were 227 persons on board the two ships, 27 of whom were Moravians; the others, except a few English, were Lutherans. In storms and hurricanes, when others were in great fear and dread of death, these adherents of the Augsburg Confession sang praises in the full consciousness of that faith which is the anchor of the soul, sure and steadfast.

They reached Charleston early in March, 1734, and on the twelfth of March landed at Savannah, Ga. At Ebenezer they set up "A stone of help", amid prayers and songs of rejoicing. There, twenty-five miles from Savannah, they built a church, which remains to this day. History records the fact that "Their beautiful house of God, built near the Savannah River, was turned into a stable for the horses of the British soldiers, and sometimes served as a Lazaretto for the sick and the wounded".

But God finally delivered them from their troubles, and a glorious record followed. One may be justly proud of the claim, "I am a descendant of the Salzburgers."

The ministers and churches at that time in this part of the South felt the inconvenience of their isolation, the great need of cooperation and of a closer bond of union, the better to accomplish the object of their mission as heralds of the Cross in a needy land.

This naturally led to the taking of the first steps towards the organization of a district synod. At that time (1810) the following ministers were laboring in Lexington County, with one from Orangeburg County:

Rev. John P. Franklow.
Rev. John Y. Meize.
Rev. Godfrey Dreher.
Rev. Michael Rauch.
Rev. Jacob Moser.
Rev. Samuel Herscher (from Orangeburg).

Rev. Godfrey Dreher opened the meeting, which convened in St. Michael's Church, Lexington County, on January 14, 1824, and he proceeded to outline "the rites and titles which were established by our ancestors in the year 1788, and sanctioned by the Government of the State, for the benefit of the Evangelical Lutheran Churches within the limits of its Jurisdiction".—This reference to "rites and titles established by our ancestors", and the "sanction of the Government of the State", has evident allusion to the agreement entered into by "The Corpus Evangelicum" in 1787 and 1788, and to the articles of the constitution adopted by that body, August 12, 1788. That organization, though not ideal, was nevertheless an important step towards the formation of our synod.

The lay delegates present at the initial session of the synod were: John Dreher, Sr., St. Michael's Church; George Lindler, St. John's Church; Christopher Wiggers, Bethel Church;

Samuel Oswald, Salem Church, and Henry Bookhardt, Orangeburg County.

Rev. Samuel Herscher was ordained, and Rev. John C. A. Schoenberg, from Pennsylvania, was licensed.

Rev. Godfrey Dreher was elected president and Rev. Samuel Herscher secretary, and at the next convention, November 18, 1824, Rev. Godfrey Dreher was elected treasurer, and Rev. John Bachman president.

REV. JOHN BACHMAN, D.D., LL.D.

Thus the organization of the synod was completed at the second session in St. John's Church, Lexington County, South Carolina, November 18, 1824. At this session the names of Rev. John Bachman, from Charleston, and Rev. C. F. Bergman, from Ebenezer, Georgia, appear on the roll of ministers, and the lay delegates were: Capt. J. H. Margart, Charleston; George Rast, Santee, Orangeburg County; Jacob Kelly, Zion, Lexington County; Samuel Oswald, Salem, Lexington County; Jacob Rauch, St. Peter's, Lexington County; John Counts, St. John's, Lexington County; Herman Aull, Bethlehem, Lexington County; Samuel Wingard, Nazareth, Lexington County; John Bouknight, Bethlehem, Newberry County.

The synod was now made up of eight ministers and nine delegates:

Rev. John Bachman, President.
Rev. Godfrey Dreher, Treasurer.
Rev. Samuel Herscher, Secretary.

The roll of churches was as follows: Santee congregation; Salem; St. Paul's, Newberry; St. Peter's, Piney Woods; St. Michael's; Bethlehem, Broad River; Zion; St. Jacob's; St. John's; Bethel; Bethlehem, Newberry; St. Peter's, Meetze's; and St. Paul's, Hollow Creek.

At this convention the first parochial table appears, giving as the membership of the churches a total of 251; the first delegate to the North Carolina Synod was elected in the person of Rev. Samuel Herscher; catechization was urged; and the first note was sounded in the interest of home missions.

In view of the fact that churches from southern states other than South Carolina were to be included in the organization, the title adopted was, "The Evangelical Lutheran Synod of South Carolina and Adjacent States."

It will now readily be seen that the synod was fully organized by November, 1824, and began a historic life which is worthy of the highest commendation, and which will be more fully sketched under appropriate headings.

Chapter II

DOCTRINAL HISTORY

IT should be borne in mind that the years preceding the organization of the synod were days which tried men's souls; and while some were weak in the faith, they were not necessarily or intentionally opposed to the faith. Theological training and scholarship were not up to our present standard, nor were our people so well educated as in this age of general and special knowledge. The exigencies of that period of spiritual destitution often made it necessary to put men in the pastoral office whose education was extremely limited, and they could hardly be expected to grasp the finer shades of doctrine easily apprehended by the thoroughly trained mind. And yet many of the fathers were spiritual giants, well grounded in the Scriptures and in the Confessions of the Church.

At the first convention of the synod, by resolution, "the Augsburg Confession of Faith" was made "the point of union in our churches"; and no reference whatever was made to any modified acceptance of the Confession or of the Holy Scriptures. Very few ministers had access to the Symbolical Books of the Evangelical Lutheran Church; and not until the learned and distinguished Dr. Socrates Henkel published the Book of Concord in 1851, did any of our ministers possess an English copy of our Confessions.

The synod at its first session adopted the following rule: "Every candidate for ordination to this synod should be well acquainted with the phraseology, doctrines and books of the Holy Scriptures, and the evidences of Christianity; that he should be able to read the Scriptures in their original languages, and also have a knowledge of the German language; and that he should have a competent knowledge of natural and moral philosophy, and Church history; and, in particular, of the peculiar doctrines of the Evangelical Lutheran Church."

An exception of some branches of learning was made, provided the candidate applying "possessed qualifications peculiarly fitting him for the Gospel Ministry".

As further evidence of the synod's insistence on "Order and Sound Doctrine", we find in the proceedings of the Ministerium of 1833 a firm deliverance against "such practices as are not in harmony with the established forms and usages of our venerable and beloved Church".

As far back as 1831 the synod went on record as a constitutional body and provided for a general form of Church Discipline.

Having previously adopted the Augsburg Confession of Faith as their point of union, the Holy Scriptures as their rule of faith and practice, and insisting that all candidates for ordination should have "a competent knowledge of the peculiar doctrines of the Evangelical Lutheran Church", the synod seems to have regarded that as a sufficient doctrinal basis. Nor is the fact surprising when we duly consider the peculiar circumstances surrounding these scattered Lutherans. It was doubtless taken for granted that all confirmed Lutherans had been duly instructed in the word of God and the doctrines of the Church. Later on, however, when conditions demanded it, clearer doctrinal statements were made from time to time, and the synod finally adopted the following doctrinal basis:

THE DOCTRINAL BASIS.

(a) This Synod receives and holds the canonical Scriptures of the Old and New Testaments as the inspired Word of God, and as the only infallible rule and standard of faith and practice, according to which all doctrines and teachers are to be judged.

(b) This Synod accepts the three ecumenical creeds—namely, the Apostles', the Nicene and the Athanasian—as important testimonies drawn from the Holy Scriptures, and rejects all errors which they condemn.

(c) This Synod receives and holds the Unaltered Augsburg Confession as a correct exhibition of the faith and doctrine of the Evangelical Lutheran Church, founded upon the Word of God; and acknowledges all churches that sincerely hold and faithfully confess the doctrines of the Unaltered Augsburg Confession to be entitled to the name of Evangelical Lutheran.

(d) This Synod recognizes the Apology of the Augsburg Confession, the Smalkald Articles, the Large and Small Catechisms of Luther and the Formula of Concord, as in the harmony of one and the same pure scriptural faith.

About the year 1835, and subsequently, unfortunate misunderstandings came into the life of the synod and of our Southern Church, which form the only real shadow in our historic life. Doctrinal issues were injected into it, but at the beginning of that sad controversy, *it was not a question of doctrine.* The persons with whom the trouble began belonged to this synod, and their doctrinal views and practices were the same.* We thank God that in His own time and through His mercy the storm-cloud passed away, and the most beautiful harmony now pervades the life of our beloved Church.

*   *   *   *   *   *   *

The following action of the synod, taken at its convention in 1922, marks the consummation of the reunion long desired and devoutly prayed for, and naturally filled every heart with deep gratitude to God. When the nineteen delegates from the congregations received, and their pastors, surrounded the chancel and were joyfully welcomed by the whole synod, the scene was very touching and will linger throughout life in the minds of all who were present.

REPORT OF COMMISSION TO CONFER WITH THE SOUTH CAROLINA
CONFERENCE OF THE UNITED SYNOD OF
NORTH CAROLINA.

Your Commission held a meeting with the Committee representing the South Carolina Conference of the United North Carolina Synod. It was evident that the time had come when all the congregations in this state were ready to hold membership in one synodical body. Methods of transfer were discussed and plans arranged for the consummation of this transfer at this convention of our synod. The congregations represented by this Committee have submitted letters of dismissal from the United North Carolina Synod together with application for membership in this body. Copies of congregational constitutions accompany these applications, the same having been considered and approved by your Commission. We would recommend the following:

1. That these congregations be now accepted into full membership in this synod.

---

*One of the pastors of this synod and several congregations withdrew from the Synod and later connected themselves with the Tennessee Synod, which synod subsequently merged with the Synod of North Carolina.

2. That the pastors serving these congregations be received and their names placed on our clerical roll.

3. That as a synod we express our gratitude to God for His guidance in bringing us to this happy issue, by engaging in a special service of thanksgiving.

Respectfully submitted,

C. A. FREED,
V. Y. BOOZER,
CHAS. J. SHEALY,
S. J. DERRICK.

The report was adopted unanimously and in the special service which was held the greetings of the synod were extended to the nineteen congregations by Dr. S. J. Derrick; response was made by Judge C. M. Efird.

The applications of the following congregations with the accredited representative of each congregation were presented:

Congregation.	Representative.
St. John's	John A. Summer
Mt. Hermon	M. N. Kleckley
Zion	C. M. Efird
St. Thomas'	J. C. Fulmer
St. Jacob's	R. F. Cumulander
Cedar Grove	J. Ansel Caughman
St. James'	R. E. Shealy
St. Paul's	J. L. Sease
Grace	E. C. Davis
Holy Trinity	Fred G. Hartley
St. John's	G. O. Schumpert
Emmanuel's	Marshall Roof
Pilgrim	D. F. Efird
St. Peter's	G. B. Wingard
Mt. Tabor	P. I. Sox
St. Andrew's	J. O. Eargle
Bethlehem	C. H. Bouknight
Mt. Horeb	W. A. Ballentine
St. Peter's. Chapin	L. B. Frick

By motion the representatives were received as commissioners and given the privilege of the floor. By the unanimous vote of the synod the congregations were received into the synod and their respective commissioners were declared members of synod.

By motion, Revs. W. H. Riser, W. D. Wise, R. M. Carpenter, H. A. Kistler and J. M. Senter, pastors of the congregations just received into the synod, were unanimously received and their names placed on the clerical roll of the synod.

Chapter III

MISSIONARY HISTORY

THE missionary history of the synod begins with the second convention, held November 18, 1824. A strong desire was expressed for the appointment of a missionary to be sent to the vacant and destitute congregations in the synod, and in other states. This, however, had to be deferred with regret, because of a lack of funds, until the next convention of synod, at which time the same need was felt and considered. At the fourth convention, November 24, 1826, Rev. John Bachman sounded the keynote in a sermon on the "Macedonian cry", and a committee was appointed to engage two missionaries of this synod. Accordingly Mr. J. D. Scheck was secured and licensed to perform ministerial acts; he was therefore the synod's first regularly constituted Home Missionary. Several ministers statedly visited destitute congregations, and thus the urgent need was temporarily met.

Mr. Henry Muller, reporting for the mission committee, most highly commended the work of Rev. J. D. Scheck and said, "In two months the missionary rode nearly nine hundred miles, preached forty-seven sermons, and baptized twenty-six persons."

A Committee on Missions was therefore constituted early in the life of the synod and soon became an established part of the work of this body. As far as we can gather from the records, the first committee appointed to serve for the ensuing year was in November, 1827; and this action established a precedent which has prevailed to the present day.

It will be of interest to state that the first committee appointed for annual service was Messrs. Dreher, Caughman, Muller, Metze and Haltiwanger (initials not in the record).

The missionary spirit of the synod continued to grow and in 1837 led to the formation of a Synodical Society, with officers separate and distinct from those of the synod. This was styled, "The Foreign Missionary Society of the Synod of South Carolina and Adjacent States," and it cooperated with a similar society of the General Synod of the Evangelical Lutheran Church in the United States.

The South Carolina Synod had united with the said General Synod in 1833, under such restrictions as left the South Carolina Synod free in the legislation of its own affairs, and in the maintenance of our own Theological Seminary.

Under this synodical arrangement our district synod through a series of years made contributions to the foreign work through cooperation with the said General Synod, reserving the right to enter any foreign field that Providence should open up to us.*

The officers of this Synodical Missionary Society were elected as follows: Jacob F. Mintzing, President; Dr. J. Bachman, Mr. W. Caughman and Mr. T. Purse, Vice-Presidents; Dr. E. L. Hazelius, Corresponding Secretary; Mr. Joseph Wingard, Treasurer; Rev. J. C. Hope, G. Haltiwanger, W. Berly, L. Bedenbaugh, and Messrs. H. Muller, J. Eichelberger and T. Schuler, Executive Committee.

This society continued to do effective mission work up to 1873, when, upon the adoption of a new constitution, the synod in its organic law regulated all the committees and funds coming into its treasury.

An Executive Committee on Missions was therefore made responsible for the missionary operations of the synod during the interim of its regular conventions; and this committee has grown in efficiency and importance until it has long since become one of the most valuable agencies in the work of the synod.

It is a matter of historic interest to record the fact that this synod as far back as 1841 took an active part in the establishment and support of the Guntur Mission, India, under Father Heyer. This synod in 1841, through the Foreign Missionary Society of the Pennsylvania Synod, contributed $696.04, and this money was used in the erection of a mission house. Other sums were subsequently given for "the completion of the missionary buildings", and were so acknowledged by Father Heyer himself. It will thus be seen

*(See Minutes of 1833, pp. 11-13.)
 (See Minutes of 1837, pp. 9-13.)

that the Guntur Mission is interwoven into the life of this synod, and that we were contributors to its early life and success.*

In 1845, Rev. John Bachman, then president of the synod, gave credentials to Boston Drayton, a colored man, to go as a missionary to Africa. Nor has this synod ever faltered in its efforts to aid in the world's evangelization.

This synod entered upon what may be called the greatest stage of its home and foreign mission activities when its women and children were organized into societies for increased interest in the work of missions. This movement was carried on largely by Rev. W. P. Swartz in 1884 and 1885, under the direction of the Board of Home and Foreign Missions and Church Extension of the United Synod of the Evangelical Lutheran Church in the South.

The Board reported that about forty auxiliary societies had been organized, with nearly one thousand members, some sixty children's foreign missionary societies, and four synodical societies.

The organizing operations of Rev. W. P. Swartz, the missionary-elect, ended early in July, 1885, and on the twelfth of that month he left New York for Guntur, India, the farewell meeting being held in Grace Church, Winchester, Va., July 6, 1885. The missionary reached India, October, 1885, but by April 27, 1887, he had returned to this country, and on August 31 he resigned, and subsequently united with another denomination.

The Board of Missions of the United Synod at that time was made up wholly of ministers and laymen from South Carolina, five of the seven being members of this synod and thus linking us very closely with the foreign mission work. Japan now became the objective of the Board. Rev. James A. B. Scherer was called, and examined by a committee of the South Carolina Synod, upon recommendation of the United Synod's Board. He was ordained in St. John's Church, Charleston, November 22, 1891, and sailed for Japan February 4, 1892.

---

*(See Minutes of 1841, p. 33; 1848, pp. 36-37; 1844, pp. 11, 20, 32.)

It will therefore be seen that this synod, through all of its history, has been an active participant in the foreign mission work of our Southern Church and has been a liberal supporter of all our missionary enterprises. From her ranks other mission workers have gone to Japan; and her prayers and contributions are still going out to the land of the Rising Sun.

It will be of historic interest to state that Miss Alice M. Wulbern, of Charleston, and Miss Lottie Wyse, of Columbia, married missionaries and accompanied their husbands to the foreign field (Japan)—Miss Alice Wulbern as Mrs. Arthur J. Stirewalt and Miss Lottie Wyse as Mrs. Clarence E. Norman. Two daughters of congregations connected with the synod went out as missionaries to the foreign field and became wives of missionaries, Miss Gertrude Simpson, daughter of Dr. J. A. Simpson, of Prosperity, becoming the wife of Rev. G. C. Leonard, in the Muhlenberg Mission, Monrovia, Liberia, West Africa, and Miss Mary Lou Bowers, daughter of Rev. Dr. and Mrs. A. J. Bowers, of Newberry, becoming the wife of Rev. L. G. Gray, in the Japan Mission, Kumamoto.

Inner Missions

The work of the Inner Mission is of comparatively recent establishment in this country. It is commonly known as "the ministry of mercy". This ministry, a revival of early Christian practice, arose in the Evangelical Church of Germany toward the end of the Eighteenth and early in the Nineteenth centuries. The names of Theodor Fliedner and Johann Heinrich Wichern are associated with its inception and development. Transplanted to this country, the Inner Mission has been gaining an enlarging sphere of service, especially in the Lutheran Church. In this work of mercy the South Carolina Synod also has a part. Two Inner Mission institutions are located on its territory, in one of which the synod has a share in the way of ownership and support.

FRANKE HOME.

The Franke Home at Charleston, although not an institution of the Synod of South Carolina, is located on the territory of the synod and is doing a most beneficent work. The Home was made possible by a bequest of about $33,000, made in his will by the late C. D. Franke, of Charleston, to establish "The Jacob Washington Franke Lutheran Hospital and Home" in memory of his deceased son, Jacob Washington Franke. The bequest was made to the pastors of the Lutheran churches of Charleston "in trust for the erection, maintenance and support of a Hospital and Home for the indigent sick in the City of Charleston, to be built, and erected, maintained and supported by any Association, Society or Institution that may hereafter be incorporated by an Act of the Legislature of the State of South Carolina as and for such Hospital and Home". The contemplated corporation was chartered in December, 1892, under the name of "The Evangelical Lutheran Charities Society of Charleston, S. C." The act of incorporation was amended in 1896, and the members of the Society in the new act are named as the pastors of the Lutheran churches of Charleston and two representatives of each of said churches, chosen annually. by the respective congregations. The control and management of the Home is in the hands of this Society, with which, to supplement the income, is affiliated an auxiliary organization, whose members contribute at least one dollar per annum. Anyone contributing at least one hundred dollars is entitled to life membership. Under the administration of this Lutheran Charities Society the Franke Home has rendered and is rendering a blessed service.

THE LOWMAN HOME FOR THE AGED AND HELPLESS.

In the year 1910 Mrs. Malissa Lowman of White Rock, S. C., who had been left a widow with three incurable invalid children, offered her entire estate for the founding and maintenance of a home for the aged and helpless. This offer was first made to the State of South Carolina and was declined. Then the offer was made to the Lutheran Synod of South Carolina, and was accepted in 1911. The gift consisted of approximately one thousand acres of land, lying between White Rock and Ballentine, a lot each in the towns of White Rock and Chapin, and cash to an amount between

$1,500 and $2,000. The Church bound itself to maintain an institution for the care of the aged and afflicted in perpetuity, to take care of Mrs. Lowman and her children as long as they should live, and to sell none of the land within thirty-three years from the date of the deed.

For a short time after the transfer of this property Mrs. Lowman remained at her old home and her care and the affairs of the estate were looked after by Mr. James Shealy, a neighbor, representing the synod. The money given by Mrs. Lowman was designated as a nucleus of a fund for the beginning of a training institution for deaconesses, to be used for other purposes until such time as the Church might determine to begin that work. This provision was largely due to the influence of Rev. C. E. Weltner, D.D. The major gift was made to the Church through Rev. W. H. Greever, D.D., who was then editor of the *Lutheran Church Visitor*, and has been a member of the Boards of the institution from the beginning until the writing of this sketch, and is the present president of the Board.

The first superintendent of the Home was Rev. W. P. Cline, D.D., who retired on account of ill health at the beginning of 1923, after having served for a period of nearly ten years. During Dr. Cline's administration two residences were built at White Rock, a third one begun and a barn erected. The farms were operated with varying success, and a number of needy people were cared for, some until taken by death and some for short periods. At no time were there more than five or six persons under care. The Church, during this period, made very small and irregular contributions to the institution; the income from farm operations was small and uncertain, and no program of expansion seemed possible.

In 1914 the South Carolina Synod offered the institution to the United Synod in the South. The offer was approved. In 1915 the South Carolina Synod took the necessary legal steps to transfer the property, and upon the presentation of deed and other necessary papers to the United Synod at its meeting in 1916 the transfer was effected. Following the Merger of the United Synod into the United Lutheran Church in America, the institution was transferred again to the dis-

LOWMAN HOME

trict synods in the South, formerly belonging to the United Synod in the South. In 1924 a charter was secured from the state of South Carolina.

At the beginning of 1923 Mr. C. E. Hotinger took charge as superintendent, and a definite program of expansion was begun. The first of the permanent buildings has since been completed, old buildings have been repaired, renovated, repainted and refurnished. Plumbing and electric lights have been installed. Farming operations have been extended and

LOWMAN HOME FAMILY

improved. The raising of poultry has been successfully inaugurated, and other advances made. The number of persons under care has been increased to 15, the present capacity of equipment, and the interest of the Church at large has been secured in greatly increased measure. This institution, already of inestimable service, promises to grow into one of the greatest of the contributions of the South Carolina Synod to the Church at large.

Woman's Synodical Missionary Society of South Carolina—1885-1923

To begin the story of Woman's Missionary organization in the South Carolina Synod, we must travel back through the intervening years and wake the year 1885 from its long sleep in the arms of the past.

To make vocal the story of a still earlier past would be to tell the history of a period of time when the missionary spirit of the Church was at "low tide", and the definition of such work would be that of a faithful pioneer-preacher on horseback, riding from thirty to seventy-five miles to preach the Gospel to the pastorless churches of the highways and byways of our own state.

Into this "wilderness" of struggle for local self-support came the "voice" of Rev. W. P. Swartz, missionary-elect to India, bringing to the women of the Church the message, "The Master hath come, and is calling for thee." His story of the wrongs of heathen womanhood and their need of the Saviour touched the chord of womanly sympathy and met with quick response. At his suggestion and under his direction, women's missionary societies were organized in the churches he visited, wherever possible.

The power of direction and control of these scattered societies was in the hands of a committee of the synod, and at the synodical meeting in 1885, Revs. J. Steck and J. Hawkins, the members of this committee, made report on the women's missionary societies. In this report the following list of organized societies is given:

Grace Church, Prosperity.
St. Luke's and Colony, Prosperity.
Luther Chapel, Newberry.
Ebenezer, Columbia.
St. Paul's, Bethlehem, and St. Philip's, Pomaria.
St. Matthew's, Orangeburg.
St. Andrew's and St. Stephen's, Lexington.
Good Hope, Leesville.
Mt. Calvary, Johnston.
St. John's, Calk's Road.

Bethel, Lexington County.

Pine Grove and Trinity, Orangeburg County.

For the wonderful progress made in so brief a time, the committee commends the zeal of the women and bids them "God-speed in their work so well begun".

The money gathered from these young organizations totaled $436.50. We set up this report in the minutes of the synod, October, 1885, as the first milestone in organized missionary activity, for the reason that nine months prior to this time, on February 3, 1885, representatives of these first societies met in Luther Chapel, Newberry, and effected an organization for state-wide extension work under the name of "The Synodical Executive Committee of the Woman's Home and Foreign Missionary Society of the Evangelical Lutheran Church of South Carolina".

At this meeting officers were duly elected as follows:

President, Mrs. J. Steck; Vice-Presidents, Mrs. P. Robertson, Mrs. T. W. Holloway, Mrs. Jacob Epting; Recording Secretary, Miss Laura E. McFall; Corresponding Secretary, Miss Kate Mayer; Treasurer, Mrs. G. W. Holland.

The purpose of this organized committee to blaze a widening trail of missionary activity is positively set forth in the second item of the constitution adopted at this time, which reads: "It shall be the aim of this Society to promote the organization of Auxiliary Home and Foreign Missionary Societies in all the churches of the synod; to disseminate missionary intelligence; to cultivate a missionary spirit, and to engage and unite the efforts of Christian women, under the direction of the Board of Missions of the United Synod South, in supporting missions and missionaries in the home and foreign fields of our Church." By the fruits of the years, evidence is given that this object has been fully realized.

A resolution to hold an annual convention at or near the time and place of the meeting of synod was adopted, and at the further meetings of this Executive Committee in 1885, the plans and program for this prospective initial convention were discussed and matured.

Since the functioning of this Executive Committee gave life and direction to the women's missionary work in South

Carolina, it must be crowned as the "mother" of the movement, and the birthday of organized activity must be traced back to the year 1885, as a memorial tribute to those brave pioneer women who now "rest from their labors", while "their works do follow them".

On the foundation stone of the preliminary work so courageously accomplished, against almost overwhelming odds, in 1885 was built the first actual convention of women missionary workers of the Lutheran Church in South Carolina. This meeting was held in Luther Chapel, Newberry, October 11, 1886.

Because of failing health and removal, Mrs. J. Steck, prior to this time, had resigned the office of president, and her mantle had fallen on the first vice-president, Mrs. P. Robertson. Miss Lelia G. Rives had also succeeded Miss Kate Mayer as corresponding secretary.

There were present at this meeting, besides the eight officers and members of the executive committee, eleven delegates, representing nine societies, a total of nineteen in attendance. A notable fact is that all of these first missionary societies represented, with *three exceptions*, were in Newberry County; the exceptions being Orangeburg, Lexington and Columbia.

The opening devotional service of this *first annual* convention was conducted by Rev. Jacob Hawkins, D.D. The first address of welcome was made by Mrs. A. B. McMackin; the response by Miss Lillian Luther. The first life membership recorded was Mrs. M. C. Rawl of Lexington, and the first president's message was given by Mrs. P. Robertson.

In Item 2 of this message one can "read between the lines" the discouraging apathy and opposition which these early workers had to face and overcome in the pathetic paragraph: "I recommend, also, that we urge upon our pastors the *importance of our work* and *beg* that they will give us their assistance and hearty co-operation, presenting our claims more often and rendering all possible aid."

Mrs. Robertson served the society officially for two years, and the work under her leadership developed so encouragingly that in her report in 1887, she makes special men-

tion of St. Matthew's Society, Orangeburg County, Rev. J.
H. Wilson, pastor, which that year paid into the missionary
treasury more than $200.

In this formative period of time the banner of official
leadership was passed quickly from hand to hand. Mrs. J.
Steck, Mrs. P. Robertson, Mrs. T. W. Holloway, Mrs. C.
A. Marks, each in turn gave their best to the cause and left
abundant evidence that the work prospered under their direction, and that the growth, while "slow", was "sure". About
the same number of delegates reported at each annual convention and the ground gained was staunchly held.

An array of figures is usually uninteresting, but figures
give in a nutshell a story of substantial advancement which
would otherwise be long and tiresome.

In 1885 the total amount contributed was $ 343.25
In 1886 the total amount contributed was   604.55
In 1887 the total amount contributed was   693.07
In 1888 the total amount contributed was   647.74
In 1889 the total amount contributed was   680.95
                                            ─────────
Grand total for first five years' work $2,969.56

The Home Mission stations aided in this period were
Augusta, Ga., Knoxville, Tenn., and Winston-Salem, N. C.

The Foreign appropriation of the initial $50, and a later
one of $110, were sent through Dr. Gilbert of the Northern
Board.

For many reasons the missionary women of South Carolina longed and prayed for a satisfactory channel in their
own Southern Board, through which their gifts to foreign
missions might be applied, and in token of their faith that
their prayers would find an answer, appropriations for foreign work were put on deposit for several years.

Then Mrs. C. A. Marks, because of removal from the
state, was forced to resign the office of president. Mrs. M.
C. Rawl, of Lexington, was elected to fill the vacant chair
in 1890. No tribute of the pen could ever do justice to the
overflowing devotion of Mrs. Rawl's heart for the cause of
her Saviour. Herself a fluent writer and poetess, she put

her best talent into her annual reports, and the touch of
the Master she served made them vibrant with the power of
an irresistible appeal for the extension of the work at home
and over the seas.

At the sixth annual convention held in Grace Church,
Prosperity, the withholding of missionary money, while
countless souls were perishing uncomforted and unsaved, so
distressed the heart of the president that she uttered her protest in the original poem with which she closed her report
for 1891:

> "O Fisherman, toiling in shallows,
>   And toiling all night in vain,
> Ever seining in oft-tried waters,
>   And shunning the pathless main;
> Launch out on the fathomless ocean
>   Of sorrow and darkness and sin,
> Launch out at the word of the Master,
>   And gather the outcasts in."

This poem was later set to music, but the sweetest music
which resulted from this fine protest was the new note which
runs through her official message in the year 1893, and
sounds like the chanting of a hymn of praise. The prayers
of the Church to "the Lord of the harvest" had been heard,
and Rev. James A. B. Scherer had volunteered to go out as
a missionary of the Southern Board to the Empire of Japan.
This was the "Rising Sun" of enthusiasm and new impulse
to those who had waited long for a channel through which
their obedience to the Saviour's last command could find
proper expression.

As Rev. James A. B. Scherer went to Japan under the direction of the Board of Missions of the United Synod South, the
women of South Carolina made their yearly contribution to
the general conduct of the mission he established at Saga
until the year 1898, when with the missionary women of
North Carolina and Southwestern Virginia they united in
the joint support of Rev. C. L. Brown, a later recruit.

When Mrs. Rawl was obliged by declining health to pass
on the banner to stronger hands, the vice-president. Mrs. J.
H. Wyse, stepped into line to receive and carry it forward.

In her annual report for 1895 and 1896 she showed a deep conviction of responsibility and a wonderful grasp of the problems of the day in which she wrought. Her appeal for the distribution of more missionary literature and the observance of the Week of Prayer proved the deep concern she felt for the vital essentials of growth.

The first decade of Woman's Organized Activity closed with a record of $5,997.06 expended, and 26 societies with 496 members.

SECOND DECADE.

This period opened with the convention at St. Paul's Church, Pomaria, in 1896. It was at this meeting that Mrs. M. M. Kinard, first vice-president, became acting president, and was later duly elected for her term of service.

Again the pendulum which marks missionary advance fell into a steady, even beat. Efficient in leadership, Mrs. Kinard stressed each year the main essentials of the work, and the work prospered in her hands. Mite boxes, those "forerunners" of the present Thank-offering, came into use at her suggestion, and definite goals were named for definite objects. Mrs. Kinard's term of service ended with her resignation to the 1899 convention, which met in Grace Church, Prosperity, and again the honor of the office was transferred to the first vice-president, Mrs. Nease.

And here we pause to pay the tribute of "remembrance for what she has done" to this worker who passed from active service to rest and reward while the convention of the next year was in session. The Master she served said unto her, "It is enough. Come up higher," and she went, crowned with the glory of a young life well spent, and rich sheaves to lay at His feet.

The Week of Prayer had become a fixed annual feature of the work as early as the year 1889, but as the years multiplied, its observance became more general and its influence more vital.

A Literature Committee had also been appointed, and the appeal of the societies to this committee for light and information must have been well-nigh distracting in that period of extreme poverty in tracts and programs. This demand led to the requirement of a per capita tax to meet the condition. The story of the next decade can be more briefly told because the women of this period had but to rear the superstructure of the future years upon the strong foundation laid by their courageous sisters of the earlier days.

The "leavening power" of the work was becoming recognized as a mighty force in the "measure of meal"—the Church. When, in the year 1900, Mrs. James A. B. Scherer became president, thirty-seven societies reported at the convention held at St. Andrew's Church, and ninety-four new members were added to the roll.

In the year 1904 Mrs. James A. B. Scherer and Mrs. M. O. J. Kreps were appointed to tour the churches as an organizing committee. This tour lasted six weeks and resulted in the formation of twenty new societies and an added membership of two hundred. For this aggressive campaign an appropriation of $50 was made, and it is a notable fact that the committee returned to the treasury a sum in excess of the original expenditure, and at the same time materially stimulated gifts to the Forward Movement which at that time was being promoted.

No less a forward movement was the advance step whereby Mrs. Kate Eargle as chairman of the Literature Committee, and with the help of others, prepared and distributed to each society in 1904 a complete program booklet with all necessary helps.

This wise provision launched a movement of far-reaching importance to the whole Church, since it was quickly adopted by other states and finally became the model after which the program packets of more modern times were planned.

In 1906 two original tracts written by Mrs. M. O. J. Kreps were published under the imprint of the Synodical Society of South Carolina. These tracts were "Aunt Dinah's Starry Crown" and "Love's Offering". They were notable not only for the fact that they speedily created a large demand, and passed into greater usefulness, but also that they created an impulse to produce for ourselves and others the literature so sorely needed in the extension of the work.

The second decade closed with a financial total of $16,-
160.20. Adding to this the $1,800 contributed to the For-
ward Movement, the grand total was $17,960.20; and to this
gift of money can be added a wealth of love and devotion
which to the King of kings is a priceless offering.

THIRD DECADE.

Special Work.

In the history of the first twenty years there was no special
home mission work assigned to the women. With the mod-
esty and devotion of the woman-heart, they were content to
aid every cause adopted by the synod, without claiming the
privilege of laying the hand of the convention on any one
task and designating it as the woman's monument of love
and self-denial.

By special resolution in 1904 this old order passed away
and with the full endorsement of the Executive Committee
of the Synod, the women made special appropriation to the
erection of a mission church at Spartanburg. Mrs. M. O.
J. Kreps represented the Woman's Society at the laying of the
cornerstone, and the Society was greatly honored by having
the new church called "The Woman's Memorial Church of
Spartanburg". Larger obligations have been assumed for
the building of other churches since then, but this one is
still the only Woman's Memorial within the bounds of the
synod.

For many years there was a growing conviction that the
work of the women in each southern state would be materially strengthened and advanced by union of interest and
operation. Acting upon the suggestion of Rev. R. C. Holland, D.D., the matter was agitated and emphasized in the
Women's Department of the *Lutheran Church Visitor,* and
representatives of the synodical societies then in existence
were called to a meeting at Dallas, N. C., July 12, 1906.

This meeting resulted in the birth of the Woman's Missionary Conference of the United Synod South. This general
organization mightily broadened and deepened the tide of
missionary interest and enthusiasm in South Carolina, as in

all other states joining in the union, by the fresh courage and assurance of strength which is the unfailing result of fellowship in service.

From this time the work advanced rapidly, the Synodical Society of South Carolina contributing to the Forward Movement, the Japan School, the Silver Jubilee, and later specials, more than its proportionate share, and at the same time discharging promptly and cheerfully its obligations to the Home Board and the missionary operations of its own state work.

For many years the Children's Societies were under the direction and training of the Woman's Society, but their treasurer was a member of the South Carolina Synod, and their funds were not included with those of the Convention. As this arrangement hindered the extension and development of the children's work, appeal was made to synod to transfer all the interests of Junior Societies entirely to the women, and when this appeal met with favorable decision, these societies were transferred from the synod to the Woman's Synodical Society, thus putting the missionary training of the children and the direction of their offerings exclusively into the hands of the women.

At this time kindergarten work in Japan was being launched by Mrs. C. K. Lippard, and the children of South Carolina assumed the obligation of $12 per month for the support of this work, the rest of their annual fund being appropriated to Synodical Home Missions. A few years later, with the children's societies of other synods, they assumed their proportionate share of the salary of Rev. A. J. Stirewalt, who then became the children's missionary.

With the children enlisted in definite missionary training and practical service, the Convention turned its attention and mother-concern to the boys and girls of high school and college age. How could this youthful army be won and its unlimited capacities be turned into channels of Christian service? The practical attempt to solve this problem was made at the annual convention at Spartanburg in 1907, when, with the program for that meeting, a "Young People's Hour" was featured.

This was the "pebble in the stream" of the great uncharted river of youthful enthusiasm, which in its widening circles has speedily grown into the Young People's Federation of South Carolina. A pioneer organization of young people, it "blazed the trail" in working out its relationships to existing bodies as it developed its own strength and efficiency in service, and in the making of its wonderful history it became a beacon of inspiration and a model in efficiency.

MRS. M. O. J. KREPS

At the 1908 convention, which met in Grace Church, Prosperity, there was a "vacant chair" and a familiar face sadly missed in the official force, which for nearly eight years had remained unbroken. Because of removal to the sunset-side of America, Mrs. James A. B. Scherer resigned the office of president, and Mrs. M. O. J. Kreps was transferred from the office of recording secretary, which she had held for nine years, to the higher honors of official leadership.

At this time there were three girls of the Synodical Society who had volunteered for definite Christian service, wherever the Church should call them, and were in training under Pastor C. E. Weltner at St. Luke's Church, Olympia village. These girls were Gertrude Simpson of Prosperity, Mary Lou Bowers of Newberry, and Josephine Copeland of Ehrhardt. The equipment for this training home at Olympia was provided by the Women's Societies, and but for overwhelming obstacles this work would have been continued under the very able direction of Pastor and Mrs. C. E. Weltner.

After finishing the course, Gertrude Simpson answered a temporary call to become Field Secretary of the Woman's Synodical Society, and served with fine success until she answered a more compelling call to become a missionary to Africa. Mary Lou Bowers also gave herself to the Japan mission field, and Josephine Copeland took up Christian social service in industrial communities.

After the organization of the Woman's Missionary Conference of the United Synod South, Mrs. E. C. Cronk was appointed Chairman General Literature Committee for the whole southern territory, and the Thank-offering box became the permanent successor to the Forward Movement.

At the convention of 1910 forty-five new societies, representing all stages of life from grandmothers to the wee flowers of the growing Cradle Roll, were added. These new organizations were in large part the result of Miss Simpson's field work.

For many years the strongest note of the convention was training the children, and committees were appointed yearly to advocate and introduce missions into the regular curriculum of the Sunday Schools. Mission study also was encouraged in all possible ways, and classes multiplied everywhere and were reported in encouraging number at each convention. The forces of the Young People also mobilized like those of the Youthful Crusaders, and their high courage became infectious to the workers of more mature years. In the year 1910 the following resolution was offered by these workers to the convention:

"Resolved. That as representatives of the Young People of the South Carolina Synod, we petition the Woman's Convention to appoint an Executive Committee of five young people, naming the General Secretary and Treasurer, which Committee shall seek to advance the work among young people in all the congregations of the synod."

This was the first step in the severance of the work launched and fostered by the mother organization in behalf of its young sons and daughters—a step made necessary by the rapid growth of the younger body, which from this date became the Federation of Lutheran Young People of the South Carolina Synod, directing and controlling its work and holding annual conventions apart from any kindred body.

The third decade closed with a financial record of $35,-007.55 for both women's and children's societies. A generous share of this sum total was appropriated to extension work in the foreign field, and to buildings and equipments for the increased force of workers. A proportionate amount has been given to strengthen the work of the home field. Through the United Synod's Board, the money expended assisted in the work at Richmond, Knoxville, Norfolk, Augusta and Winston-Salem. Through the South Carolina Synod, the missions at Sumter, Orangeburg, Augusta, Ga., Spartanburg, Greenwood, Greenville, Olympia Mill, and other points, have been materially aided and encouraged.

FOURTH DECADE.

In celebration of twenty-five years of service in Japan, a Silver Jubilee Fund was launched in 1917, to build a home for the young women who had gone out in 1913—Miss Akard and Miss Bowers. The South Carolina Convention had previously assumed its share of the support of Miss Akard, and Miss Bowers was adopted by the Young People of South Carolina. The chairman of the Jubilee Fund was Mrs. Robert F. Bowe, who served in connection with a representative from other Synodical Societies of the United Synod. The campaign was efficiently and speedily accomplished, South Carolina giving $1,584.70 of the total sum.

As a tribute to that matchless leader and friend, Rev. R. C. Holland, D.D., who had laid down the robe of service for the victor's crown, a permanent scholarship was established in the Japan School to his memory in 1916. Again in the same year the convention adopted a resolution to assume its share of the increase incident to sending to Japan two more women workers, Misses Maude and Annie Powlas, who were then taking special training in New York City.

For many years prayers had been offered in South Carolina convention for the way to open for the establishment of a girls' school in Japan, and during these years all life memberships were put on deposit, from year to year, to serve as a nucleus of a girls' school fund when the way would open up.

Since the home for the women missionaries was emphasized as the *first step* in the realization of the school, the money held on deposit was put into the home, and this action was followed by a special resolution in 1910, which reads as follows: "We recommend that the Woman's Societies of the South Carolina Synod take up the work of establishing a Girls' School in Japan, as soon as the way is opened, in connection with the Woman's Missionary Conference."

Inner Mission Work at this period was gradually accorded a place all its own in the annual reports, and visions of larger service became vitally operative in consecrated hands and feet for the Master's use.

New departments were created to keep in line with each forward step, and the General Literature Committee, with Mrs. E. C. Cronk as chairman, and headquarters in Columbia, furnished splendid literature helps, and sent out generous supplies for monthly meetings and other advance work.

It was at this age and stage of the work that someone dreamed a dream of a United Lutheran Church in America, and in response to the movement of the various synodical bodies, the women too joined in the outstanding event of modern Lutheran history in America—the great Merger Meeting in New York City in 1917. The delegates to this eventful assemblage of missionary workers, from many states, were Mrs. M. O. J. Kreps, Mrs. J. A. Summer and Miss Caro Efird.

Since this time the work in South Carolina has mightily broadened and deepened its tide. New departments have been created to meet the new opportunities of a world-field of operation.

Regular funds must now flow through regular channels, but special work still beckons to Synodical Societies for special adoption. The Specials of the present period are $175,000 for a Girls' School in Japan, and $20,000 for building a church and parsonage for the Rock Hill mission, which has been chosen as the "Synodical Special" of the missionary women of South Carolina.

In the adjustments of the Merger, the *Lutheran Church Visitor* was absorbed by *The Lutheran* and passed out of existence. Since this organ of the United Synod, South, carried weekly a Woman's Missionary Department, edited for more than twenty years by Mrs. M. O. J. Kreps, the Synodical Society of South Carolina felt keenly the loss of this medium of information in the work. To maintain some line of intimate communication seemed such a necessity that in 1921 a Quarterly Missionary Bulletin was established under the imprint of the Synodical Society of South Carolina.

In very recent years the forces of the children have been rallied and united under the new name of The Light Brigade, but this change in no way effects the regular order of work, other than by different classifications, under the one head, suited to every stage of child-life. It is hoped by this the more effectively to enlist and train all the children of the Church. There are fifty-four Light Brigades in the South Carolina Synod, with eighteen hundred children enrolled.

Catching the inspiration from the Piedmont societies, which were organized into a conferential district society, under the leadership of Mrs. Kate Eargle, in the Autumn of 1922, like societies were later formed in each of the conference districts of the synod. By and through the functioning of these "wheels within wheels" it is hoped to broaden contacts and better connect up all phases of activity.

When Rev. Charles L. Brown, D.D., went home to God from the distant fields of Africa, a second memorial was established by the Woman's Society; this tribute to be a gift to the interior furnishing of the Brown Memorial Chapel in Japan.

Behold! The pebble cast into the river thirty-eight years ago in 1885 is moving the waters of a mighty stream of activity, its current still reaching outward and onward.

Looking backward the Synodical Society can claim a generous share in every advance movement at home and abroad.

To those earlier gifts to mission churches in the years gone by, it adds similar gifts to Clinton, Immanuel, Ridge Spring; Incarnation, Shandon; and St. James', Saxe-Gotha.

To the work mentioned specifically in the former pages of this history, it can add a large sum given to the erection of Kyushu Gakuin, and to churches and homes for our missionaries and kindergartens.

The roll of presidents and their terms of office are as follows:

Mrs. J. Steck ....1 year.
Mrs. P. Robertson ....2 years.
Mrs. G. W. Holloway, V.-P. ....1 year.
Mrs. C. A. Marks ....2 years.
Mrs. M. C. Rawl ....4 years.
Mrs. J. H. Wyse ....2 years.
Mrs. M. M. Kinard ....2 years.
Mrs. S. L. Nease ....1 year.
Mrs. J. A. B. Scherer ....8 years.
Mrs. M. O. J. Kreps ....15 years.

To these official leaders of past years should be added the names of Mrs. Kate Eargle, Mrs. Laura Wise and Miss Lillian Luther, who have wrought from earliest beginnings and still work on with unfaltering zeal and devotion, asking no other reward than the Master's "Well done" when they shall come to the end of the way.

And memory recalls the many consecutive years of service as treasurer, given by Mrs. George W. Holland and by Mrs. Jacob Epting as vice-president. To these faithful ones, who now "rest from their labors", history must pay the tribute of the immortelle of grateful remembrance.

SUMMARY.

Today, marching in line with the missionary forces of the United Lutheran Church, the women and children of South Carolina are rapidly advancing the cause of Christ under the Stars and Stripes, and touching with the transforming power of the Gospel the lives of the Christless in India, Africa, Japan, South America, and the Islands of the Sea.

Many thousands of consecrated dollars have flowed out from the Synodical treasury in the years which are now history, but the priceless gift of the past, and the heritage it extends to the future, is the educational and inspirational blessing of the missionary work to the heart of the whole Church.

The fortieth milestone looms up in the path ahead, and the pen of the future is poised. Hanging above the pen is a question mark. What history will be made from the foundation of the years behind? Only God can answer.

If in the thirty-eighth year the annual gift of more than $10,000 for women and children is in excess of the first ten years' *total*; if the societies have grown from the original twenty-four in 1885 to the eighty enrolled in 1923, and the membership from 318 of the first convention to the 2,075 of 1923, the prospect for a brighter future is a challenge to speed the promise to fulfillment.

The fourth decade will close in 1925. Eight years of that period have passed into history; and the financial record made in that incomplete period of time is, at a conservative estimate, $60,220.27, with advance along other lines which shows marvelous progress.

COMPARATIVE TOTALS BY DECADES.

1885—1895	$ 5,997.06
1895—1905	17,960.20
1905—1915	35,007.27
1915—1923 (8 years)	60,385.08
Grand Total	$119,349.68

Attention is called to the fact that the above figures represent *only* the money which passed through Convention treasurer's hands. If the "Special Gifts", inspired by the convention, but sent direct to various objects, could have been tabulated, the total would swell like a mighty river of blessing. Attention is also called to the remarkable fact that the sum total of only eight years of the last decade exceeds the combined totals of the first three decades of service.

History serves its purpose only when it is woven into the finer pattern of an advancing order of progress. So this history of thirty-eight years of missionary operations will be worthless, unless those for whom it is written read between the lines the sublime challenge of Him whose Resurrection message is "Go quickly, and *tell* the disciples that *I go before you*".

"Prize what is yours, but be not quite contented;
  There is a healthful restlessness of soul,
By which a mighty purpose is augmented
  In urging you to reach a higher goal.

"So when the restless impulse rises, driving
  Your calm content before it, do not grieve;
It is the upward reaching and the striving
  Of God in you—to still achieve—achieve!"

Chapter IV

EDUCATIONAL AIMS AND ACHIEVEMENTS

THE educational history of this synod began at its second convention, November, 1824. The foundation was laid in special action looking to the religious training of the children and youth of the Church. By a special resolution the duty of the ministers connected with the synod regularly to deliver lectures to young persons and others, was clearly defined; and the doctrines and duties of religion were to form the chief element of such instruction. Parents and heads of families were urged to cooperate with their pastors in this important work.

The Catechism was named as the proper textbook to be used, and "the principles of religion" were to be instilled into the minds of the young—drawn, of course, from the Holy Scriptures.

The next objective was to secure "well educated Lutheran ministers to supply our vacant churches, or to labor as missionaries within the bounds of the synod".

Theological Seminary and Classical School

The lack of ministers to meet the increasing demand of the destitute congregations and outlying mission points was so great that Rev. John Bachman expressed the feeling of all concerned when he said at the convention of 1828: "It is to be feared that we will never be supplied with a suitable number of clergymen until we afford them the facilities of an education nearer home. Let us make this subject the object of our reflection, our reading and our prayers." This proved to have been the starting point of a wave of educational influence which will finally touch the utmost shores of time and find its full fruition in the world to come. At this meeting of synod a series of resolutions was presented and unanimously adopted, provision being made for the raising of funds for the establishment and support of such an institution as would meet the needs of our Southern Church.

The earnest purpose of the synod is seen in the fact that a committee of twenty was appointed by resolution and "authorized to receive any donations and legacies which may be presented" towards the creation of a fund for such institution as was contemplated.*

At the convention of 1830 the special committee appointed to raise funds for the proposed Theological Seminary reported "considerable progress in obtaining funds", upon which the synod resolved, "in humble reliance on the Divine blessing, to establish a Theological Seminary, consecrating our efforts to Him who is the great Head of the Church, the Shepherd and Bishop of Souls—God over all, Blesesd forever."†

It was also resolved to connect with that school of the prophets a Classical Academy, under the direction of the professor of theology. At once such professor was elected in the person of Rev. J. G. Schwartz, who accepted this important position; and so Rev. John Bachman, whose great soul had so earnestly plead for an institution in which our young men could be trained for the ministry, was at last to see "the work of the Lord prosper in our hands".

The record of the Seminary is not full in the published proceedings of the synod of 1830, but the fact is given, in an appended statement on page 28, that applicants for admission were to meet the Standing Committee of the Board on the second Tuesday in January, 1831, at the residence of Colonel John Eichelberger in Newberry District; and the professor, Rev. J. G. Schwartz, gave notice that for the year 1831 he would receive such students as should have been approved by the Standing Committee of the Board. The first Monday in February of that year was named as the opening of the Seminary in his residence, which was the home of the said Colonel John Eichelberger. He also announced that he would give "a liberal course of classical study" to a limited number of young men. Hence, before the Theological Seminary and Classical Academy had a permanent location, its exercises were conducted in the Eichelberger home

*(See Minutes of 1829, pp. 8, 11.)
†(See Minutes of 1830, p. 13.)

near Bethlehem Church, Newberry County; and that home is still standing.

There Professor Schwartz died, August 26, 1831, to the great sorrow of the synod, and more especially of Rev. John Bachman, who had trained this young minister and who, better than anyone else, knew his ability and great worth. Naturally his distinguished preceptor mourned for him as a beloved son in the Lord. The funeral discourse delivered by Rev. John Bachman on September 11, 1831, is published in full in the minutes and covers twenty pages. It gives a sketch of the brilliant career of this young man and breathes the deep affection of his spiritual father.

GABLE END OF. EICHELBERGER HOME

At the convention of 1831 the necessary steps were taken for the location of the Theological Seminary and the Classical Academy; but final action was "deferred till the next meeting of the synod".

Then at the convention of 1832, after the most careful and conscientious consideration, Lexington village, S. C., was chosen as the location.

The synod then expressed the firm conviction that "our prayers have been answered and our efforts blessed; and now that we have succeeded by our own exertion, accompanied by the approving smiles of Heaven, in establishing an institution, which, we trust, will supply our Southern Zion with talented and faithful watchmen;—now, if ever, we feel that we have abundant cause for thankfulness to the Great Head of the Church, and the confident assurance that He will never leave and never forsake us."*† These prayers and hopes of the synod have been realized.

The location of the Seminary having been definitely settled, a most gratifying number of young men offered themselves as students for the ministry, and the following were accepted: Messrs. Frederick Harris, David Bernhard, William Berly, Levi Bedenbaugh, Elijah Hawkins, Samuel Bouknight, David Hungerpeler, and Henry Stoudenmeyer. To this number Jesse Bates was also added.

The first Board of Directors—ten in number—was constituted as follows: Revs. John Bachman, Godfrey Dreher, W. D. Strobel, S. A. Mealy, and C. F. Bergman; with Messrs. West Caughman, Henry Muller, Col. J. Eichelberger, Henry Horlbeck, and Major Jacob Swygert.‡ Rev. John Bachman was chairman, and Mr. Henry Muller was treasurer. Subsequently we find that Rev. John C. Hope was appointed secretary, but the record is not clear as to the person who first acted in this capacity.

The next step in this far-reaching movement was that of securing a professor of theology and a suitable person for the Classical Department of the institution. The synod was careful to state that, "Whereas the Teacher will be required to prepare young men in their Classical Studies for admission into the Theological Seminary, he be a man of piety, as well as possessed of approved classical attainments."

---

*(See Minutes of 1831, p. 15; of 1832, pp. 8, 9, 10, 11, 14 and 15.)

†The institution when so located was chartered in 1832 as "The Board of Directors of the Theological Seminary of the Evangelical Lutheran Synod of South Carolina and Georgia" (Statutes at Large, Vol. 8, p. 376).
   In 1851 the name of the institution was changed by act of the General Assembly to "The Classical and Theological Seminary of the Evangelical Lutheran Synod of South Carolina and Adjacent States". (Statutes at Large, Vol. 12, pp. 115, 116.)

‡(See Minutes of 1830, p. 14.)

At the session of 1833, held in Lexington village, at the place of the location of the Seminary, it was reported that Rev. E. L. Hazelius, D.D., of Hartwick, N. Y., had been elected professor of theology, and Rev. Washington Muller principal of the Classical Department.

REV. E. L. HAZELIUS, D.D.

As Rev. E. L. Hazelius, D.D., was present, he was at once made a member of the synod, and took an active part in the further proceedings of the body. The first Monday in January, 1834, was fixed as the opening day, and all necessary details were arranged for the prosecution of this work, so dear to the hearts of all our people in the Southern Lutheran Church, and from which such wide streams of light and holy influence have gone out into many parts of the American Lutheran Church.

The convention of 1834 was held in Ebenezer Church, Effingham County, Georgia, beginning November 15, at which the first annual report of the Board of Directors of the Theological Seminary was read.

The president of the synod in his address said: "Thus far the Theological Seminary has fully equalled our most sanguine expectations;" and he also reported that "The Preparatory Institute has fully equalled the expectations of its friends".

In the report of the Directors of the Seminary we learn that the institution opened on January 6, 1834, under favorable circumstances. On April 28 the first examination of the students was held, and proved highly satisfactory to the Board. On April 30, 1834, Rev. E. L. Hazelius, D.D., was inaugurated as first professor of theology; and nine young men has been duly matriculated and were pursuing their studies. Rev. George Haltiwanger and Rev. F. F. Harris were ordained at this convention of the synod.

At the convention of 1835, held in St. Nicholas' Church, Barnwell County, November 14-18, it was reported that the work of the Seminary was gratifying, and that already there had been an increase of ministers in "the extension of the borders of our Zion".

Messrs. Herman Aull and Robert Cloy were ordained to the office and work of the Gospel ministry; and Messrs. Jas. P. Ring, Edwin A. Bolles, David Bernhard and Levi Bedenbaugh received license to the same office and work.

At the Spring session of the Theological Seminary a Junior Class was formed, made up of six probationers: George Haltiwanger, Jr., Jacob Crim, George Harter, Stanmore Shepherd, H. E. Hartridge, and J. Boyd.

The synod also took action looking to securing the cooperation of the North Carolina Synod in the support and management of the Theological Seminary, which was consummated, and so reported at the convention of 1836.*

In the third annual report of the Board of Directors of the Seminary, 1836, we are again assured of the continued and useful operation of the institution, and that the first class of students which entered the Seminary had now been grad-

---

* (See Minutes, pp. 17, 18, 20 and 21.)

uated. These were Messrs. Frederick Harris, Edwin A. Bolles, Levi Bedenbaugh, David Bernhard, Henry Stoudenmeyer, William Berly, Philip A. Strobel and Elijah Hawkins.

This School of the Prophets had by this time gone beyond the experimental stage, had fully justified all the claims and efforts of its founders, and the stamp of Divine approval had been fixed upon it. From now on its prosperity is clearly marked and its usefulness established beyond question. The report of the Directors for 1837 informs us that twelve students, coming from several states, had been directly and indirectly connected with the Seminary that year.

It was found necessary to build a lecture room on the seminary grounds, since it was not desirable to have the Classical School and the Seminary holding recitations in the same building. The necessary action was taken to secure such addition to the institution, which object was accomplished.*

It will be of interest to state that while classical work was associated with the Theological Seminary from the beginning of its existence, "a permanent Classical School in connection with the Seminary" was not fully established until the synod of 1840, when plans were adopted for the consummation of this long cherished purpose.

Rev. C. B. Thummel, of Wadmalaw Island, was chosen as the head of said Classical School, which position he accepted and became a member of this synod at the convention of 1841. He was formerly a member of the Synod of New York. Subsequently he supplied the place of Dr. Hazelius in the Seminary from April to October, 1841, while the latter was on a visit to Germany.

At the close of 1841 a library of 1,837 books had been collected, and the Seminary was exerting a "salutary influence" upon the Church, and gave promise of greater achievements in the future.

At the convention of 1843, the president, Rev. J. C. Hope, reported that Dr. E. L. Hazelius had returned from Germany near the close of 1842, and had been greatly encour-

* (See Minutes of 1838, pp. 22, 23.)

aged on his visit by the missionary zeal of our brethren across the sea. A special resolution of thanks was adopted with reference to the able and satisfactory manner in which Rev. C. B. Thummel had presided over the institution in the absence of Dr. Hazelius, and the Board of Directors of the Theological Seminary expressed sincere pleasure at the safe return of Dr. Hazelius from his tour to Germany, and declared "its satisfaction and pleasure that his ability and faithfulness are not impaired by his advanced age". The entire confidence of the Board was thus put on record. In October, 1843, Rev. C. B. Thummel resigned and moved to Ohio.

But by the convention of 1846 the devout and consecrated Dr. Hazelius felt the need of an assistant in the prosecution of his arduous labors. This was left to the choice of Dr. Hazelius himself, and at the next convention of the synod, 1847, he reported that he had employed Rev. J. F. W. Leppard, who had "given satisfaction to all concerned"; but it was not until December, 1849, that another regular professor was elected in the person of Rev. Lewis Eichelberger, of Virginia.

In 1848 the first expressions of dissatisfaction were heard as to the present location of the Seminary, but at that time the synod did not share in that opinion, and declared at the convention of 1847 that in the nearly twenty years of its location at Lexington, it had prospered, that the number of our ministers had increased sevenfold, the congregations proportionately, and that little sickness, and no death had occurred. In fact, it was reported that scarcely a case of illness had come into the institution. Mention was also made, 1848, of a donation of $4,000 by Mr. Henry Muller, of Sandy Run. The Board reported (1849) that a "pious layman, Brother John Rauch", had been secured to take charge of the Academy to instruct the preparatory students.

Then at the convention of 1850 it was reported that Rev. Lewis Eichelberger, the assistant professor and principal in the Classical Department, had entered upon his duties on the twenty-second of September of that year. His resignation, however, is reported in November, 1850, so that his term of service at that time was of short duration. Subsequently Rev. William Berly was elected to this position, and on January, 1851, he entered upon his duties. In the report announcing his election the declining health and resignation of the venerable professor, Dr. E. L. Hazelius, are also stated, to the deep regret of the Board and the Church in the South.

Shadows were thus falling over this institution, which meant so much for the Church, and especially for the South Carolina Synod; and yet the sun was still shining above the clouds, and larger things were to come in answer to the earnest prayers of the Church.

When the convention of 1852 opened in St. Mark's Church, Edgefield County, November 12, it was reported that Dr. Hazelius, "though laboring under the weight of advancing age and increasing infirmities, had continued to conduct the Theological Department with his accustomed diligence and punctuality." Then, incidentally, the synodical record gives the information that Rev. Lewis Eichelberger had again been elected as professor of theology in the Seminary, and was present at the synod; and in the report of the Board of Directors it is said, "The Board regrets the necessity of accepting the resignation of our venerable professor, Rev. Dr. Hazelius, assures him of their continued affection and regard, and that such provision will be made for his future support as his long and faithful services so justly deserve."

Rev. Lewis Eichelberger entered upon his duties on the first Monday in November, 1852. For some time before this, Rev. William Berly had been carrying forward both departments of the institution in consequence of the failing health of Dr. Hazelius; therefore, the coming of Rev. Lewis Eichelberger to the institution was a real blessing.*

The president's report, November 11, 1853, gives the information that Rev. E. L. Hazelius, D.D., had gone to his heavenly reward, having died on the Lord's Day evening, February 20, 1853. For thirty-eight years he had served the Church in the capacity of professor of theology, twenty years

---

*(See Minutes of 1852, p. 227.)

at Lexington, and his whole life had been given in Christian service. In the period of his professorship in the Seminary Dr. Hazelius wrote three books whose publication was a valuable contribution to the scant Lutheran literature of the time in the English language. These books are valuable for reference to the present day. They are: Discipline, Articles of Faith and Synodical Constitution, As Adopted by the Evangelical Lutheran Synod of South Carolina and Adjacent States. 1841. A History of the Christian Church from the Earliest Ages to the Present Time, 1842 (to be published in four volumes, of which, however, only the first volume appeared). History of the American Lutheran Church from its Commencement in the Year of Our Lord 1685 to the Year 1842. 1846.

Dr. Hazelius died in his 76th year, full of good works, and his remains rest in Lexington, near the Seminary in which he had served so long and faithfully.*

At its convention in 1922 the synod directed that a tablet to the memory of Dr Hazelius be placed in the Seminary and appropriated $300 for the purpose.

The necessity of employing another teacher induced the Board of Directors of the Seminary to engage the services of Mr. Simeon E. Caughman, a well known educator, who rendered very satisfactory work in the institution.

It was evident, however, that a crisis had come in the life of this School of the Prophets and that important changes were inevitable. Already in 1848 the matter of removal had been agitated, and now in the convention of 1854 the president in his annual report announced the fact that the Board, at a meeting in June of that year, had taken notice of rumors of an intention to find another location.

Sooner than was expected that issue was clearly drawn; and in the Board's report to the synod the following preamble and resolutions were adopted:

"Inasmuch as our Institution at Lexington is evidently in a languishing condition, and owing, no doubt, in part at least, to local circumstances, which the future does not promise to obviate; therefore, be it

---

*(See Minutes of 1853, pp. 6, 67-70.)

1. RESOLVED, That, in the opinion of synod, there is a necessity
for its removal to a more eligible situation, and that the Directors be, and are hereby, instructed to take the necessary steps
to effect the removal to such place in South Carolina as may
promise a more eligible location.
2. RESOLVED, That the Directors be also instructed to obtain from
the Legislature of that State such amendments in the Charter,
as to constitute it a regular College, with the power of con-
ferring degrees.
3. RESOLVED, That the Institution, with its new Charter, shall be
called ....College of South Carolina."

The convention of the synod of November, 1855, was held
in Bethlehem Church, Newberry County, at which time it
was reported that the Board of Directors, on the twenty-sev-
enth of June, 1855, had appointed the necessary committee
to receive proposals for the location of the institution.

Proposals from Walhalla and Newberry were presented,
the question of removal was definitely settled, and Newberry
was chosen as the place of location.

The treasurer's report showed that the Fund of the Classical Academy and Theological Seminary had now reached
the sum of $23,386, which included cash and bonds, notes
and stocks.

The Board of Directors reported that Mr. M. Whittle had
been engaged in the English Department, and that Dr. Lewis
Eichelberger was assisting Prof. William Berly in the Classical Department.

Theological Seminary and Newberry College

We now reach one of the most important periods in the
history of the Classical and Theological institution of the
synod. The convention of 1856 was held in Mount Calvary
Church, Edgefield County, and to this convention of the synod
the Board of Directors reported that a suitable location had
been selected for the college site, the land purchased and
titles secured. Two agents had been employed to collect additional funds—Col. John R. Leavell and Rev. T. S. Boinest,
the latter being subsequently elected general agent for the
college. Architectural plans, submitted by a Mr. Walker
of Columbia, had been adopted, provision made to secure

an amended charter, and the necessary action was taken to safeguard the funds given for special purposes, that none should be paid out for any purpose other "than that for which it was originally contributed".

The charter was presented to synod and by resolution provided that eighteen names should make up the Board of Trustees, twelve to be members of our Church, and six to be citizens of the town of Newberry and vicinity. This Board was thus constituted:

Revs. J. Bachman, E. B. Hort, N. Aldrich, T. S. Boinest, J. P. Margart and J. H. Bailey. Messrs. Dr. G. Muller, W. K. Bachman, Matthias Barre, Dr. P. Todd, J. K. Schumpert, J. P. Aull, Henry Summer, N. A. Hunter, Gen. A. C. Garlington, Dr. O. B. Mayer, Col. S. Fair, and Maj. John P. Kinard.

These trustees were constituted the building committee and empowered to appoint such sub-committees from their number as they might deem best. Ten members of the Board constituted a quorum at all meetings.

The Board was authorized to proceed in the erection of of the building, provided the cost, including the land, should not exceed $21,000, and that the synod should not be made liable for any debt in the progress of the work.

The charter adopted provided that the Board of Trustees be elected annually at the meetings and by the members of the synod.

It was resolved at the convention of 1855 that the institution be known and designated as "Luther College and Theological Seminary", but at the convention of 1856 this was reconsidered and the name Newberry College adopted.*

We now reach the transition period in the history of this dual institution—a time of peculiar and conflicting emotions. A tree which had taken deep root in dear old Lexington was being pulled up to be transplanted in another soil. Many hearts were sad, while others rejoiced; but the loyal devotion of our people was shown in their continued support of the institution and in the oneness of their desire to build up the Church of God and advance His cause.

---

*(See Minutes of 1855, pp. 24-30, and Convention of 1856, pp. 22, 23, 26 and 27.)

Soon after the meeting of the synod in 1856 a contract was let for the erection of the college building, to cost $18,000, Osborne Wells and Wallace A. Cline being the contractors.

The cornerstone was laid July 15, 1856, with addresses by Rev. J. J. Brantley, Baptist pastor at Newberry, Dr. John Bachman, Maj. Henry Summer and Gen. A. C. Garlington. At the convention of October 29, 1857, it was reported that the walls of the first story were nearly completed, and that the building was to be finished by October, 1858.

By July, 1858, one wing of the college building was sufficiently completed to admit of its being occupied, and accordingly the Board decided to open the Preparatory Department on the first Monday of October. Rev. M. Whittle, a graduate of Roanoke College, was elected to the principalship of that Department, and the prospects were bright. The term opened with over fifty students; $28,000 had been raised by the sale of scholarships, and by donations.

After the convention of synod in 1857, Rev. Lewis Eichelberger, D.D., resigned his professorship in the Theological Department, which resignation took effect July, 1858. The Board elected Rev. William Berly temporarily to fill this position. He entered upon his duties in September, and reported at the convention of October 30, 1858, that he had discharged the twofold duties of the office—teaching both theology and the classics.

The report of the trustees closes with the information that Rev. Theophilus Stork, D.D., had been elected president, and his reply was looked forward to with the hope that he would accept. The report also stated that the necessary arrangements would be made for the removal of the institution to Newberry.

Accordingly, it was reported to the synod in 1859 that the College and Seminary had opened in the large and substantial new building at Newberry, and that Dr. Theophilus Stork, the president of the College, and Rev. J. A. Brown, D.D., professor of theology, were present. These brethren were elected members of the synod.

Then, at 2 o'clock in the afternoon, October 29, 1859, the synod proceeded in a body to the college, where Rev. Theophilus Stork, D.D., and Prof. Robert Garlington delivered their inaugural addresses before a large assembly. On the next day, October 30, at 11 o'clock, Rev. J. A. Brown, D.D., was inaugurated professor of theology, he having entered upon the duties of his office in February, 1859.

At the close of the synod in 1859, about 135 students had been enrolled, and the following assistant teachers had been added to the college faculty: Messrs. M. Whittle, J. A. Sligh, J. D. Boozer and Mr. Hard. Before the end of the term, however, Mr. Hard resigned, and Mr. A. P. Pifer was elected as the head of the Preparatory Department.

Thus it will be seen that the year 1859 closed with a most encouraging outlook for the future of the College and Seminary.

When the synod met on October 25, 1860, the increasing prosperity of the institution was hailed with special pleasure and devout gratitude; but, unexpectedly, Rev. T. Stork, D.D., had resigned the presidency because of ill health, and it became necessary to make some changes in the teaching force in the College. Rev. J. H. Bailey was elected principal of the Preparatory Department, Rev. C. F. Bansemer, by arrangement of Dr. Stork, had had charge of Latin and Greek, but subsequently Rev. J. J. Brantley, D.D., Baptist pastor at Newberry, was elected to this position. Rev. Dr. J. A. Brown had also been asked to act as president of the College during the unexpired term of Dr. Theophilus Stork's incumbency. Prof. A. P. Pifer was elected principal of the Classical Department and adjunct professor of the Latin language, Rev. M. Whittle having resigned.

Other vacancies occurred, and Rev. James M. Schreckhise was made professor of Latin and Greek; he also taught in the Primary Department.

When the convention of 1859-1860 began, the brightest hues colored the horizon; one hundred and fifty students were in attendance; the teaching force was characterized by a commendable zeal and all hearts throbbed with buoyant

"THE OLD PATH," NEWBERRY COLLEGE

hope. The dream of years was being realized, and the seed-time promised an abundant harvest.

But very soon a storm cloud rose in the distance; war was borne on the breeze; cannon boomed over the hills; students marched to the beat of martial airs; political elements of generations were forming a volcano from whose fiery crater only death could come; and, ere long, the dreams and toils of our fathers seemed to lie in ruins.

The synod did not meet until January 16, 1862. At this convention the Board reported that on the fifteenth of February, 1861, the college was placed under the supervision of Prof. Robert Garlington, Rev. J. A. Brown, D.D., having resigned and left the state. Then on the fifth of February Rev. Josiah P. Smeltzer, of Salem, Va., was elected president, pro tem., and professor of theology in the Theological Seminary. He accepted and entered upon the duties of his dual position April 8, 1861. At the Board's June meeting, 1861, Rev. Webster Eichelberger was elected adjunct professor of Languages and principal of the Preparatory Department, several professors having joined the army; but he was not able to enter upon the discharge of his duties until October, 1862, having been in actual war service.

For lack of students in the Theological Department that arm of the service was suspended, to be resumed in September, 1861, but even then no students of divinity presented themselves. Nor was that Department again fully opened until October, 1866, only one student being mentioned in the intervening years between 1861 and 1865.*

At the meeting of synod in October, 1863, the noteworthy fact is mentioned that the secretary of the Board, Henry Summer, Esq., heard lessons in Latin, History, Composition and Rhetoric "each afternoon of the teaching days, from the twenty-third or twenty-fourth of March to the close of the session in June" of that year.

The real crisis in the life of the College extended from 1863 to 1865, culminating in the occupancy of the building by Federal soldiers under Brigadier General Van Wyck in

---

*(See Minutes of 1863, p. 31.)

July, 1865, which use and abuse of the college finally led to the ruin of the building. When the synod met in October, 1864, the suspension of the exercises of the institution seemed inevitable, for there were then only thirty students in the College,—four in the College proper, seven in the Preparatory Department, and nineteen in the Primary Departments. Such had been the havoc wrought by the War Between the States.

Naturally and inevitably there followed what the president in his annual report, October, 1865, styled a "partial suspension of the college at Newberry"; and the same was true of the Theological Department, for he says, "Not one escaped." They had either fallen in battle or died from disease.*

By special resolution the Board of Trustees was instructed to meet on the first Wednesday in November to open the College and appoint professors. Under this action, Rev. John Bachman, D.D., moved the reelection of the same Board then in office, which was adopted.

At the meeting of the synod, October, 1866, the Board reported that "a nucleus of a school" had been continued under the supervision and instruction of Rev. J. P. Smeltzer, D.D.; and here we find a verification of the old truth that great crises bring out great heroes. This sainted man of God stood by the College in this darkest hour of its existence, taught almost without pay, and conducted a bakery in his home, working with his own hands, that he might support his family and maintain the institution until the dawning of a brighter day.

At that meeting of the synod the necessary legal steps were taken to recover damages for the injury done to the building by Federal soldiers; this end was not attained, however, until 1898, when the Government at Washington paid over to the college authorities $15,000. The net amount received, after paying contingent fees, attorney's fees, etc., was $10,-500. Of this amount $500 was spent in repairs on Smeltzer Hall and $10,000 was constituted a memorial to Rev. Dr. G. W. Holland, known as the Holland Memorial Fund.

---

*(See Minutes of 1865, p. 48.)

CAMPUS, NEWBERRY COLLEGE

The College opened on the first Monday in October, 1866, under Rev. Prof. J. P. Smeltzer, D.D., Prof. A. P. Pifer and Prof. Robert Garlington. There were twenty-three students in the College and two in the Theological Department—H. S. Wingard and S. T. Hallman.

REV. J. P. SMELTZER, D.D.

But the clouds had not yet passed. There was a debt of $19,180.65 hanging over the College, and the walls of the building were slowly, but surely, crumbling. Finally the college property was surrendered. Its creditors subsequently gave up their claims, and the debt was thus canceled. The building, however, had become unsafe, and so, after the convention of 1867-1868, the College found a home in Walhalla, where it lived and prospered. At the opening of the session in 1877 the College came back to Newberry, whose people received it with warm hearts and open hands, having erected a splendid building for its permanent occupancy.

There it now lives—the pride and glory of our Church in South Carolina.

In 1867 the College and the Theological Seminary, in a sense, began to part company as a dual institution. At the convention of 1867 the president informed the synod that, by her action, the General Synod in the South had taken over the Seminary; but that our synodical Seminary Fund does not cease to be our property, and her alumni are not to be deprived of their Alma Mater. This action was sustained by a resolution adopted by the General Synod in May, 1867. Rev. Prof. J. P. Smeltzer was elected professor of theology, and Rev. A. R. Rude was elected as an additional professor of theology.

The Seminary in its changed relation continued with Newberry College through the scholastic year, which closed June, 1868, and after that was in charge of Rev. A. R. Rude, D.D., for a short while in Columbia. Subsequently it was removed to Salem, Va.

There is what may be termed "a missing link" in the life of the Theological Seminary. In 1867 the South Carolina Synod made overtures to the General Synod in the South to take over this School of the Prophets and locate it as seemed best to that body. The desired action was taken, and a Board was elected from all the synods constituting the General Synod; but when the General Synod met in Charleston, S. C., April, 1884, the Seminary was discontinued by a vote of twelve against eleven dissenting votes.*

The South Carolina Synod then held a called meeting May 27, 1884, and took over the Seminary, connected it with Newberry College, and put it under the faculty of the College, Mr. C. W. Dingle, of Charleston, being then treasurer of our Seminary Fund.

The College Board, under the action of synod, elected Rev. A. C. Voigt professor of Modern Languages in the College. He was also elected professor of theology in the Seminary and served in this dual capacity from 1885 to 1889. Rev. Mr. Voigt removed to Newberry from Mt. Holly, N. J., where

---

*(See Gen. Synod Minutes of 1884, pp. 23, 35, 38, 39.)

LUTHERAN THEOLOGICAL SOUTHERN SEMINARY

he was serving a pastorate. Resigning his professorship in
1889 he became professor in and acting president of Thiel
College, Greenville, Pa. He returned to the Seminary of
the synod at Newberry in 1891 and served as professor until 1898, when he resigned to become pastor of St. Paul's
Church, Wilmington, N. C. In 1903 he was recalled by the
Board of the Seminary, now the institution of the United
Synod in the South, as Professor and Dean, and has continued in that position to the present time. Dr. Voigt has proved
himself worthy of all the honors conferred upon him. His
profound scholarship and ecclesiastical statesmanship are
universally recognized.

When the General Synod in the South abandoned the Seminary they retained control of their Seminary Fund. The
South Carolina Synod also had its Seminary Fund, which
can never be diverted from the original purpose of its donors,
the interest, however, being available for theological education. This fund, of which Dr. Geo. Y. Hunter is treasurer,
now amounts to upwards of $13,000, and is still held and
administered by the South Carolina Synod.

In the formation of the United Synod in the South in
1886, that body named as one of its objects "Theological
Seminaries"; and so, in due time, that action developed into
the establishment of its Theological Seminary. Under pro-
visional arrangements, it opened in Newberry College, the
professors of that institution giving the needed instruction.

Thus the South Carolina Synod's Theological Seminary
again became the Seminary of the General Body, and the
"missing link" was restored.

The work of the Seminary at Salem, Va., was carried on
for a decade with more or less success. Discouragement
caused its discontinuance by the General Synod in 1884.
But the South Carolina Synod resumed the work in 1886, in
connection with Newberry College, as has been said.

This year was marked by the founding of the United Synod
of the Evangelical Lutheran Church in the South, and this
body promptly took into consideration the establishment of
a central theological seminary, a plan which was not realized until 1898, when, by the generosity of the Lutherans

PROFESSORS' HOUSES, SOUTHERN SEMINARY

at Charleston, a home was given to the institution at Mt. Pleasant, S. C., and an endowment fund of $30,000 was raised throughout the United Synod. Meanwhile the theological school of the South Carolina Synod at Newberry had been adopted by the United Synod in 1892. The location at Mt. Pleasant proved unsatisfactory, and the liberal offer of a site of six acres and a large cash donation drew the institution to the city of Columbia. A granite building was erected in 1911, at a cost of more than $50,000. The cornerstone was laid on January 10, and the building was dedicated on October 11, 1911.

In 1918 the United Synod merged with other bodies to form the United Lutheran Church in America, and transferred the institution to its component synods, asking them to elect trustees. The new Board of Trustees met and organized in Columbia in January, 1919. In 1921 a charter was secured and the institution was incorporated.

There are 153 living alumni of the Seminary, graduating between the year 1866 and 1923, inclusive. Of these, 133 are serving pastorates in the Southern Church. Five are foreign missionaries, three serving in Japan, one in India and one in Africa. The Faculty at present consists of Rev. Andrew G. Voigt, D.D., LL.D., Dean; Rev. Charles K. Bell, D.D., Rev. John W. Horine, D.D., Rev. Walton H. Greever. D.D. Rev. Charles A. Freed, D.D., is president of the Board of Trustees. The synod's representatives on the Board of Trustees are Revs. M. O. J. Kreps, D.D., C. A. Freed, D.D., and Messrs. A. H. Kohn, W. G. Allworden and C. M. Efird, Esq.

We devote so much of our space to the College and Theological Seminary because of their far-reaching influence and the large part they have played in the building up of the Church and in creating higher ideals of life and duty.

After full sixteen years of ardent devotion to the College and of self-sacrificing toil, Rev. J. P. Smeltzer, D.D., was succeeded by Rev. G. W. Holland, D.D., whose noble life was a benediction to thousands, an unceasing power for good in the College and in the Church at large. For twenty-one years he was connected with the College, seventeen years as its efficient and successful president, from 1878 to his death in 1895, and his dying prayer, "God bless Newberry College," has been and ever will be abundantly answered.

The mind of the synod then rested upon the Hon. George B. Cromer, an able lawyer of the Newberry bar. He was unanimously tendered this responsible position, October, 1895, and, conscientious Christian that he is, he believed this call to be one from the Church, left his chosen profes-

REV. GEO. W. HOLLAND, D.D.

sion, and entered upon the presidency of the College. He performed the duties of this office with marked ability and success for about seven years, when he resigned, to the deep regret of the synod. Because of his scholarship and marked ability, the degree of LL.D. was conferred upon him by Wittenberg College and by Muhlenberg College.

Rev. James A. B. Scherer, Ph.D., was elected his successor, and during his term of service materially increased the endowment of the College from the year 1904 to 1908, when

HOLLAND HALL, NEWBERRY COLLEGE

he accepted a position in another field of labor. It was through his influence that Mr. Andrew Carnegie gave $10,000 to the College, and Dr. D. K. Pearson $25,000, which, together with other gifts from many friends, put the College in better financial condition than ever before in its history.

At a special meeting of the Board of Trustees, held in Columbia in 1908, Rev. J. Henry Harms, D.D., an alumnus of the College, was elected to the presidency of the institution, which he administered successfully and efficiently for ten years, resigning May 9, 1918. His connection with the College was efficient and highly profitable. He resigned that he might return to pastoral work.

At once the mind of the Board and of the Synod turned to another of our own men, one who had abundantly shown his loyalty to the institution and his ability as one of its professors. That man is Professor S. J. Derrick, who was elected president June 3, 1918, and has proved himself to be a worthy successor of the strong men who preceded him. Under his management and control of the institution the College is steadily growing in service and power of influence, and a very bright future lies before it. He has been honored by Lenoir College with the degree of LL.D., which he worthily bears.

In summing up the history of Newberry College it is only just to say that no college in the South can show a combined force of abler and better men than those who have taught in its classic halls during the sixty-eight years of its existence. Their labors and influence will live down to the end of time. From their instruction have gone out over 759 graduates, and hundreds of others, who took special courses. These have done honor to all callings and professions, and have materially aided in making this a better world in which to live.

With all the trials incident to its life it has moved slowly upward financially, and now has an endowment of $175,000 and a property value of $150,000,—a grand total of $325,000, with the facilities for thorough collegiate training. With 11,000 volumes in its library, and other sources of information at hand, no fears need be entertained as to

NEW DORMITORY, NEWBERRY COLLEGE

the training which young men may receive in Newberry College. True to the Word of God, thoroughly sound in a pure, scriptural faith, and standing for the highest, noblest and best in life, we can in all conscience, say, "God bless Newberry College."

Summerland College

The establishment of a college for women by the Lutherans of South Carolina had its origin in the Joint Conference composed of the South Carolina Conference of the Tennessee Synod and the Central Conference of the South Carolina Synod. At a meeting of that body, held at Bethel Church, Lexington County, April 3, 1909, a committee was appointed "to take into consideration the advisability and feasibility of the establishment of a female college within our state".

Two years later, April 29, 1911, the same body in session at St. Michael's Church, only a few miles from the former place of meeting, endorsed a movement for the establishment of such a school, and appointed a committee to take up the matter in conjunction with a committee from the South Carolina Synod and from the Tennessee Synod. The Conference Committee was composed of Dr. E. J. Etheredge, Rev. C. P. Boozer, Rev. J. A. Cromer, and Hon. C. M. Efird. The South Carolina Synod appointed as its representative Rev. S. P. Koon; Rev. B. D. Wessinger was the representative from the Tennessee Synod.

The committee organized in Columbia, December, 1911, and announced itself ready to receive bids for the location of the proposed school. Various meetings were held from time to time, and it was unanimously decided on the first ballot to recommend the Summerland Inn property, which was proffered by the citizens of Batesburg and Leesville.

The next meeting of Conference was held at Bethlehem Church, Irmo. Here the recommendation of the committee was sustained, with a resolution to offer said Summerland Inn property to the South Carolina Synod for the establishment of a college for women. A called meeting of synod was held at Summerland May 28, 1912, when the property was accepted by the synod for the purpose named. At this meet-

MITCHELL HALL, SUMMERLAND COLLEGE

ing six members of the Board of Trustees were elected, as
follows: Rev. S. C. Ballentine, Rev. C. P. Boozer, Rev. S.
P. Koon, Dr. E. J. Etheredge, Dr. J. I. Bedenbaugh, Mr. H.
S. Black.

As a result of much faithful labor and in answer to many
earnest prayers, Summerland College was auspiciously
opened October 1, 1912, for the higher education of the
daughters of our beloved Church.

The old dormitory is a large building equipped with all
modern conveniences, including electric lights, steam heat,
hot and cold water, sewerage, and special fire protection.
Every room is an outside room, insuring good light and ven-
tilation. This building will be remodeled in the near future,
and will be used as an administration building.

The recitation hall is a substantial brick building within
fifty feet of the dormitory, and is well suited for the work.
The class rooms are large, airy and well lighted.

In November, 1919, Summerland College united with
Newberry College in an effort to raise a three-hundred-thou-
sand-dollar educational fund. Their object was ably supported by the Lutheran Synod of South Carolina, to which
they belong, and as a result their campaign met with the
greatest success.

In October, 1920, at a meeting of the Board of Trustees
of Summerland College, a building committee was appointed,
which secured the services of Scroggs & Ewing, architects
of Augusta, Ga. On August 19, 1921, the plans of these
architects were submitted to the Board of Trustees and
adopted. On the same day the contract was let for the erection of a new dormitory to the General Building Company
of Boston, Massachusetts, for the sum of $70,000. On
August 31, 1921, ground was broken for this new building,
which was completed April 20, 1922.

This brick building, modeled upon the most modern architectural plans, is one of the finest dormitories in the state.
Only the best quality of material has been used in the construction, and nothing has been spared for the safety and
convenience of the students. Among the particularly note-

MITCHELL HALL. FRONT VIEW OF SUMMERLAND COLLEGE MONROE HALL

worthy features may be mentioned: the protection against fire; the fresh air and sunlight in every room, facing, as it does, the campus; the excellent plumbing facilities, affording one bath room and shower to every four students, and a lavatory in every room; the two closets in every room, assuring ample room for clothing and trunks; and the separate system for drinking water with its refrigerator in the basement. To these may be added the faculty suites, with their private baths, and the spacious parlors on each floor. This building was furnished and in readiness for occupancy at the opening of the session, September 14, 1922.

Rev. S. P. Koon served as president during the first session, 1912 and 1913. Rev. P. E. Monroe, D.D., served as president 1913 to 1924. Upon the resignation of Rev. P. E. Monroe, D.D., at the close of the session (May, 1924), Rev. F. Grover Morgan, of Hickory, N. C., was elected president. He accepted and prepared to enter upon his duties September 1, 1924.

In the twelve years of Summerland College's existence, it has never taken a backward step in attendance or financial income. Every year has been a little better than the preceding one. The College now has a select library of three thousand volumes, which it hopes to increase to five thousand by the opening session of 1924. The College has a well equipped laboratory, music department, equipped largely with Stieff pianos.

In its financial management the College has never made a current expense debt to be carried over from one year to the next.

The faculty at the 1923-1924 session is composed of the following:

Rev. P. E. Monroe, D.D., President and Teacher of Bible and Ethics; Mrs. P. E. Monroe, Matron; Mrs. Mattie Kneece, Mathematics and Pedagogy; Miss A. R. Marriotte, Science and German; Miss Greta Cunningham, English and Latin; Miss Mary Bosse, French and Assistant in English; Miss Irene Palmer, History; Miss Margaret Benner, Piano and Voice; Miss Blanche Fincke, Piano; Miss Bessie Wilt, Expression; Mrs. W. D. Wright, Assistant Matron.

The student body is distributed over five states, viz., Georgia, Mississippi, North Carolina, Virginia, South Carolina.

Views of Summerland

Chapter V

THE PUBLICATION CAUSE

THE publication cause of the Southern Church, as represented in its varied activities, has been associated almost invariably with the work of the South Carolina Synod. Here on its territory was established the first weekly periodical after the district synods in the South became a separate organization due to the exigencies of the Confederate War. This intimate relation was continued throughout the many vicissitudes and changes which imperiled the existence of the church paper until the development in its wider sphere of usefulness in the decade immediately preceding the merging of the publication cause, together with all the other interests of the United Synod, into a central management under the fostering care of the United Lutheran Church in America.

Nearly a year elapsed after the severance of the relations with the General Synod in 1861 before any action was taken looking toward the establishment of a weekly church periodical in the South. The South Carolina Synod took the initial step in this respect when at its convention held at St. Paul's Church, Pomaria, in January, 1862, a publication committee, charged with the oversight of *The Southern Lutheran*, was appointed. The paper was established with its publication office in Charleston, with Rev. A. R. Rude as editor with his office in Columbia. Rev. W. S. Bowman of Charleston was associated with Dr. Rude as editor for a time. One of the most useful laymen in the Southern Church, Mr. Robert G. Chisolm of Charleston, assumed the entire financial responsibility for the publication of *The Southern Lutheran* at its inauguration and his interest in the cause never lagged but was maintained until the day of his death in 1907. He was among the first to make a contribution to the publication cause after it was established officially in Columbia in 1908, and his gift was most liberal and cordial.

The General Synod of the Confederate States (the name of the general body as it was organized at Concord, N. C., in 1863) assumed no financial responsibility in the publi-

cation of the new church paper, but in the same year gave its
hearty endorsement to the enterprise. It is a notable fact
that although more than a century had elapsed since the organization of the first Lutheran synod in America, *The Southern Lutheran* was the second English Lutheran Church paper
which was established on this continent. Prior to the inter-
ruption of relations with the General Synod of the Evangelical Lutheran Church in the United States, *The Lutheran
Observer*, as the first English Lutheran paper in this country,
having been established in 1831, served the congregations as
their medium of intelligence.

The Southern Lutheran continued its existence throughout
the period of the war, probably until 1866. It frequently
appeared in half-sheet form of two pages and sometimes an
issue was missed entirely on account of the inability to secure
paper on which to print it, such being the common experience
of all publications in the South during the period of 1862-65.
During the interval between this period and the establishment of *The Lutheran Visitor*, the Church in the South de-
pended as a medium of information to a large extent upon
The Evangelical Lutheran, of which Rev. Nicholas Aldrich
had begun publication in 1866 in Charlotte, N. C. However, on account of some dissatisfaction with the management
of this paper, it did not receive an endorsement as an official
organ by the Southern General Synod (then known as the
General Synod of the Evangelical Lutheran Church in North
America), and this condition of affairs created a demand for
a church paper which the synod could recommend to its congregations.

The publication of such a church paper was one of the important questions which came before the Southern General
Synod when it met at Newberry, May 21-26, 1868. The
synod after thoroughly discussing the matter decided to give
its endorsement to such an enterprise. A monthly publication, under the name of *The Lutheran Visitor*, had been conducted by Rev. J. I. Miller, D.D., at Staunton, Va., since
1866, and it was decided to adopt, in part, this title as the
name of the new weekly church paper. It appeared in September following, under the name *The Lutheran and Visitor*.

Subsequently the connecting "and" was dropped and the paper continued as *The Lutheran Visitor* until September, 1904.

In the establishment of the paper at Columbia the General Synod assumed no pecuniary responsibility, it being stipulated that the editor, Rev. A. R. Rude, with whom Rev. J. I. Miller was associated in an editorial capacity, should publish the paper "at his own risk". However, the General Synod commended the paper to all its constituents and it was finally called, "The church organ, *The Lutheran Visitor.*" At the convention of 1873 the General Synod said that "although not directly the organ of the General Synod, yet as the paper is our recognized medium of church intelligence, it has claims upon us as such", it being acknowledged that *The Visitor* was a true exponent of the doctrines as represented by the synod.

At the convention of 1874, Rev. A. R. Rude offered to transfer unreservedly the paper with all its assets and liabilities to the General Synod. This offer was accepted and from No. 33 of the volume of 1874-75 the synod published the paper. Rev. T. W. Dosh, D.D., pastor of St. John's Church, Charleston, Rev. Jacob Hawkins of Orangeburg, and Prof. E. J. Dreher, Lexington (professor at Newberry College) composed the editorial staff.

In 1876 Rev. T. W. Dosh was continued as editor and Rev. Jacob Hawkins was appointed associate editor, the latter having at that time assumed charge as pastor of St. Michael's and St. Andrew's churches, Lexington County. The editors were charged not to make any transfer of the editorial management without the consent of the General Synod. Rev. J. H. Honour of Charleston, who had been business manager for a number of years, finally resigned, the synod expressing its earnest regret at being deprived of the excellent qualifications for the position which he had thus relinquished.

When the General Synod met at Newberry in May, 1878, the interests of the paper received earnest consideration with the view of increasing its efficiency to as large a degree as possible in its service to the Church. The result was that Rev. Jacob Hawkins was appointed editor-in-chief, Dr. Rude having asked the synod to relieve him of the editorship. It was decided that the paper should be issued from Columbia as the place of publication. The paper had never been issued from its own printing plant and prior to this time (1876-78) it had been printed at Salisbury, N. C. However, Dr. Hawkins made favorable arrangement with W. J. Duffie, of Columbia, the publisher of the Book of Worship, by which the latter assumed full financial responsibility, including the payment of a moderate, yet satisfactory editorial salary, the General Synod having again provided in the conduct of the paper that it would "assume no financial responsibility".

At the convention of the General Synod at Richmond, Va., in May, 1880, Dr. Hawkins reported that he had made arrangements with Mr. J. J. Quantz, of Salisbury, N. C., a former publisher of *The Lutheran Visitor*, and Mr. W. P. Houseal, of Newberry, S. C., hereafter to have the paper published at Prosperity, S. C. These plans were approved by the synod and Dr. Hawkins was made permanent editor. This arrangement had materialized upon the earnest desire of the patrons of the paper that better service in its publication should be inaugurated. The church news was especially hampered under the plan by which the paper had been heretofore issued, with the editorial office twelve miles from Columbia (the publication office), which was the nearest post-office, and the printing office at least one hundred miles distant at Due West, where the paper was issued from the office of the *Associated Reformed Presbyterian* on account of an advantage secured in the cost of printing by using approximately two pages of its matter each week.

In May, 1880, having been established for the first time in its existence in its own printing office at Prosperity, the paper was continued there until the spring of 1881 when Dr. Hawkins found that it required too much of his time in connection with his work as pastor of Grace Church, to give the paper the necessary business oversight. Negotiations with Mr. W. P. Houseal (who had severed cordial relations with the office September 1, 1880, on account of business reasons) to take charge of the paper, removing the office to Newberry, were concluded in March of that year, and the paper began publication again accordingly at Newberry April 21, 1881. The subscription list at that time was 1,080, which was increased to 3,750 while under the management of Mr. Houseal.

The General Synod at its convention in 1882 sanctioned the appointment of Rev. F. W. E. Peschau, D.D., pastor of St. Paul's Church, Wilmington, N. C., as associate editor. It was again mentioned at the convention in 1884 that Dr. Hawkins was sole editor and that "the office had been sold (January 1, 1882) to Mr. W. P. Houseal, the present publisher, he having added about $1,000 worth of material, the whole office costing him more than $2,000". During the period from April to December, 1881, the paper was printed on the slow and cumbersome Washington hand press, capacity of 200 copies an hour, in the office of the *Newberry News* (it was also using the same kind of slow press), the same process that had been employed in the office at Prosperity. Decided improvement was effected January 1, 1882, when the publisher made an arrangement with his friend and former employer, the late Thomas F. Greneker, whereby the use of a power press was secured. In order to take advantage of this better arrangement it was necessary to carry the type "forms" up and down a narrow stairway twice a week and transport them on a wheelbarrow a distance of two blocks to Mr. Greneker's printing office. After a year of such extremely arduous work, *The Visitor* was removed to another office and was printed on a new power press in connection with the *Newberry Observer*.

The formation of the United Synod in 1886 made a condition, as other papers were being published in its territory, by which no one of them could be recognized as the official organ. This left *The Lutheran Visitor* solely as an individual enterprise in the control of Dr. Hawkins as permanent editor and Mr. W. P. Houseal as owner. It was under these circumstances that Rev. S. T. Hallman, D.D., was appointed associate editor by Dr. Hawkins, with the concurrence of Mr. Houseal. Dr. Hallman had been a regular contributor to the paper during eight years previously and upon the death of Dr. Hawkins in July, 1895, he became editor-in-chief.

Until relinquishing entirely editorial connection with the paper in 1905, Dr. Hallman had served the publication cause continuously during a period which embraced thirty-four years.

The editorial staff in 1887 embraced also Rev. A. B. McMackin, pastor of Luther Chapel congregation, Newberry. Rev. A. G. Voigt was also a member of the staff for a year or more at a period beginning about 1892.

A stock company was formed in 1888, with a paid up capital of $1,500, under the name of *The Lutheran Visitor Company*, composed of Rev. Jacob Hawkins, Rev. W. C. Schaeffer, and Messrs. E. H. Aull and W. P. Houseal, to publish the paper in the office of the *Newberry Herald and News*, the ownership of which Aull & Houseal acquired as partners in March, 1887. Dr. Hawkins withdrew within two years, Mr. Aull in December, 1894, and the company was continued by the remaining members, Dr. Schaeffer and Mr. Houseal, the stock of the former retiring when the paper was removed to Columbia in 1904.

In December, 1903, a proposition was accepted from Rev. W. H. Greever and Rev. C. A. Freed, pastors of St. Paul's and Ebenezer congregations, respectively, to remove the paper to Columbia, it being provided that they secure thereby a financial interest in the enterprise to serve the Church with the purpose of making the paper more acceptable in issuing it in the best possible mechanical form.

This new arrangement was accomplished and *The Lutheran Visitor* made its appearance in improved form in Columbia under the date of January 7, 1904, with Rev. S. T. Hallman, D.D., as senior editor; Rev. W. H. Greever and C. A. Freed as associate editors, and Mr. Houseal as managing editor.

June 15, 1904, the Lutheran Visitor Company was dissolved, being succeeded by the United Synod Publishing Company, and it submitted a proposition to the United Synod at its convention at New Market, Va., through the committee on Consolidation of Church Papers, which had been appointed at the convention at Staunton, Va., in September, 1895, for the purchase of *The Lutheran Visitor* and *Our Church Paper* (the latter established at New Market, Va., in 1873, in the

interests of the Tennessee Synod, by Henkel & Company),
the editorial staff and management of the paper to be constituted as follows: Editor-in-chief, Rev. W. H. Greever,
D.D.; contributing editors, Revs. S. T. Hallman, D.D., and
C. A. Freed; managing editor, Mr. W. P. Houseal; business
manager, Rev. Mr. Freed; assistant business manager, Mr.
Houseal.

The proposition of the United Synod Publishing Company
to effect the consolidation of the two church papers was accepted by the United Synod, which forthwith appointed a
publishing committee, charged with this duty and the oversight of the publication cause, the committee being constituted as follows: Rev. W. L. Seabrook, Rev. R. C. Holland,
D.D., Dr. George B. Cromer, Rev. J. W. Horine, D.D., and
Hon. C. M. Efird, all members (including the paper's staff)
of the South Carolina Synod except Mr. Efird, who was a
member of the South Carolina Conference of the Tennessee
Synod.

The Publishing Committee met July 30, while the United
Synod was yet in session in New Market, and decided, in
consultation with the managers of *The Lutheran Visitor* and
Our Church Paper, that the proposed consolidation should be
effected September 1, 1904, and that the name of the new
paper should be the *Lutheran Church Visitor*, a combination
of the names of the two existing papers.

In the formation of the United Synod Publishing Company, it was also contemplated that the company should have
charge of the publication of the new hymnal which had been
issued with the Common Service that year. The publication of the Common Service had been in charge of the
Lutheran Board of Publication, which was organized at Newberry in May, 1898, during the convention of the United
Synod, with Mr. E. H. Aull, as superintendent. It was the
pioneer organization of its kind in the Southern Church and
performed valuable service. However, it readily transferred
its assets to the United Synod Publishing Company, including
The Southern Lutheran, and ceased existence as soon as its
affairs could be arranged satisfactorily.

When the United Synod met at Dallas, N. C., July 10-15, 1906, the publishing committee reported that the consolidation of the church papers (*The Lutheran Visitor* and *Our Church Paper*) had been accomplished under the name of the *Lutheran Church Visitor*. The synod accepted unanimously the offer of the United Synod Publishing Company to transfer the *Visitor*, *Tidings* and all other possessions and interests of the company to the United Synod for direct ownership and control at the first cost of the consolidation, in the amount of $3,950, the synod assuming the liabilities of the company and becoming the beneficiary of the assets, which were reported as being $750. A large part of the consolidation had already been secured and the committee was authorized to proceed in raising the remainder, together with $1,500 additional, in order to provide an amount necessary for the support of the paper during the first year under the management of the United Synod. It is significant that no similar action providing financially for the maintenance of the official church paper had ever been authorized in the Southern Church.

At the same convention the publication committee reported a plan for the purchase and improvement of a certain property in Columbia for the establishment of a regular publishing house. It was represented that a splendid property could be brought into the possession of the United Synod without involving the synod financially and without appealing to the Church for any of the purchase funds. This proposition was a new thing and was considered remarkably generous on the part of the members of the United Synod Publishing Company, a novel proposition, especially in church finances, and the idea seemed to some the suggestion of a "gold brick" scheme. However, it was shown to be possible by the fact that the rentals from parts of the building not occupied by the publishing business would furnish an income over and above interest, taxes and insurance, which would create a sinking fund sufficient to pay for the building in ten or fifteen years.

The offer of the property was accepted by the United Synod, but it adhered to the custom which its predecessors had reserved in such cases and inserted the resolution, the usual "safety" clause, "provided it could be done without any financial responsibility upon the part of the synod." It is certain that no part of the Lutheran Church in America had ever been so fortunate in the establishment of a publication house as was the United Synod in this case. No better piece of property was available in Columbia. Such an enterprise could not have been successful in any other city within the territory of the United Synod at that time, and the leading business men of the city expressed their opinion that it could not have been accomplished except in the remarkable manner by which it was achieved. Opportunity knocked once in this instance, as is proverbially the case, and the door was opened and success, standing upon the threshold, entered and was made the welcome guest. The conclusion reached at that convention as to the church paper was: "The *Visitor* which had floundered so long in deep water, now feels secure upon the solid rock." At that time the circulation of the paper amounted to 4,000 copies and in subsequent years the increase in the number of subscribers was gratifyingly large.

Upon the establishment of the paper in Columbia (January, 1904) the members of the Lutheran Visitor Company had financed the enterprise with their private funds. It was necessary to increase the subscription price at that time from one dollar to $1.50 (from which it had been reduced several years previously in a special campaign which had guaranteed a large increase in subscribers by the various congregations) in order to meet increased cost of publication in the improved mechanical appearance of the paper.

Success in raising the consolidation fund ($3,950) which the United Synod had authorized at the Dallas convention during the interim (1906-07), added interest to this movement, which interest manifested itself in the fact that the contributors to this fund numbered one hundred individuals, twenty-three congregations and one Sunday School, the amounts contributed ranging from fifty cents to $350.

The current maintenance fund of $1,500, which it had been considered also at the Dallas convention to be necessary to the immediate success of the publication cause, enrolled sixty-eight congregations and thirty-one Sunday Schools as its contributors.

Yet another fund had been authorized—the amount of $10,000 for the employment of the publication secretary, Rev. E. C. Cronk, whose chief duty was the canvass of the Church in the effort to increase the circulation of the *Lutheran Church Visitor* and *Tidings*. The individual contributors to this fund numbered ninety-one, nearly a score of whom were leading business men of Columbia, representing all denominations, including both Catholics and Jews. Congregations responding to this appeal numbered 130, besides several conferences of the district synods, and five Sunday Schools, the amounts ranging from fifty cents to one of $1,000 (the latter sum given by that liberal-hearted Lutheran layman, the late J. E. Cooper, of Grace Church, Winchester, Va., who gave nearly his entire income to various causes of the Church), the total of all contributions to this purpose being $5,227.32.

The Southern Lutheran had been established as a monthly parish paper in 1894 by Rev. L. E. Busby at Asheville, N. C., where he was a home missionary pastor. It later entered the larger field as a monthly church paper. However, being transferred to Rev. Henderson N. Miller, Ph.D., it was published subsequently as a Sunday School paper at Mt. Pleasant, N. C. Dr. Miller sold it to Mr. E. H. Aull in 1897. Rev. S. T. Hallman, D.D., became the editor. Rev. W. H. Greever was afterwards the editor, and Rev. W. L. Seabrook was serving as editor when the paper was acquired among the assets of the Lutheran Board of Publication by the United Synod Publishing Company, when its name was changed to *Tidings*, with Mrs. E. C. Cronk, of Columbia, as editor. Mrs. Cronk served efficiently in that capacity,—*Tidings* having enlisted the hearty support of the Sunday Schools and the missionary societies of the Church,—until the paper terminated its existence soon after the merger of the various synods into the United Lutheran Church in America.

Dr. Hallman retired as contributing editor of the *Lutheran Church Visitor* in 1905 and Rev. C. A. Freed relinquished

his connection with the paper March 1, 1908. his position
at that time being that of treasurer of the publishing company.

The plan of the publication building to be erected in Columbia provided for a three-story brick structure with stone
front, to be erected at 1626 Main street, in the heart of the
business district of the city, which itself at that time was ex-
periencing the largest growth in its history of 120 years.
The eligible lot had been purchased for the sum of $14,000
and the building was erected at a cost of $25,743, the loans
and interest until May, 1908, making the entire cost of the
enterprise, $43,143.

The late W. J. Winesett came from Bluefield, W. Va.,
where he was a communicant member of the Lutheran
Church, especially to supervise the erection of the building,
and to him and Mr. P. C. Price, of Columbia, was said in the
Lutheran Church Visitor, upon its completion, that to them
"the Church owes a special debt of gratitude and their services and sacrifices for this cause will never be fully known".

A decided expansion of the publication cause was mani-
fest upon the completion of the building in the Fall of 1907.
Many of the congregations and Sunday Schools gave their
support to the distribution of Sunday School supplies and
the circulation of church literature generally and the sales
of the new hymnal were encouraging.

The history of the publication of the Book of Worship, as
its name stood until 1888, forms an interesting record at this
time. The first hymn book to be published under the auspices of the Southern Church was the Book of Worship as it
was authorized by the General Synod of the Confederate
States at its first regular convention which was held in Concord, N. C., May 20-26, 1863. The Book of Worship was
adopted by the synod as it had been outlined serially by
Rev. D. M. Gilbert, D.D., in *The Southern Lutheran*, having
been prepared by committees which had been appointed
by the preliminary meeting of the delegates from the various
synods at the convention which was held at Salisbury, N. C.,
in January, 1862,—so great was the need for such a book by
the Southern Church that no time was to be lost in waiting

for the regular organization of a general synod in the South. The Book of Worship was most favorably received by the Church upon its publication and obtained a wide circulation, an edition of 8,000 being reported by the publishing committee at the convention of the General Synod at Newberry in May, 1868, with sales of 2,500 copies.

The publication of the Book of Worship upon its adoption by the General Synod was financed within the territory of the South Carolina Synod. This was made possible by interesting a publisher who would assume this responsibility. This publisher was the late W. J. Duffie, a bookseller of Columbia, himself a Presbyterian, as no Lutheran business man was available who could engage in the work at that time. Mr. Duffie sold a farm in order to secure additional capital by which to publish the book. It is said here to his credit that in all his transactions with the General Synod in the publication of the Book of Worship, the synod had no cause for complaint in any particular. The various styles in which the editions were issued proved most satisfactory, being finished in substantial character both for use in pew and pulpit.

The Southern Church had never engaged extensively in any publication enterprise prior to the consolidation of the church papers in 1904. An organization, under the name of the Southern Book Company, was proposed at the convention of the General Synod at Concord in 1863, but there is no record that the movement ever materialized. Neither was an almanac and clerical register, also proposed at the same convention, ever published, most probably due to the difficulties and vicissitudes which confronted the Church on account of the war.

The South Carolina Synod published a leaflet in 1883 especially to commemorate in a measure the celebration of the 400th anniversary of the birth of Martin Luther. In view of the love of the Reformer for children, as evidenced in his own household, the author of the leaflet, the late Dr. O. B. Mayer, Sr., of Newberry, chose as its title, "Luther and the Children." It was written in his well-known interesting and inimitable style and was largely circulated and freely

LUTHERAN PUBLICATION HOUSE, COLUMBIA

distributed at the celebration of the anniversary by the synod at its convention at Bethlehem Church, November 10, 1883. Dr. Mayer himself was present at that time and was a member of the special choir which led in the singing on that occasion, Luther's battle hymn, "Ein' Feste Burg ist Unser Gott."

At the convention of the United Synod in Savannah, October, 1908, the Lutheran Board of Publication was organized, the United Synod Publishing Company then ending its existence, and the former was charged with the oversight of the church paper and the conduct of the publication interests of the synod.   Dr. Greever continued as editor of the paper and general manager until 1914, when he resigned to give his time to the *American Lutheran Survey*. He was succeeded by Rev. John W. Horine, D.D., who with Mr. Houseal as associate editor, continued in charge of the paper until it was consolidated with *The Lutheran*, May 1, 1920.   It was a significant coincidence that Mr. Houseal in concluding his connection with the paper, wrote his valedictory April 21, 1920, filling exactly a continuous service of thirty-nine years.

A further development occurred in the publication cause when the building on Main street was sold for $80,000, an advance of about $37,000 on its cost, and a building, better equipped for its special requirements, was erected at 1617 Sumter Street.   It was occupied in 1912.   It is a commodious four-story building, the first floor of which is at present occupied by the Southern Branch of the Publishing House of the United Lutheran Church in America.   The second, third and fourth floors have a profitable rental value as an apartment house.   It is connected with an annex, which was built in 1910 to accommodate the printing office when the *Lutheran Church Visitor,* which had been printed by contract in the city since 1904, began to be issued from its own presses.   This annex is now being rented as a printing office and used by a Columbia firm.   It all grew from an exceedingly small beginning when the business was begun at Columbia in 1904.   Mr. R. C. Counts, who became associated as cashier with the Lutheran Board of Publication in 1912 is the present manager of the Southern Headquarters of the Board of Publication of the United Lutheran Church in America which is housed in the same building.

The founders of the church papers in the South "like our fathers", as a writer of our Church has expressed it, "were men of profound convictions, far-seeing in their vision, laying the foundations for our Church deep and strong, and building wisely for the future.   They believed it was the im-

perative duty of the Church to provide the literature for its
members, and they well knew that the Church, failing to
do so, would soon cease to make history," and that in providing "literature which breathed the spirit of the Gospel,
it also taught their readers to appreciate and love their own
Church institutions. . . . The literature of a Church repre-
sents the thought and conclusions of a Church in its most vital
relations and practical activities. . . . showing the onward
trend of its theology and life."

Speaking for the United Synod in 1908, one of the leaders in the Church, voicing the above sentiments, wrote as
follows for the special edition of the *Lutheran Church Visitor*, concerning what had been accomplished by the Publication Cause until that time since the beginning of the work
in Columbia in 1904: "We take extremely little of the
credit for what has been done. Three men are entitled to
the thanks of the United Synod for taking hold of the Publication Cause when it was almost dead at New Market and
making it a thing of living power: W. P. Houseal, C. A.
Freed, W. H. Greever. The last named man especially has
borne financial burdens and undertaken unselfish ambitions
that would have dismayed all but one in a thousand. Yet
Mr. Houseal, with veteran devotion, and Mr. Freed, with
his well-known solidity of judgment, have given indispensa-
ble support; and there are consecrated business men in Columbia and elsewhere without whose sanctified generosity
the work would be at a standstill. As it is, I, for one, am
amazed at what has been accomplished under Mr. Greever's
leadership. His proposition at Dallas sounded almost like
a 'gold brick' scheme to those who did not know him, but
he has more than made it good. The committee, without ex-
ceeding instructions, will be able to make a report at Savannah that will gratify the United Synod more than Mr. Greever's proposal surprised it. His most daring and important
achievement, perhaps, is in the engagement of a secretary.
For this he provided the means, because there are laymen—
as well as ministers—who believe in him. Mr. Cronk accepted the place, and seems just the man for the position.
By keeping a representative constantly before the people,

who will constantly keep this work before them, the Publication Cause is expected to develop to that point which the highest interests of our growing work demand."

Chapter VI

FINANCIAL GROWTH

THE financial life of the synod constitutes one of the most remarkable features of its history. Those of our fathers who formed the chief element in the early history of the synod had been brought up under a system which was in no sense conducive to the development of a spirit of liberal giving. They had never been trained to give, and time was required for the cultivation of that part of their religious life. Then, too, they had lived a life of struggle in this "new world" and were not able to give large sums.

But in tracing this branch of service in our synodical history, we note a steady and commendable growth. At the organization of the synod nothing whatever is said about funds to carry on its work. In fact, no treasurer was elected until the second meeting, and the donations reported were less than $100. The next year the total was nearly $300, and at the sixth convention the contributions footed up, to that time, $2,285.12½. The bond of the treasurer was fixed at $2,000; and the synod's liberality steadily increased until the figures given in later reports show that our people were not unmindful of the important duty of caring for the financial operations of the Church.

The examination by years and by decades reveals the fact that this ratio has been maintained through all the years of the synod's life, and the figures have gone up into tens of thousands, and even hundreds of thousands; and we now have to our credit properties which do honor to our Church, and give evidence of the loyal devotion and liberal spirit of the Lutherans of South Carolina.

Apart from the raising of liberal sums for the Theological Seminary, first located at Lexington, and the collections made for the building of Newberry College in 1856 and 1859, the real advance along financial lines did not begin until the synod resolved to secure funds for the establishment of what is called, "The Bachman Endowment Fund." Sundry efforts had been made to raise funds for the maintenance and better equipment of the College, but these were only partially successful. In 1875 Rev. J. A. Sligh, speaking for the Board of Trustees, proposed that such monument be erected to the memory of Rev. John Bachman, D.D., LL.D., and this the synod adopted.*

The agency under this plan was accepted by Rev. S. P. Hughes, ordained in 1876, and Colonel O. L. Schumpert was elected the first treasurer. The agent began his canvass in Mt. Lebanon and St. Matthew's Churches, Orangeburg, and his first general report was rendered October, 1877. Up to this point the grand total of that agency was $12,172.50, in cash and bonds. Not all of this was fully paid, but the tide moved on with varying degrees of success.

Next came the Holland Memorial Fund of $10,000, and subsequently the Semi-Centennial Endowment Fund, including the gift of $25,000 from Dr. D. K. Pearson of Chicago, Ill., the $10,000 from Mr. Andrew Carnegie; and then the Newberry-Summerland College Educational Fund, an achievement of such importance as to deserve special mention.

The Board of Trustees of Newberry College and the Board of Trustees of Summerland College, in joint session, petitioned synod to authorize and organize a campaign for the raising of a fund of $300,000 from its members for the two colleges, credit subscriptions to be payable in three equal annual instalments, and to be evidenced by good bankable notes.

The South Carolina Synod in extra convention in St. Paul's Church, Columbia, August 14, 1919, launched an educational campaign for $300,000. Newberry College and Summerland College were named as the beneficiaries of the fund, Newberry College receiving two-thirds and Summerland College one-third. October 19 to October 31 was the date set for subscriptions.

Synod appointed a Central Campaign Committee of thirty-five to inaugurate and have control of the campaign. The Central Committee met in the Jefferson Hotel, Columbia, August 20, to organize and outline plans for the campaign.

---

*(See Minutes of 1875, p. 27.)

At this meeting an Executive Committee was appointed to have supervision of the execution of the plans. This committee was composed of Rev. H. A. McCullough, D.D., Prof. S. J. Derrick, Rev. P. E. Monroe, D.D. Mr. R. C. Counts was elected treasurer. The Executive Committee at a subsequent meeting elected Rev. S. L. Blomgren of Charleston as Executive Secretary. Mr. Blomgren immediately accepted. Headquarters for the campaign were opened in the building of the Lutheran Board of Publication. The campaign met with phenomenal success. About $275,000 was subscribed and payments of the pledges were reasonably good. Of the amount subscribed upwards of $170,000 has been paid to the treasurer. Unfavorable conditions, which have prevailed in the state, have delayed the payment of the subscriptions in full.

Moreover, the fact should be considered that the synod has contributed many thousands of dollars for missions, for the relief of the sufferers over the seas, etc. A fact worthy of note is that through the wise judgment and far-seeing vision of Mr. Jacob F. Schirmer, long the treasurer of our Seminary Fund, much of that Fund was saved in the period of the War Between the States and materially aided the dual institution—the College and Seminary.

On the face of the record of our financial life as a synod, stands the fact that with our small constituency—even now numbering only about 18,000, the synod has a church property valuation of $1,163,265, a college endowment of $175,000 and college properties totaling $325,000; the whole constituting an educational equipment of which we are proud, and one which promises great things for the future of our Church in the South.

Numerical and Financial Growth

NOTE.—*The variation in some of the figures is doubtless due to the failure of pastors to hand in their parochial reports.*

1824-1833

Year.	Congregations.	Members.		Receipts.
1824	22	257	$	78.69
1825	16	564		282.94
1826	23	1,301		310.50
1827	17	1,306		352.65
1828	24	1,594		529.60
1829	23	1,442		490.06
1830	26	1,452		471.15
1831	27	1,748		716.00
1832	27	1,752		391.15
1833	30	1,899		517.62

Increase 8   1,642 Total .... $ 4,140.36
Average annual in-
crease   .8   64.8 Annual average $ 414.03

1834-1843

Year.	Congregations.	Members.		Receipts.
1834	28	1,703	$	847.55
1835	31	1,840		954.97
1836	28	1,896		705.63
1837	24	1,574		532.22
1838	27	1,566		375.64
1839	32	1,514		473.70
1840	34	1,622		417.46
1841	28	1,915		495.48
1842	34	2,177		247.19
1843	37	2,383		236.39

Increase 9   680 Total .... $ 5,286.23
Average Increase ... 1   68 Annual average   528.62

1844-1853

Year.	Congregations.	Members.	Colored Members	Receipts.
1844	36	2,434		$ 268.38
1845	39	2,533		519.36
1846	46	2,629		477.26
1847	47	2,639	439	457.49
1848	39	2,644	394	400.51
1849	47	2,659	402	248.49
1850	46	2,874	424	482.92

Year.	Congregations.	Members.		Receipts.
1851	44	2,933	432	461.51
1852	46	3,326	635	496.92
1853	50	3,853	683	526.16
Increase	14	1,419	Total	$ 4,339.00
Average Increase ... 1.4		142	Annual average	433.90

1854-1863

Year.	Congregations.	Members.	Col'd Members.	Receipts.
1854	52	4,019	789	$ 588.38
1855	47	3,796	815	531.11
1856	52	3,948	764	616.12
1857	51	4,138	851	523.99
1858	43	3,838	832	613.86
1859	49	3,897	969	615.07
1860	48	4,056	952	846.82
1861	44	4,120	954	652.96
1862	40	3,387	845	793.95
1863	36	3,108	740	779.48
Decrease	16	911	Total	$ 6,561.74
Average Decrease ... 1.6		91	Annual average	656.17

1864-1873

Year.	Congregations.	Members.	Col'd Members.	Receipts.
1864	40	3,216	825	$ 1,587.50
1865	30	2,197	585	158.39
1866	41	4,135	383	530.03
1867	40	4,129	212	649.66
1868	39	3,289	144	513.55
1869	45	4,560		1,157.68
1870	43	4.488		776.41
1871	40	3,954		951.27
1872	43	4,833		687.06
1873	45	4,911		857.79
Increase	5	1,695	Total	$ 6,869.34
Average Increase 5		169	Annual average	686.93

1874-1883

Year.	Congregations.	Members.	Receipts.
1874	50	4,219	$ 868.14
1875	43	4,301	742.45
1876	46	5,344	761.89
1877	46	5,065	740.88
1878	47	5,112	748.91
1879	48	5,444	947.69

Year.	Congregations.	Members.	Receipts.
1880	52	5,566	1,182.64
1881	53	5,670	1,518.30
1882	55	5,972	910.14
1883	55	5,802	1,613.21
Increase 5		1,583 Total	$ 9,272.43
Average Increase .5		158 Annual average	927.24

1884-1893

Year.	Congregations.	Members.	Receipts.
1884	60	6,033	$ 1,369.61
1885	61	6,642	1,777.12
1886	58	6,738	2,731.77
1887	55	6,705	1,979.75
1888	59	6,336	2,004.00
1889	59	6,521	1,793.16
1890	61	6,879	1,961.31
1891	61	7,040	1,800.64
1892	62	7,392	1,938.16
1893	64	7,486	1,848.65
Increase 4		1,453 Total	$19,204.17
Average Increase .4		145 Annual average	1,920.41

1894-1903

Year.	Congregations.	Members.	Receipts.
1894	66	7,918	$ 1,919.64
1895	66	8,131	1,585.26
1896	59	7,923	2,268.64
1897	64	8,408	2,411.98
1898	60	8,255	3,181.27
1899	63	8,421	3,171.20
1900	68	8,712	2,921.84
1901	63	9,801	2,822.05
1902	71	9,503	4,166.26
1903	67	9,889	4,374.78
Increase 5		1,941 Total	$28,922.92
Average Increase .5		194 Annual average	2,892.29

1904-1913

Year.	Congregations.	Members.	Receipts.
1904	72	10,162	$ 5,294.25
1905	72	9,535	5,319.59
1906	76	10,089	6,019.02
1907	75	10,393	7,011.94

Year.	Congregations.	Members.	Receipts.
1908	76	11,080	7,401.64
1909	77	10,731	9,011.97
1910	70	10,599	9,000.27
1911	80	10,889	11,882.28
1912	83	10,860	15,620.25
1913	69	9,752	6,190.15
Decrease 3		410 Total	$82,751.36
Average Decrease 3		41 Annual average	8,275.13

1914-1923

Year.	Congregations.	Members.	Receipts.
1914	82	10,802	$ 7,471.85
1915	85	11,323	14,907.93
1916	75	10,618	13,838.70
1917	86	12,243	14,811.84
1918	86	12,529	13,228.44
1919	86	12,767	19,775.39
1920	87	11,805	22,372.11
1921	89	13,636	25,603.74
1922	89	13,695	29,473.18
1923*	109	17,445	45,399.44
Increase 20		6,643 Total	$206,882.66
Average Increase ... 2		664 Annual average	20,688.26

*In 1922 the South Carolina Conference of the United North Carolina Synod had been merged with the South Carolina Synod.

Chapter VII

LAY ORGANIZATIONS

THE history of the Woman's Synodical Missionary Society has been set forth in the chapter on the "Missionary History" of the synod, and in connection therewith the children's societies at least received mention. A group picture of the lay organizations of the synod would be incomplete without the presence in it of the Luther League and Men's Federation.

Luther League

The possibility of organizing a Young People's Missionary Society had its birth in the minds of a few young people of the South Carolina Synod. These young people discussed among themselves the feasibility of organizing a federation of Lutheran young people, and decided to send a resolution to the Woman's Synodical Missionary Society, which met in St. Paul's Church in Columbia, November, 1910. At this meeting a young people's service was held on Sunday evening, at which time this resolution was offered:

"RESOLVED, That as representatives of the young people of the South Carolina Synod, we petition the Woman's Convention to appoint an executive committee of five young people, naming the treasurer and general secretary, which committee shall seek to advance the work among young people in all the congregations of the synod."

This resolution was adopted by the Synodical Convention, and on the committee were appointed Rev. G. P. Voigt, Mr. C. C. Habenicht, Misses Elberta Sease, Gertrude Simpson and Rosalyn Summer. Through the untiring efforts, the earnest prayers and the consecrated work of these young people, there was organized at the Woman's Convention in 1911, in the Lutheran Church in Orangeburg, the Federation of Lutheran Young People's Societies of the South Carolina Synod. Twenty-five delegates, representing nineteen societies, were present. At this meeting the treasurer reported that $500 had been raised during the year. This sum was in answer to a challenge from the young people of North Carolina, and was used to purchase a memorial room in Kyushu Gakuin, our Japan school.

Mr. C. J. Shealy was elected first president of the Young People's Federation, and for three years the work grew and prospered under his efficient leadership.

Already this body of youthful workers was reaching out into larger fields. The Federation began to work in the home and foreign fields, contributing in the second year of its organization to the support of Miss Mary Lou Bowers, one of our own South Carolina missionaries to Japan, and the home mission stations in Greenville, S. C., and Jackson, Miss.

During the following year the work of the Federation grew to such proportions and the societies increased so rapidly that it was thought expedient to hold the annual meetings at a time and place separate from the Woman's Convention. This was a grave undertaking, for it was through the interest, encouragement and wise direction of these women and the providence and blessings of God, that the Federation had thus far prospered. The first convention apart from the Woman's organization was held in Grace Lutheran Church, Prosperity. The interest and enthusiasm manifested at this meeting afforded great inspiration. As the forces increased and the opportunities for service grew, the necessity for a more thorough knowledge of the fields became apparent. So there was begun the study of Bible and Missions. In six years there has been an increase of 489 young people engaged in these study classes. This gratifying increase has been marked not only in the line of Bible and Mission Study classes, but in membership as well.

In 1912, the first meeting of the permanent organization, there were represented at the Federation 16 societies with 283 members; in 1922 there were enrolled 58 societies with 2,282 members.

The young people have certainly proved that they have not withheld their means from God's service. The first pledge, made in 1910, was $500. The treasurer's report for 1922 shows a total income of $2,794.38. That the people of South Carolina may know something of the work that has been done by the Luther League, there is herewith given a review of the benevolence side of the balance sheet:

1911—Memorial room in Kyushu Gakuin.

1912—Support of Miss Mary Lou Bowers.

1913—Support of Miss Bowers.
    Work in China.

1914—Miss Bowers' equipment.
    Work at Greenville.

1915—For support of Miss Bowers.
    For Jackson, Miss., Mission.
    Church at Greenville.

1916—Support of Miss Bowers.
    Support of Missionary at Jackson, Miss.
    Support of a Bible woman.

1917—Greenville Mission.
    Support of Miss Bowers.
    Jackson, Miss., Mission.
    Support of Bible woman in Japan.

1918—Support of Miss Bowers.
    Support of Greenville Church.
    Support of Jackson, Miss., Mission.

1919—Support of Miss Bowers
    Support of Greenville Church.
    Support of Jackson, Miss., Mission.
    General Foreign Mission work.

1920—Support of C. E. Norman, Japan.
    Support of Jackson, Miss., Mission.
    Furnishings of Greenville Church.
    Building Fund, St. Barnabas', Charleston.
    Special Offering for Miss Bowers.
    Offering for the Norman Relief Fund.

1921—Seminary Library Fund (first of a series of ten annual payments of $100).
    Orphan Home.
    Home Missions:
      Macon, Ga.
      Pelion Pastorate.
      St. Barnabas', Charleston.
    Students' Aid (for helping a student at Newberry and Summerland College, respectively, who is preparing for active Christian service).
    Hymn books furnished to:
      Silver Street, at Silver Street.

Church of the Incarnation, Columbia.
St. James', Sumter.
Church at Laurel, Miss.
Foreign Missions.
Contribution to European Relief.
1922—Church of Incarnation, Columbia, heating plant and piano.
Macon, Ga., church debt.
Seminary library and equipment.
Services, Rock Hill.
Salem Orphanage.
Students' Aid.
West Indies' Board Scholarship.
St. Barnabas', Charleston.
Kumamoto, Japan,—on chapel.
For work at Buenos Aires, South America.
On salary Miss Mary Lou Bowers.

Our young people have given not only of their time and means, but five of them have answered the call to service in foreign fields:

Mrs. Lewis G. Gray, *nee* Miss Mary Lou Bowers, stationed in Kumamoto, Japan; Mrs. G. C. Leonard, *nee* Miss Gertrude Simpson, of Prosperity, now in Liberia, Africa; Rev. C. E. Norman, of Concord, N. C., and Mrs. Norman, *nee* Miss Lottie Wyse, of Columbia, in Japan; and Rev. Carl B. Caughman, of Mississippi, in India.

For ten years known as the Young People's Federation of South Carolina, at the convention of 1921, it was deemed wise to change the name to the Luther League of South Carolina, in view of affiliating with the Luther League of America, which has been chosen by the United Lutheran Church as the national organization of Lutheran young people. In 1922 this change in name was effected. The connection with this general body does not change the work in any way, its object being education, missions, and life service, the three objects it has been working for since its foundation.

This, in brief, is the story of the Luther League of South Carolina. It is the story of a vision, of a strong desire for service, of a constant and unswerving devotion to ideals, of an active faith, of a hope ripening rapidly into fruition. The young people are grateful for the opportunities for service that have come. They crave greater usefulness. They realize that the most urgent need is always just ahead, and their unending prayer is that they may be equal to the harvest.

Federation of Men

At the meeting of synod in Leesville, 1921, the laymen rendered a program consisting of the following addresses: The Layman's Opportunities and Duties (a) In the Sunday School, Mr. E. H. Schirmer, (b) In the Congregation, Prof. E. O. Counts, (c) In the Synod, Judge C. J. Ramage. At the close of the service a Synodical Brotherhood was organized with the following officers: President, Hon. J. D. Cappelmann, Vice-President, Dr. S. J. Derrick, Secretary-Treasurer, Mr. B. H. Barre.

After serving the church two years, the laymen decided to change the name and form of the Brotherhood. This action was taken at the convention of synod held in Zion Church, Lexington County, November 13, 1923. The men of the synod were again given a place on the program. This period was designated as "Laymen's Period". It was at this time that the men of the synod deemed it desirable to change the form of the organization as well as the name. The question was referred to a committee of five, consisting of Dr. S. J. Derrick, Prof. Jas. C. Kinard, G. M. Eleazer, D. F. Efird and R. C. Counts. The committee extended a call to the Brotherhoods, Bible Classes, Church Councils, and Superintendents of Sunday Schools. The meeting was held in the Sunday School building of St. Paul's Church, Columbia, December 28, 1923. An organization was effected and the following officers elected: D. F. Efird, president; R. C. Counts, secretary; G. M. Eleazer, treasurer. A constitution was adopted and the name of the organization called Federation of Men of the South Carolina Synod. Forty-two congregations of the synod were represented at this meeting. The Federation is increasing in size and strength. Its history lies largely in the future, but it promises to be one of which the men of the Federation will be justly proud.

Chapter VIII

HISTORY OF CONGREGATIONS

St. John's Church, Charleston

ST. John's Church was organized in 1743, although Lutherans were in Charleston as early as 1734. The pastors are listed as follows: Reverends John George Friederichs, H. G. B. Wordmann, John Nicholas Martin, John Severin Hahnbaum, Frederick Daser, Christian Streit, John

ST. JOHN'S CHURCH, CHARLESTON

Charles Faber, Matthew F. C. Faber, John Bachman, William W. Hicks (assistant to Dr. Bachman), John H. Honour (supply), Thomas W. Dosh. Edward T. Horn. John W. Horine, C. Armand Miller and George J. Gongaware, the present pastor.

The following is a list of Lutheran ministers who went out from St. John's Church: John G. Schwartz, William D. Strobel, Philip A. Strobel, Stephen A. Mealy, Elias B. Hort, John P. Margart, Thaddeus S. Boinest, Edwin A. Bolles, James P. King, John B. Haskell, T. H. Strohecker, Henry A. Schroder.

The first ten named in this list were largely trained for the holy ministry by Dr. John Bachman, who also instructed Rev. Washington Muller in his preparation for the ministry.

INTERIOR ST. JOHN'S CHURCH, CHARLESTON

Dr. Bachman also organized a negro congregation, to which the north gallery of the church was assigned for their exclusive use.   From among them he trained three as ministers of the Gospel; Boston Drayton, who was sent to Africa as a missionary; Bishop Payne, who afterwards united with the Methodist Church, by which he was made a bishop, and John Jones, who settled in the North.   There were at one time 190 negro communicants.   Dr. Bachman also organized for the negro children a Sunday School consisting of about 150 scholars, who were regularly instructed by thirty-two white teachers.

In 1830 Dr. Bachman induced the synod to establish our Theological Seminary, the first professor of which was Rev. John G. Schwartz.

Two flourishing congregations in Charleston went out from St. John's Church during Dr. Bachman's pastorate: St. Matthew's Church in 1841, and Morris Street (now St. Andrew's) Church in 1857. St. Barnabas' Church, which had its inception in 1883 upon the initiative of Rev. Edward T. Horn, then pastor of St. John's Church, must be credited to S.t John's Church in connection with the other Lutheran churches of Charleston.

St. John's congregation throughout the period of its long history has been a loyal and liberal supporter of the synod. In this regard the name of Robert G. Chisolm, its president for 37 years, should be held in special honor. Its Ladies' Society, for many years under the presidency of Miss Kate Bachman, has furnished beneficiary aid to several theological students each year (when students were available) almost since the time of its organization in 1825. The corporate name of St. John's Church is The Lutheran Church of German Protestants. The presidents of the corporation have been:

1785—George Hahnbaum	1850—Elias Horlbeck, M.D.
1795—Daniel Strobel	1855—Jacob F. Schirmer
1807—Jacob Sass	1869—Henry Cobia
1836—Jacob F. Mintzing	1870—John H. Steinmeyer
1842—John Strohecker	1878—Robert G. Chisolm
1849—B. F. Dunkin	1915—John F. Ficken

St. Matthew's Church, Calhoun County

The exact date of the organization of this congregation can not now be definitely fixed, but there are recorded facts which go far towards determining the approximate date.

German and Swiss colonies settled in that section of the state in 1735 and 1737, and history records the fact that Rev. John Ulrich Giessendanner preached in Orangeburg

village and Amelia township about that period. He died
in the fall of 1738. It seems certain, then, that his ministry there began with those early settlers between the dates
named. His nephew, bearing the same name, became his
successor, and although this young man preached for a term
of years as a Lutheran pastor, he finally went over to the
Episcopal Church and carried with him the congregation in
the town, which numbered about 200 souls. Had he then
been in charge of the Lutheran people of Amelia township
he would most probably have carried these with him also.

ST. MATTHEW'S CHURCH, CAMERON

This view of the case justifies the fixing of the date of
organization at about 1737, the time when the second group
of arrivals of Swiss and German Lutherans settled in that
part of the state.

It is fair to state, however, that the younger Giessendanner
preached in Orangeburg from 1738 to 1749 as a Lutheran
minister, and in 1749 united with the Episcopal denomination under an unjust law of England which would not allow
the church to hold property without the Episcopal ordination

of the pastor. If we credit him with the organization of St. Matthew's congregation, the date would necessarily be about 1740. After him came Rev. John George Friederich until 1760. Then there was a vacancy which seems to have extended to 1786. From 1786 to 1799 Rev. Frederick Daser was pastor. From 1799 to 1814 Rev. John Philip Franklow was pastor. Rev. Michael Rauch preached there once each month from 1814 to 1822, but November, 1813, and February 16, 1814, Rev. David Henkel preached there also and received some members; however, Rev. Michael Rauch was pastor of the church. From 1822 to 1826 Rev. Samuel Herscher was pastor in charge but Rev. Godfrey Dreher dedicated a new church on July 2, 1826, he being a prominent officer of the South Carolina Synod and its first president. From 1827 to 1833 Revs. Jacob Wingard, J. D. Sheck, John C. Hope and George Haltiwanger served the congregation, but the term of service is not definitely stated. The pastors then were: Rev. David Bernhardt, 1835-40; Rev. John P. Margart, 1841-47; Rev. George H. Haigler, 1847-58; Rev. Paul Derrick, 1859-71; Rev. George A. Hough, 1872-74; Rev. S. T. Hallman, D.D., 1875-80. Reverends William Stoudenmire and J. F. Probst supplied for a short while, and then the following succeeded each other as the regular pastors: Reverends J. H. Wilson, D.D., Jacob Hawkins, D.D., John H. Wyse, James A. B. Scherer, D.D., H. A. McCullough, D.D., J. D. Kinard, D.D., J. W. Oxner, J. L. Yonce, and Charles J. Shealy, the present incumbent.

Rev. George H. Haigler was a son of this congregation, entering the ministry in 1843.

Rev. Charles J. Shealy, the present pastor, writes: "The original St. Matthew's church was located on Lyons Creek, some three or four miles from the present site of the town of St. Matthews. However, when a new church was dedicated by Rev. Godfrey Dreher in 1826, it was moved to the present site, on the Monck's Corner road. The church here was rebuilt and dedicated under the leadership of Rev. H. A. McCullough. In 1841, when Rev. J. P. Margart became pastor, the council of St. Matthew's agreed that their pastor should hold services at a log schoolhouse called Pine

Grove, five miles from St. Matthew's Church towards Santee River. This was the beginning of what is now Pine Grove Church, which in turn was the parent of Trinity, Elloree. In the course of time it was deemed expedient to build a church in Orange Parish on Four Holes Swamp, for the accommodation of the members residing in that direction, and with a view of still further extending the Church. Accordingly, a building was erected, chiefly by the contributions of the Haigler family, and, being ready for service, was dedicated on Sunday, March 25, 1843, Rev. J. F. W. Leppard assisting Rev. J. P. Margart. This church received the name of Mt. Lebanon. Also in these latter years, members of St. Matthew's Church cooperated in the building of Epiphany in the town of St. Matthews. Thus it is seen that the desire to extend the Church has always been in the hearts of the people of St. Matthew's congregation.

"However, at the present time, the church is rather weak numerically. The erection of Resurrection Church at Cameron has drawn some of the larger leading families into it. Yet there is a sufficient constituency to maintain the church, and the outlook is such that it may safely be predicted that the old church will for many years take its place among the churches of the synod.

"A responsiveness to the calls of the Church at large has characterized this country congregation for the last quarter of a century. Its members have given liberally to the work of the synod, to the support of Christian education and to foreign missions."

Mt. Pleasant Church, near Ehrhardt

The organization of this church dates back to 1750, and an earlier date may well be assumed. Ramsay, in his history of South Carolina, mentions Lutheran churches in Barnwell District prior to that date, and these must have been St. Bartholomew and St. Nicholas' Churches, for Shiloh Church was not organized until late in 1830.* Shiloh has long since ceased to exist.

---

*(See Minutes 1830, Page 17.)

St. Bartholomew is the present Mt. Pleasant Church. It
was located about one mile south of the present site. When
the second church was built in 1835, the name and location
were both changed.

Pastor A. W. Ballentine gives the following information:
"Some of the very old people have seen this old building,
with its roof fallen in. In this building it is supposed that
Rev. Isaac Bamberg preached from 1798 until his death in
1800. One of his descendants, now an old lady, had the

MT. PLEASANT CHURCH, EHRHARDT

grave pointed out to her when she was a child. The old
church ground and graveyard have no markers and have
been all but forgotten. The second church was built and
dedicated in 1835 at the present location under the pastoral
care of Rev. Robert Cloy, who died May 4, 1853. Most
of the old people remember this old building distinctly. The
third building on the same grounds was constructed and dedicated in 1873 during the pastoral care of Rev. C. P. Boozer.
The forty-ninth convention of the Synod of South Carolina
was held here in October of the same year. October 26,

1909, this congregation with the Ehrhardt congregation united to form the Mt. Pleasant-Ehrhardt Pastorate. With the exception of the year 1864, Sunday School has been held in Mt. Pleasant Church since the year 1800."

The following pastors have served this church: Reverends Isaac Bamberg, 1798-1800; W. D. Strobel, about 1830-31; J. D. Sheck; David Hungerpeler; Robert Cloy, about 1835; W. G. Harter, about 1836-40; P. A. Strobel; C. F. Bansemer; Paul Kistler, about 1852; G. R. Haigler; B. F. Berry, 1856-68; C. P. Boozer, 1872-73; Barney Kreps, about 1873-76; J. B. Haskell, supply in 1877; J. F. Probst, 1877-81; I. P. Hawkins, about 1883; E. A. Wingard, 1886; J. H. Wilson, D.D., 1888-1902; P. E. Monroe, D.D., 1902-08; D. B. Groseclose, 1908-13; E. F. K. Roof, 1914-17; P. D. Risinger, 1917-22; A. W. Ballentine, 1922-24.

The roll of members is now 161, with 168 in the Sunday School. The property value is $2,000.

St. Paul's Church, near Pomaria

This is one of the oldest congregations in Newberry County, if not the very oldest, and its history has been hard to trace; however, with the assistance of Pastor S. P. Koon, we have in the following sketch a reasonably accurate account of its origin and development.

It was no doubt organized about 1761, and not later than 1764. Its organizers were some of the early settlers. Tradition places the organization when Joseph Boone was Governor of South Carolina, which would fix the date between 1761-1764.

The land belonging to the church is a tract of sixty-eight acres, and must have been granted by George III of England. Mr. John Bulow Campbell, of Atlanta, Ga., writes: "My records indicate that Rev. Joachim Bulow founded the Lutheran Church in Newberry District in 1765," and he furnishes evidence to show that the said Mr. Bulow was preaching at St. Paul's Church in 1775. He owned two hundred acres of land on Crim's Creek and had a mill on Bush River, which accounts for his ability to furnish supplies to the American Army during the Revolution. The same authority says that Rev. Mr. Bulow was buried under St. Paul's Church, but no trace of the grave has been found.

The first building was constructed of logs. This building gave place later on to a second church, which stood until about 1830, in the ministry of Rev. Michael Rauch, when a new and better structure took the place of the old church. The dedicatory service was conducted by the pastor assisted by Rev. J. G. Schwartz. This building has since been remodeled, and is still in use by a flourishing congregation.

ST. PAUL'S CHURCH, POMARIA

The first parsonage was built during the pastorate of Rev. J. D. Stingley (1853-55). The contract is still preserved in the church records and bears the date 1853.

In November, 1905, Mr. A. H. Kohn stated in the public prints that Rev. Bernard Michael Houseal of Reading, Pa., preached at St. Paul's Church during a visit to his brother before the American Revolution. Pastor S. P. Koon has a copy of a receipt given by Capt. William Frederick Houseal, brother of Rev. B. M. Houseal, to Rev. Joachim Bulow for supplies to General Sumter, thus proving that Rev. Mr. Bulow was the first pastor of this historic church.

The next pastor was Rev. Frederick Joseph Wallern. He was preaching here in 1787, being then a young man 28 years of age. He made his home here, and lived until 1818. There is evidence that he was preaching up to 1815; thus he was active in the ministry almost to the time of his death. He was buried near his home, but in 1917 his body was brought to St. Paul's cemetery, where his tomb may still be seen.

GRAVE OF REV. AND MRS. F. J. WALLERN

The bodies of Rev. and Mrs. Wallern were removed to this place from their family burying ground by A. H. Kohn and J. J. Epting. The tombstone bears the following inscription: "To the memory of Frederick J. Wallern, who was born April 6, 1759, and departed this life Oct. 6th, A.D. 1818, aged 58 years and 6 months. He was a preacher of the Gospel in the Lutheran Church and we now hope is removed to the rest prepared for the servant of God."

Rev. Mr. Wallern was followed by Rev. J. Yost Meetze, and he was preaching here before the organization of the South Carolina Synod in 1824.

Coincident with and following the year the synod was organized, pastors served St. Paul's Church as follows:

Rev. S. Herscher 1824-
Rev. Michael Rauch 1825-1827
Rev. Jacob Wingard 1828-1829
Rev. Michael Rauch (again) 1830-1833

Rev. J. C. Hope 1834-1838
Rev. W. G. Harter (following a va-
cancy of two years) 1840-1841
Rev. William Berly 1841-1850
Rev. J. B. Anthony 1851-1853
Rev. J. B. Stingley 1853-1855
Rev. J. P. Margart 1855-1858
Rev. D. M. Blackwelder (following a
vacancy of one year in 1859, when
ministers from Newberry College
supplied) 1860-1865
Rev. J. A. Sligh 1865-1912
Rev. Y. von A. Riser 1912-1916
Rev. S. C. Ballentine, temporary sup-
ply during portion of 1916
Rev. S. P. Koon, present pastor since ...1916.

The services of Rev. J. A. Sligh, D.D., as pastor extended over a period of forty-six years, one of the longest and most fruitful in the history of the Southern Church. Dr. Sligh took charge in 1866, and in 1912 resigned on account of advancing age, having Rev. Y. von A. Riser as associate pastor one year before he relinquished the work.

During the term of Rev. S. P. Koon, the present pastor, a new parsonage has been built at a cost of more than $5,000. In this parsonage work St. Paul's Church was assisted by St. Philip's and Bachman's Chapel Churches. These two churches now belong to the St. Paul's charge. St. Paul's congregation at present numbers about 350 communicants.

The following sons of St. Paul's Church have entered the ministry: Revs. Herman Aull, William Berly, Elijah El-more, J. E. Berly, M.D., M. J. Epting, D.D., S. T. Riser, G. A. Riser, R. E. Livingston, W. K. Sligh, T. B. Epting, H. P. Counts and E. K. Counts.

Rev. S. P. Koon, pastor, gives some interesting matters in the following letter:

"Since writing you, I have seen a plat of Rev. Joseph Bulow's land. He took out an original grant. The survey was made May 12, 1773. The grant was made in 1774.

It was recorded November 12, 1774. The location of his house is also given. I have all the boundaries of this two hundred acre tract. It was on Crim's Creek, and could not have been far from the home of Rev. Mr. Wallern. He also owned a mill on Bush River.

"I understand from receipts which he gave that he went to Charleston after the Revolution, and remained there some years. He gave these receipts when he received pay for supplies furnished the army. I understand that he had a daughter named Ann, who married a Mr. Gettis and through her Mr. Campbell is descended. Mr. A. S. Salley, Jr., Secretary of the South Carolina Historical Commission, deserves credit for much of this information."

Rev. J. A. Sligh, D.D., is buried in the cemetery of St. Paul's Church, near Pomaria.

Bethel Church (High Hill), Richland County

This is one of the old historic churches of the synod, and it deserves more than a passing notice. It was organized in 1770, but under whose ministry it has not been possible to determine. The first building was constructed out of pine logs, and not until 1846 was a better house of worship erected. This congregation seems to have been among those incorporated in 1788, and was no doubt part of "The Corpus Evangelicum". It is one of the congregations included in the organization of this synod in 1824.

Some years ago Mr. J. J. Dreher furnished a sketch of this church, which states that Rev. Godfrey Dreher, with Rev. J. Y. Meetze as "co-preacher", served this church, but this could not have been prior to October 23, 1810, when the former was licensed, and the latter not until October 19, 1812. Mr. J. J. Dreher furnishes the reliable information that Reverends Godfrey Dreher and J. P. Franklow preached and performed other ministerial acts there as far back as 1815, the one preaching in German, the other (Pastor Dreher) preaching in English.

The faithfulness of these preachers of the old times is indicated by the following incident: Rev. J. Y. Meetze was crossing Saluda River at Dreher's Ford, on his way to fill his appointment, when his horse blundered and the rider fell in the stream, one of his feet hanging in the stirrup. The horse immediately made for the shore, pulling the rider out and thus saving his life.

BETHEL CHURCH, HIGH HILL

The list of pastors is uncertain. These are mentioned: Reverends Frederick Joseph Wallern, C. E. Bernhardt, H. Winkhouse, Paul Henkel, David Henkel, C. A. G. Storch, J. P. Franklow, Godfrey Dreher, M. Moser, Michael Rauch, G. Haltiwanger, Jr., J. D. Stingley, J. B. Lowman, J. N. Derrick and W. A. Houck. The last named died January 18, 1874. A long list of pastors served the church in the ensuing fifty years.

The present building was erected in 1881, improvements having been made in 1908.

Out of Bethel Church St. Michael's Church grew, and these two constituted a pastorate during a considerable part of the life of these congregations.

St. John's Church, Pomaria

By precept issued by Egerton Leigh, Surveyor General, on January 1, 1763, to John Pearson, deputy surveyor, a tract of land of one hundred acres was surveyed and certified to the Surveyor General June 27, 1763. October 5, 1763, a grant was issued in the name of King George III, by Thomas Boone, Governor in Council, to John Adam Epting and Peter Dickert, elders of the dissenting congregation and their successors, for one hundred acres on Grames Creek (now Crim's Creek) between Broad and Saluda Rivers, in trust for a glebe and building, a meeting house to the min-

ST. JOHN'S CHURCH, POMARIA

ister of the said congregation for the time being, bounded on the westward by lands of Melchior Lyner and Rev. John Capert, to the northward vacant land, to the eastward vacant land and part on land laid out to Henry Hertley, and to the southward part on land belonging to John Sweetenburg and part vacant.

The plat on which this grant is based has located on it several roads now open and a house located thereon called a meeting house, which, according to the roads laid out and those now used, is the same location of the present house. This house must have been built prior to 1763 or else it would not have been shown on the plat. Some time after the Revolutionary War there was some impression that the grants made by King George III were not good, and Major William Summer, on November 4, 1826, had this tract of land surveyed and measured as 111 acres. December 4, 1826, he obtained a grant from the state for the same. He conveyed this land to Uriah Mayer, William Chapman and Nicholas Summer, as elders, trustees and wardens in trust for Lutheran St. John's Church, January 13, 1827, in consideration of "the attachment I bear to the protestant Lutheran St. John's Church".

It has been the impression to some extent among some of the older people of this church that John Adam Epting had the original grant to the church land and that it was in possession of his granddaughter, Mrs. Davenport. By the kindness of friends a photographic copy of the grant held by Mrs. Davenport has been secured. This copy did not indicate the book in which it was recorded and upon examination it could not be found even indexed, but one of the clerks of the Secretary of State's office and the writer made a search of a book about the date of the grant and found it. This grant conveys by King George II, by the hand of James Glen, Governor in Council, to John Adam Epting in fee, two hundred and fifty acres in the forks between Broad and Saluda Rivers on a creek called Crim's Creek, bounded southward, partly on land laid out to Nicholas Pressler and partly on vacant land and on all other sides by vacant land. The deed accompanying this plat was certified by George Hunter, Surveyor General, November 28, 1749, and the grant is dated August 27, 1751. The plat of this two hundred fifty acres locates Crim's Creek as running practically through the middle of the tract, flowing from the west toward the east.

So the grant held by Mrs. Davenport, given by George II, is not the grant to the St. John's Church land.

It is supposed that Rev. Frederick Joseph Wallern served this church from about the time of the Revolutionary War until his death. It has not been possible to get any information as to who was the pastor previous to that time. After the death of Mr. Wallern the next pastor that we know of definitely was Rev. Jacob Moser, followed by Rev. Godfrey Dreher; also in the first part of the 19th century, Rev. John C. Hope, who was reared near the church, preached there frequently.

OLD COMMUNION SERVICE IN ST. JOHN'S CHURCH (LOCALLY KNOWN AS THE WHITE CHURCH), NEAR POMARIA

Tradition says that this set was brought to America from Germany by some of the early settlers, who organized the church about 160 years ago. The flagon, baptismal bowl and wafer plate have F. F. W., 1766, engraved on them. The cup or chalice is of a later date.

The small plate shown was made out of silver coins by a member of the congregation named Setzler. The only tools used were his hammer and anvil. He was locally known as the "wizard gunsmith".

The Bible shown in the engraving was purchased about 1800, and bears date of 1796. It has been in use and in the church for nearly a century and a quarter.

Following is information which has been furnished by an officer of St. John's Church, and some additional facts have been gleaned from authentic sources.

This church, located near Pomaria, was incorporated in 1763, but must have been organized about 1750. The original members came from Germany, a few came from Pennsylvania. They brought their pastor, Rev. Mr. Luft, with them, and he was no doubt the founder of St. John's Church.

His ashes rest in the churchyard. Following him are the names of Revs. Waterman, Froelich and Theus. The first churches were built of logs, but in 1808 a better structure was reared, which, with some improvements, still remains. The nails and hinges used were forged by John Summer.

Reverends Lewis Hockheimer and John Nicholas Martin also served this congregation. Rev. Mr. Hockheimer died here and Rev. J. N. Martin moved to Charleston in 1787. In 1787 Rev. Frederick Joseph Wallern was known to be the pastor, and his ministry extended to 1815, just three years before he died. Rev. Jacob Moser was pastor here about eleven years, and Rev. Simeon Scherer, from North Carolina, also preached here, but no record appears as to the length of service he rendered. Rev. Godfrey Dreher and Rev. Jacob Moser both preached here by a mutual arrangement, but how long can not now be determined. The record is clear from 1850, at which time Rev. Daniel Efird became pastor, and continued until 1882. Then Rev. J. K. Efird, 1882-92; Rev. S. L. Nease, 1892-94; Rev. A. R. Beck, 1894-1900; Rev. B. D. Wessinger, 1900-01; Rev. E. J. Sox, 1901-10; Rev. J. L. Cromer, 1914-15; Rev. J. C. Wessinger, 1915-17; Rev. B. L. Stroup, 1918-20; Rev. W. H. Riser, 1921-22.

About the year 1835 an unfortunate misunderstanding came into the life of the congregation, after which, by agreement, ministers of the South Carolina and Tennessee Synods preached here for many years, on alternate Sundays, until time and the grace of God ended the strife and brought a new era into the life of our Southern Church. The two congregations finally joined hands in the same synod.

The following ministers of the South Carolina Synod preached here under the agreement referred to:

Reverends George Haltiwanger, Sr., J. D. Stingley, John P. Margart, D. M. Blackwelder, T. S. Boinest, G. W. Holland, S. S. Rahn, H. S. Wingard, S. T. Hallman, J. H. Wyse, J. D. Bowles, J. J. Long, I. E. Long, J. A. Linn, S. C. Ballentine, Enoch Hite, H. A. Kistler and J. B. Haigler.

Sandy Run Church, Calhoun County

This is known as one of the oldest Lutheran congregations in the state, but the exact date is shrouded in uncertainty. An act of incorporation, quoted in Bernheim's Lutheran Church in the Carolinas, furnishes the proof that it was included in that act of 1778, under the name, "The German Lutheran Church of Salem, Sandy Run." There is no historic clue to the date of organization, but it is certain that this church formed a part of the "Corpus Evangelicum". Under its incorporated name, "Salem," it stands among the

SANDY RUN CHURCH

churches entering into the formation of this synod in January, 1824. Then at the convention of November, 1825, we find a list of donations from Sandy Run Church, the church, however, then being vacant. Its early pastoral supply is more a matter of conjecture than of historic fact.

The first really authentic information comes in the minutes of November, 1826, when Sandy Run is given as in the charge of Reverends Yost Meetze and Godfrey Dreher.

Dr. E. L. Hazelius, in a translation of what is designated
"Actum, Sandy Run, August 12, 1788", names Reverends
Daser, Theus, Bamberg, and Wallern as having assembled
in Salem Church, Sandy Run, and, no doubt, some one of
these was instrumental in the organization of this congregation, but further than that it is useless to surmise. This,
however, does fix the date back of 1788—possibly about
1765. In 1828 Rev. Jacob Wingard was the pastor; also
in 1829. Then Rev. J. D. Scheck was pastor in 1830, and
was succeeded by Rev. C. F. Bergman, 1831; Rev. J. C.
Hope, 1832-33; Rev. George Haltiwanger, 1834-43; Rev. J.
F. W. Leppard, 1844-51; Rev. J. H. Bailey, 1852; Rev. J.
B. Anthony, 1853-58; Rev. J. P. Margart, 1859-60; then a
vacancy seems to have followed up to 1864, when Rev. J.
H. Cupp took charge, but resigned before the convention of
1865. How long the congregation remained vacant, or how
supplied, we can not determine by the records; but in due
time Rev. William Berly took charge and served the congre-
gation until about 1873, when he ceased to be mortal. Then
Rev. J. H. Bailey became pastor and continued up to 1883.
In 1888 Rev. M. O. J. Kreps took charge and served to
October 5, 1885.

The next name associated with this historic church as pastor is that of Rev. S. S. Rahn, 1888, but at the end of
the synodical year he resigned and the vacancy was filled by
Rev. P. H. E. Derrick. He, too, resigned in 1892 and transferred to the Georgia Synod. He was followed by Rev. R.
E. Livingston in 1892-1903; 1904 vacant; Rev. R. E. Livingston, again, 1905-09; 1910 vacant; Rev. R. E. Livingston, again, 1911-18, when he passed to his heavenly home.

In 1919 Rev. J. W. Oxner took charge as supply pastor
for the synodical year, but has been induced to continue up
to 1924.

This congregation has lost very much by death and removals, but her people have been heroic and faithful, and
a brighter day will surely come. There are about fifty members on the roll, thirty in the Sunday School, with a property
value of $3,700.

Bethlehem Church, near Irmo

There seems to be no source of reliable information with reference to the organization of this congregation and the time when its first house of worship was built. The present pastor places the organization in 1788. Credible tradition has it that the first church was built farther up the river than the church known as Bookman's Church. This was an old log structure and some of the logs remained until a few years ago.

This first organization and house of worship was known as the Ellisor Church. The late D. A. Richardson, who was a close friend of David Bookman, said that David Bookman told him that the majority of the congregation wanted to move the church lower down the river in order to interest the Swygerts and Loricks in that locality, these families being prominent in that section in those days. The minority did not want to make the change, but the church known as Bookman's Church was built by the majority of the congregation at a date which has not been ascertained. The nearest information is an entry in the Journal of Rev. Godfrey Dreher: "Preach at the new church on Broad River June 6, 1819." The first church was called Ellisor's Church because it was in a neighborhood composed of families principally of that name. The second Bookman's Church was so called because located in a neighborhood populated largely by Bookmans. This old house of worship finally gave place to the new edifice near Irmo, which building is now used by the congregation.

From 1819 or 1820 until 1851 this church was served principally by Rev. Godfrey Dreher, and from 1851 or 1852 until 1882 by Rev. D. Efird. Then followed: Reverends J. S. Koiner, J. P. Smeltzer, D.D., W. L. Darr, Jacob Wike, James F. Deal, O. B. Shearouse, Enoch Hite, W. J. Roof, J. L. Cromer, and J. M. Senter, the present pastor, who writes: "The cornerstone of the present building bears this inscription: 'Bethlehem Church, June 30, 1901. Incorporated 1788.' "

St. Jacob's Church, Chapin

Definite information is not available as to the date of the organization of the congregation or the erection of the first building. It was probably organized in 1760. The only authentic information is that it was one of the churches assisting in the organization of the Corpus Evangelicum, November 13, 1787, and that it was incorporated February 29, 1788.*

ST. JACOB'S CHURCH

It is safe to assume that at this date it had a house of worship. Mr. D. A. Richardson remembered that in 1847 he attended service with this congregation in an old dilapidated log house standing upon the site of the present building, and that on the side of the house on which he sat during service the pins holding several of the logs between two windows had rotted off and the logs had fallen out.

In 1853 a sanctuary was built under contract by Levi Seay of Lexington. It was the house used by the congregation

*(South Carolina Statutes at Large, Vol. III, pp. 144-145.)

until 1905, and was the first church in that section of the country that had a gallery in it, which attracted considerable attention from the people of the surrounding country. This old building was remodeled in 1905, and is now being used by the congregation.

The first pastor of whom it has been possible to obtain any definite information is Rev. Jacob Moser, who served the congregation in the first part of the Nineteenth century. Rev. Godfrey Dreher preached in this church in 1819, but he seems not to have been elected pastor until 1836. He served the congregation until 1852. Rev. Daniel Efird was then the pastor until 1882. Since that time the congregation has been served by Reverends J. S. Koiner, J. P. Smeltzer, W. L. Darr, Jacob Wike, J. F. Deal, Enoch Hite, O. B. Shearouse, J. C. Wessinger and R. M. Carpenter.

Zion Church, Lexington

From the best information obtainable at this time, this church was organized some time between 1740 and 1750. The first house of worship was built some time after its

ZION CHURCH, 1792

ZION CHURCH, 1922

organization, located on Twelve Mile Creek near the home
of Godfrey Dreher, Jr., which stood very near the present
location of the mill now owned by Corley Brothers. November 13, 1787, the Corpus Evangelicum was organized in this
old building.

The land for the first building was given by Godfrey
Dreher and his brother, John Dreher. The church was incorporated in 1788. January 9, 1788, Rev. J. G. Bamberg
was ordained in this building by Reverends Senior Daser
and Frederick Augustus Wallburg.

Previous to 1787, Zion, St. Peter's and Bethel (on High
Hill Creek) had been formed into a pastorate, known as the
Saluda Pastorate, but how long this organization continued,
there is no definite knowledge.

In 1792 a frame house was built very near the river close
to what was then known as Younginer's Ferry. In 1856 an
addition was made to this building and this served the purpose of the congregation until 1922, when the brick edifice
on top of the river hill on the Columbia road, about half a

mile from the second building, was erected, and now is used by the congregation.

It is possible that this congregation was connected with the North Carolina Synod previous to 1824. At that time it assisted in the organization of the South Carolina Synod. In 1853 it united the Tennessee Synod. In 1921, with the union of North Carolina and Tennessee Synods. it became connected with the United Synod of North Carolina. In 1922 it united again with the South Carolina Synod.

From tradition and from what records can be gathered at the present time, it seems that commencing about 1760 this congregation was served by the following pastors: Reverends John Nicholas Martin, Lewis Hockheimer, J. G. Bamberg, C. E. Bernhardt, John Nicholas Marcord, Michael Rauch, J. P. Franklow, J. Y. Meetze, Godfrey Dreher, R. J. Miller, Daniel Efird, Adam Efird, A. L. Crouse, E. L. Lybrand, J. A. Cromer. Rev. H. A. Kistler is the present pastor.

The lands for the second house on the river were donated by Godfrey Dreher and John Dreher and for the third building by S. M. and W. L. Corley and G. C. Ehrhart.

The South Carolina Synod met in this church November 12-15, 1923. This proved to be one of the most pleasant and profitable conventions in the history of the synod. A noteworthy fact is that two of the grandsons (Hon. C. M. Efird and Mr. D. F. Efird) of Rev. Godfrey Dreher were present as members of the synod and added much to the pleasure and success of the meeting.

Salem Church, Leesville

This congregation was organized in 1792. It is greatly to be regretted that in the preparation of this sketch of its history the data were not available. Two marble slabs in the church bear the following inscriptions:

> "In blessed memory of our Fathers and Mothers in the true faith by whose prayers and sacrifices Salem Evangelical Lutheran Church was founded, 1792."

"In grateful memory of the worthy Sons and Daughters whose contributions rebuilt and painted Salem Evangelical Lutheran Church, 1890-1891."

SALEM CHURCH

In the 132 years of its existence many pastors have served this congregation. Among the remembered names are those of Reverends David Shealy, Jesse Lowman, Drewry Kyzer, J. Q. Wertz, A. W. Lindler, B. Kreps, A. D. L. Moser, C. P. Boozer, L. E. Busby, H. P. Counts, James D. Kinard, D. B. Groseclose, S. C. Ballentine, W. E. Schuette, V. Y. Boozer. The present pastor is Rev. W. D. Wise.

St. Peter's Church (Piney Woods), near Chapin

In 1793 Peter Shumpert and Uriah Mayer, then members of St. John's Church on Broad River, found a vacant piece of land of 112 acres on which the St. Peter's Church now stands. It was surveyed February 15, 1794, and grant obtained from the state May 5, 1794. These men and others in the neighborhood then belonged to St. John's, to which church some of them walked in attending the services. A congregation was organized by Rev. Frederick Joseph Wallern and incorporated December 17, 1794. A house was built of hewn logs and ceiled on the inside, with planed pine boards. It stood across the road on the south side of the present building. One or two of the old ceiling boards of this church are now in possession of J. J. Frick, grandson of Thomas Frick, who helped to organize the congregation and build the first house of worship.

ST. PETER'S CHURCH (PINEY WOODS)

In March, 1834, the congregation decided to build another sanctuary and Jacob Wheeler, Jacob Mayer, Jack Harmon, John Sease and Jacob Bower were appointed a building committee. The amount of $633 in cash was subscribed for the building. The old house was sold and was bought by Thomas Frick. This new house of worship, a frame structure, forty feet by sixteen feet, was dedicated November 29, 1835, by Rev. E. L. Hazelius, D.D., and Rev. Godfrey Dreher.

Following is the list of pastors: Reverends Frederick Joseph Wallern, Harman Winkhouse, Michael Rauch, Godfrey Dreher, Daniel Efird, J. K. Efird, J. G. Schaid, A. R. Beck, B. D. Wessinger, E. J. Sox, M. L. Pence, B. L. Stroup, W. H. Riser. Rev. D. L. Miller is the present pastor.

St. Peter's Church united with the Tennessee Synod in 1852 and with the other congregations of the same synod in

South Carolina joined in the formation of the United Synod of North Carolina in 1921, and subsequently in 1922, in similar manner, united with the South Carolina Synod.

St. Nicholas' Church, Fairfax

The date of organization of this church is recorded in the list of churches as 1800, but this is by no means certain. At the convention of the synod in November, 1829, a petition was sent up from the *two churches in Barnwell District* for ministerial services the next year, and provision was made

ST. NICHOLAS' CHURCH

accordingly. The two churches referred to were evidently St. Bartholomew and St. Nicholas', for "Shiloh Church in the fork of the two Edistos", was not organized until late in 1830. There is at least presumptive evidence that St. Nicholas' Church was associated with Bartholomew (now Mt. Pleasant) earlier than 1800, but since there is no available record of the date of the organization and the building, the exact date must remain uncertain.*

The synod met in this church in 1835. In the early history of this church the records show the following pastors: Reverends William D. Strobel, J. D. Scheck, R. Cloy, W. G.

* (See Minutes of 1830, p. 26.)

Harter, C. F. Bansemer, G. R. Haigler, George Haltiwanger, Jr., Paul Kestler and B. F. Berry, 1860-70; C. P. Boozer, 1870-74; B. Kreps, 1875-77; J. F. Probst, 1878-81; I. P. Hawkins, 1881-84; E. A. Wingard, 1884-87; J. H. Wilson, 1887-1903; P. E. Monroe, 1903-08; D. B. Groseclose, 1908-12; E. F. K. Roof, 1913-16; P. D. Risinger, 1917-21; A. W. Ballentine, 1922-24. Rev. George Harter was a son of this congregation.

The present house of worship is the third in the history of this congregation, having been built in 1910. The Fairfax congregation is a daughter of St. Nicholas' Church.

This congregation now has ninety-five confirmed members, and ninety-nine in the Sunday School. The property value is $4,000.

St. Paul's Church, Gilbert

No definite information as to the exact date of the organization of this congregation is obtainable, but some of the older people are of the opinion that it was about 1800. In July, 1803, Jacob Roll and George Roll conveyed to the officers of the German Protestant Church named St. Paul, in Orangeburg District, on the waters of the Little Hollow Creek, a tract of land (7¾ acres) to be used for a church and schoolhouse for the use of the German congregation of "Lutherans and Calvinists" (or as some styled them, "Presbetirains"). A log house was built on this land—presumably about the date of deed—which served the congregation until 1851. Then the second house, which is still standing, was built, and used until 1889. The congregation in this time having outgrown the old building, the present edifice was erected and the cornerstone laid with services conducted by Rev. E. L. Lybrand, pastor, assisted by Rev. L. E. Busby and Rev. J. A. Cromer. There is an old log house still standing near the second church in the edge of a field, which is said to be the first house, which was sold to Captain Lewie and which he utilized for a tenant house. In 1909 the congregation purchased of the heirs of Mrs. H. A. Griffith one acre to be used as a cemetery adjoining the seven acres. It has not been possible to ascertain the names of the pastors of this congregation previous to 1837, but from that date to 1851 the congregation was served by Rev. Godfrey Dreher and such assistants as he could secure from time to time. From that time to the present the pastors have been: Reverends Daniel Efird, Adam Efird, A. L. Crouse, J. K. Efird, E. L. Lybrand, W. H. Roof, E. J. Sox, B. D. Wessinger, J. L. Cromer, G. A. Stoudemayer, L. L. Lohr, and T. C. Parker, the present pastor.

Nazareth Church, Lexington County

This church was organized in the early Nineteenth century, some say in 1803, others 1810. One thing, however, is certain, and that is that Nazareth was represented when the organization of this synod was completed in November, 1824, Mr. Samuel Wingard being the delegate from Nazareth Church.

NAZARETH CHURCH

In 1826 it is entered in the minutes of the synod as being under the pastoral care of Rev. Yost Meetze and Rev. Godfrey Dreher, but no mention is made of the numerical strength of the congregation. In 1827 it was definitely stated that Rev.

Godfrey Dreher was then pastor, and in 1828 he was still the pastor, but in the records of 1830 Rev. William D. Strobel is the pastor. In 1831 Rev. Mr. Dreher's name again appears as the pastor. The same is true in 1832, but in 1833 the name of Rev. George Haltiwanger, Sr., appears, as also in the minutes of the nine years next following. In 1843 no pastor is mentioned, but in 1844 the name of Dr. Hazelius appears as having charge of Nazareth.

The first church was a log house (such buildings were common in that day), located near a spring of good water. The second building was on the present site, on which the third house of worship also stands.

Apart from those already mentioned, the following served this congregation in the years after the long pastorate of Rev. George Haltiwanger, Sr., Reverends David Shealy, Emanuel Caughman, Jesse B. Lowman, Drewry Kyzer, J. H. Bailey, A. D. L. Moser, Barney Kreps and J. D. Shealy; then, George S. Bearden, 1901-04; J. W. Nease, 1905-06; B. W. Cronk, 1907-09; P. D. Risinger, 1912-16; and O. B. Shearouse, from 1917 to the present time.

The membership is now 120, with a total Sunday School enrollment of 97. The property value is $3,200.

St. Peter's Church (Meetze's), near Lexington

No authentic information is available as to the date of the organization of this church. Tradition is to the effect that an old log house near Eighteen Mile Creek, on lands recently owned by G. E. Roberts, was the first house of worship.

This congregation participated in the organization of the Corpus Evangelicum at Zion Church, November 13, 1787. It was incorporated February 19, 1788.* The congregation was also a part of the Saluda Pastorate, which it composed together with Zion and Bethel on High Hill Creek, in existence in 1788.

This old structure was abandoned about 1857, when a new house of worship was erected about half a mile from the site of the old building. This building was completed about

---

*(South Carolina Statutes at Large, Vol. III, pp. 144, 145.)

1859, and is the one now used by the congregation. It has been recently repaired.

ST. PETER'S CHURCH (MEETZES)

There is some doubt about the early pastors of this church, but the following ministers held service there: Reverends Hockheimer, Winkhouse, Wallburg, Bamberg, Bernhardt, and Wingard. Beginning with 1800 it was served by Revs. Michael Rauch, J. Y. Meetze, Jacob Kleckley and Godfrey Dreher.

St. Michael's Church, Irmo

This is one of the historic churches in the synod, and will ever remain memorable in the life and history of our Southern Church. It was organized in 1814, and was under the care of Rev. Godfrey Dreher, whose name is indelibly written in the history of this synod.

Mr. Jacob F. Schirmer, writing of this church, said: "We find that the first service was held here in 1814, and it was then attached to the North Carolina Synod. Rev. Godfrey Dreher was then their pastor. A record book was found in

1813 entitled, 'A Book of the School House Church.' In this school house services were held for some time; the members were mostly from Bethel Church, and are said to have left it in consequence of not having English preaching."

Reverends Godfrey Dreher and J. Y. Meetze served them for some time. Soon after, a piece of land was given by Mr. John Dreher, and a church was built on the same site where the present church now stands. In 1831 Rev. J. G. Schwartz was the pastor, and we find a pastoral letter written by him in August, 1831, which was about the last letter he wrote previous to his death.

ST. MICHAEL'S CHURCH (BLUE CHURCH)

At this distance in point of time, it is not possible to obtain an accurate list of pastors, but the following are known to have ministered in St. Michael's: Reverends Godfrey Dreher, 1814; J. C. Hope, 1834; George Haltiwanger, Jr., and J. D. Stingley, 1850; J. B. Lowman, 1853; J. H. Bailey, 1854; D. M. Blackwelder, 1861; J. N. Derrick, 1867; W. A. Houck, 1872; J. E. Berly, 1877; W. A. Deaton, 1891; H. J. Mathias, 1898; S. L. Nease, 1902; V. C. Ridenhour, 1905;

W. P. Cline, 1907; M. D. Huddle, 1914; R. R. Sowers, 1919; and J. W. Mangum, the present pastor, from 1922 to this time.

The initial organization of the South Carolina Synod took place in this church January 14, 1824, and the organizers were John P. Franklow, John Y. Meetze, Godfrey Dreher, Michael Rauch, Jacob Moser and Samuel Herscher. The lay delegates were John Dreher, Sr., St. Michael's Church; George Lindler, St. John's Church; Christopher Wiggers, Bethel Church; Samuel Oswald, Salem Church; and Henry Bookhardt, Santee Church. These ministers and laymen elected as the officers Rev. Godfrey Dreher, President, and Rev. Samuel Herscher, Secretary.

The old building was torn down and another erected about 1880, and this too gave place to a highly creditable, modern structure in 1919.

It is said that there was a pipe organ in the church in its early history, but as to its size and structure there is no information.

Besides the church building, the congregation owns a comfortable parsonage, having a combined property value of $11,000. The membership is 111. The Sunday School has an enrollment of about 153.

Bethlehem Church, near Pomaria

From information furnished by Rev. J. C. Hope some years before he died, this congregation was organized and the church built in 1816, and was dedicated with services conducted by Reverends Godfrey Dreher and R. J. Miller. From written data it is certain that Mr. Herman Aull, assisted by the congregation, laid the foundation, and one John Carr finished the building. Mr. Aull himself entered the ministry in the fall of 1831 and became an efficient minister of the Word.

The fact was gathered from the diary of Rev. Godfrey Dreher that he had charge of this congregation from 1816 to 1824, and therefore must have been the organizer of the congregation. Reverends Godfrey Dreher and Michael

Rauch served the congregation jointly for several years, and Rev. Mr. Rauch seems to have continued his labors up to 1830. Then followed Reverends J. G. Schwartz, J. C. Hope, William Berly and G. Haltiwanger, Jr. The lamented Schwartz passed away August 26, 1831, and the funeral discourse was preached by Rev. Godfrey Dreher, using Rev. 14:13 as the text of his sermon. Rev. Godfrey Dreher then preached occasionally in Bethlehem Church. He held communion services there in 1831 and 1832. In 1832 Rev. J. C. Hope became pastor and continued his labors in that capacity until 1837.

BETHLEHEM CHURCH, POMARIA

Rev. J. B. Anthony then became pastor. He was followed by Rev. T. S. Boinest, who labored there until his death in 1871—a continuous ministry of more than twenty years.

The following ministers succeeded each other: Reverends George W. Holland, D.D.; S. S. Rahn, D.D.; H. S. Wingard, D.D.; S. T. Hallman, D.D.; J. H. Wyse; J. D. Bowles; J. J. Long, D.D.; J. D. Shealy; I. E. Long; J. A. Linn; R. H. Anderson; S. C. Ballentine; Enoch Hite; H. A. Kistler, and J. B. Haigler, the present incumbent.

This has been one of the prominent churches of the synod in all of its history and has a goodly record for benevolence and loyalty to all the enterprises and institutions of the Church.

St. Mark's Church, Leesville

The exact date of the organization of this church can not be definitely settled. Some say 1820, but a careful examination of the early minutes of the synod reveals the fact that it was not mentioned in the proceedings of this body until November, 1827, and then in connection with the missionary operations of Rev. J. D. Sheck, under the direction of a special committee, of which Rev. Godfrey Dreher was chair-

ST. MARK'S CHURCH

man. The record says: "On Monday he preached at Wise Schoolhouse, and found the people very destitute—and they are both able and willing to build a place of worship and support a minister." This is believed to have been the origin of St. Mark's Church, and the date of organization should be 1827, for at the very next convention a petition was sent up from St. Mark's Church, Edgefield District, requesting the services of Rev. J. C. Hope. However, inasmuch as Mr. Hope was going to Gettysburg for further study, the churches named in the petition were placed under the care of Reverends Godfrey Dreher, M. Rauch and J. D. Sheck. This also explains the fact that Rev. Godfrey Dreher was the first pastor. At the convention of synod in 1829, St. Mark's is in Rev. Mr. Dreher's charge, and ever after that it has been one of the recognized churches of this synod.

From that date it was served by Reverends J. G. Schwartz, 1830; Godfrey Dreher, 1831-33; Herman Aull, 1834-39; S. R. Shepherd, 1840-53; Samuel Bouknight, 1854-69; Paul Derrick, 1870-76; C. P. Boozer, 1876-84; J. D. Bowles, 1884-91; C. P. Boozer, 1891-92; O. B. Shearouse, 1892-1903; D. B. Groseclose, 1904; J. L. Buck, 1904-06; J. B. Harman, 1906-11; W. A. Dutton, 1912-18; C. K. Rhodes, 1919-22; J. J. Long, 1923, the present pastor.

The present church building was dedicated in 1857. The pastor, Rev. Samuel Bouknight, was assisted in the dedicatory services by Rev. William Berly.

From this congregation the following have entered the Lutheran ministry: Emanuel Caughman, J. H. W. Wertz, J. L. Derrick, J. Q. Wertz, T. W. Shealy, Y. von A. Riser, C. M. Riser and H. J. Black.

The following ministers rest in the church cemetery: Paul Derrick, A. W. Lindler, Emanuel Caughman and C. P. Boozer.

The membership is now 255, with 125 in the Sunday School, and the property value is $4,000.

St. Matthew's Church, Newberry County

This church, located near Ashford's Ferry, Broad River, was organized in 1827. From the records of the synod, it was the result of the missionary labors of Rev. J. D. Sheck, who did extensive home missionary work under the direction of this synod.

The pastors serving this congregation in its early history seem to have been as follows: Reverends J. D. Sheck, Jacob Moser, J. C. Hope, S. R. Shepherd, William Berly, T. S. Boinest, R. J. Hungerpeler, Jacob Hawkins, and J. A. Sligh. Then followed Reverends J. D. Shirey, Z. W. Bedenbaugh, William A. Julian, J. H. Wyse, J. D. Bowles, J. J. Long, J. D. Shealy, I. E. Long, J. A. Linn, R. H. Anderson, S. C.

Ballentine, Enoch Hite, H. A. Kistler, and J. B. Haigler, the present pastor.

February 18, 1884, the church was destroyed by a cyclone, but was rebuilt under the ministry of Rev. Z. W. Bedenbaugh and dedicated May 17, 1885, Rev. J. D. Shirey preaching the dedicatory sermon. The new building, rising again from the ruins of the old through the persistent and untiring energy of the people and the zeal of its pastor, is highly creditable to the community and illustrates the power of faith and devotion to a noble purpose.

The membership numbers 125 with 44 in the Sunday School. The church has a property valuation of $1,200.

Rev. Thomas F. Suber is a son of this congregation.

St. Luke's Church, near Prosperity

This congregation was organized by Rev. J. G. Schwartz in 1828. It first worshiped in a log building, but in 1845 a better structure was erected. This was remodeled in 1886, and new pews were placed in the church. In 1916 a Sunday School room was built and suitable church furniture was placed in the main auditorium in 1924.

The following were sons of this church: Reverends Stanmore R. Shepherd, Levi Bedenbaugh, Wilson Bedenbaugh, J. S. Elmore, Jacob Hawkins, I. P. Hawkins, Z. W. Bedenbaugh, C. P. Boozer, W. E. Pugh, P. E. Shealy and J. A. Shealy.

The regular pastors have been as follows: Reverends J. G. Schwartz, William Berly, J. Moser, J. C. Hope, J. P. Margart, T. S. Boinest (assisted by Rev. J. D. Smithdeal), J. Hawkins, D.D., H. S. Wingard, D.D., J. D. Bowles, J. Hawkins, D.D., M. J. Epting, J. Hawkins, D.D., (until his death in July of the same year), George S. Bearden, H. J. Mathias, S. P. Koon, B. W. Cronk, W. H. Roof, and E. H. Seckinger, the present pastor.

The congregation has a confirmed membership of 317, with 280 in the Sunday School, and a property value of $7,500.

St. Stephen's Church, Lexington

From the best available information, this church was organized about 1830. The first building was dedicated in October, 1831, and the hallowed memories of the Theological Seminary and Classical Academy, founded at Lexington in 1832, cluster around this church. From this center streams of holy influence went out for many years and these still live, but the wanton torch of some of Sherman's vandal hordes destroyed the church in 1865, and with it went records which can never be replaced.

At the convention of synod in November, 1830, President Bachman reported that "a church, 40x50, is building at Lexington Court House, and is in a considerable state of forwardness. . . . This, when completed, will be the only church in that flourishing village. The location is favorable to the formation of a large congregation, and we feel assured that a minister of our Church would exert a highly beneficial influence upon the village and the neighborhood."*

This settles two facts, to wit: The Lutherans built the first church at Lexington, and that church was built in 1830. Missionary William D. Strobel reported at the same meeting of synod: "A large church is in a state of forwardness at Lexington Court House, and that at Nazareth will soon be completed. From the vicinity of so many members of our Church, we expect that Lexington Court House will become one of our most important stations."

This expectation was fully realized in the years following, and from that date onward the name and the influence of St. Stephen's Church has lived in the life and work of the synod. The convention of November 16, 1833, was held in this new church, and a long cherished hope was being realized.

Some of the names of the faithful pastors who served this congregation are: Reverends E. L. Hazelius, D.D., Michael Rauch, George Haltiwanger, Jr., David Bernhardt, C. B. Thummel, J. C. Hope, J. F. W. Leppard, Lewis Eichelberger, D.D., William Berly, Samuel Bouknight, J. H.

---

*(Minutes of 1830, p. 17.)

Bailey, M. O. J. Kreps, D.D., S. S. Rahn, D.D., J. G. Graichen, J. Q. Wertz, W. H. Hiller, T. S. Brown, L. A. Thomas, W. H. Riser, and A. B. Obenschain, the present pastor. While this list is correct, the order of succession may not be accurate.

This congregation has had three church buildings. Those erected in 1830 and 1870 were burned, and in 1896 a stone church was erected. A pipe organ was installed in 1922. The present church is therefore better equipped than either of its predecessors, and is highly creditable to our people in Lexington.

The membership is 287; there are 177 in the Sunday School. The property value is $26,000.

Mt. Calvary Church, near Johnston

This church was one of the fruits of the missionary labors of Rev. J. D. Sheck as far back as 1827. In 1828 a small log church was built and services were held there in the early part of 1829. In February, 1830, a formal organization was effected and the church was dedicated by Reverends W. D. Strobel and J. G. Schwartz. The congregation was supplied by them for a time and then by Reverends Jacob Moser and Herman Aull until 1835, when Rev. Levi Bedenbaugh took charge. It was soon found necessary to build a new church. Accordingly a building was erected on another site and was dedicated in July, 1837, the service of dedication being conducted by Reverends Jacob Moser and George Haltiwanger.

The following are the other pastors who have served the congregation: Reverends Emanuel Caughman, Samuel Bouknight, Barney Kreps, L. E. Busby, H. P. Counts, James D. Kinard, L. P. Boland, P. D. Risinger, D. A. Sox, P. E. Monroe, M. L. Kester and James D. Kinard (second term), pastor now in charge.

The membership numbers 284, and the Sunday School 200. Church property value is $3,000.

One son entered the ministry from this church in the person of Rev. John L. Yonce.

Trinity Church, Saluda County

This church was organized in May, 1837, under the ministry of Rev. George Haltiwanger, Sr. A church was erected at a cost of $417, and was dedicated August, 1838, the service being conducted by Rev. John C. Hope, assisted by Reverends Jacob Moser and George Haltiwanger, Sr. In 1882, under the pastoral services of Rev. C. P. Boozer, a more commodious building was erected. The dedicatory sermon was preached by Rev. Peter Miller. The membership was greatly increased, but, like many other rural congregations, the number has been reduced by death and transfers.

The following pastors have ministered to this congregation: Reverends George Haltiwanger, Sr., 1839-40; Robert Cloy, 1841-43; S. R. Shepherd, 1844-45; Robert Cloy, 1846-47; Paul Kistler, 1848-49; S. R. Shepherd, 1850; Michael Rauch, 1851-53; A. W. Lindler, 1854-57; J. H. W. Wertz, 1858-60; M. Whittle, 1861; Samuel Bouknight, 1862-63; D. M. Blackwelder, 1864-65; A. D. L. Moser, 1866; J. H. W. Wertz, 1867-70; Paul Derrick, 1871-73; C. P. Boozer, 1876-83; J. D. Bowles, 1884-88; C. P. Boozer, 1889-92; O. B. Shearouse, 1893-1900; J. M. Tise, 1901; D. B. Groseclose, 1902; J. L. Buck, 1903-04; C. J. Sox, 1905; N. D. Bodie, 1907-12; S. P. Koon, 1913; W. H. Dutton, 1915; George S. Bearden, 1917-22; John J. Long, D.D., 1922 to this time.

This congregation now has 130 members, 80 in the Sunday School, and a property value of $1,800.

Rev. W. B. Aull is a son of this congregation.

Ebenezer Church, Columbia

Steps were first taken about 1828 looking toward the establishment of a Lutheran church in Columbia. The details of dates and events in these beginnings are not at hand, but we know that by 1830 a congregation had been organized and a church building erected. Rev. Jacob Wingard, of Lexington County, was the first pastor, but his pastorate here was brief as he was taken by death in the early part of 1831. This first house of worship of Ebenezer congregation was a

neat brick structure with a shingle roof. It was provided
for mainly by Mr. Henry Muller, Sr., of Platt Springs, Lexington (then District) County, who was one of the patriarchs
of the Lutheran Church in South Carolina. This history of
the congregation affords a striking illustration not only of
foresight in church extension but also of the importance of
small beginnings. From a mere handful of loyal Lutherans,
Ebenezer has developed into one of the largest and most
active Lutheran churches in the South. During the first fifty
years there was a long period of struggle, but then a season
of steady growth set in which has continued almost uninter-
ruptedly until the present time.

The church erected in 1830 was destroyed during the night
of February 17, 1865, when Sherman's army raided the city
of Columbia. This was a great blow to the small band of
members, many of whom were then serving in the army of
the South, several being killed in battle. But the congregation, numbering not more than fifty members, set to work
to rebuild the church. December 9, 1870, the new church
was dedicated with appropriate services. The building had
cost $5,300, and at its completion all was paid except
$400. This is a fine testimonial of the love of these impov-
erished people for their church.

From this time forward the congregation made steady
progress. By the year 1900 it was found necessary to im-
prove and refurnish the old church. This was done at the
cost of about $5,000. The church was rededicated on Octo-
ber 28, 1900. This was accomplished during the ministry
of Rev. M. M. Kinard, D.D.

In 1912, during the ministry of Rev. C. A. Freed, D.D.,
the present Sunday School building was erected at a cost
of about $12,000, which was then one of the best equipped
and most commodious buildings of its kind, perhaps, in the
entire state. It was formally dedicated June 15, 1913.

However, at the present time the congregation has again
outgrown its physical equipment and new developments are
being planned to care for the continued and rapid growth
of the congregation. It is very probable that within the next

few years a larger and more adequate plant will be provided for the increased activities of the church.

This congregation has for years been prominent in the work of our Church in the South, and has the honor of having given to the ministry Rev. John C. Seegers, D.D., one of the leaders of the American Lutheran Church.

An indication of the growth of the congregation is found in the following facts. At the beginning of Dr. Kinard's pastorate the confirmed membership was 170; at its close in 1903 it was 225. At the close of Dr. Freed's pastorate in 1921 it was 525. At the present time the confirmed membership is over 700; together with the unconfirmed children it numbers about 1,000 souls. The benevolences have increased in still larger proportions, as in 1886 the total benevolence of the congregation was $102, while the latest synodcial report shows a benevolent expenditure of nearly $9,000. Rev. P. D. Brown has been pastor of the congregation since 1921.

The following pastors served this congregation from its organization in 1830, to 1843, the exact length of their services being uncertain: Reverends Jacob Wingard, William D. Strobel, John C. Hope, E. L. Hazelius, D.D., Levi Bedenbaugh, Philip A. Strobel, and William Berly. The following pastors have served since 1843: Reverends E. B. Hort, 1843-62; A. R. Rude, D.D., 1863-74; Z. W. Bedenbaugh, 1874-76; A. R. Rude, D.D., 1876-82; John B. Haskell, 1882-84; A. J. Bowers, D.D., 1884-86; M. M. Kinard, D.D., 1886-1903; C. A. Freed, D.D., 1903-21. Rev. P. D. Brown is the present pastor.

The long pastorates of four of Ebenezer's pastors are worthy of mention, namely, Rev. E. B. Hort, nineteen years; Rev. Dr. Rude, sixteen years; Rev. Dr. Kinard, sixteen years; Rev. Dr. Freed, eighteen years. These four faithful servants gave to Ebenezer congregation a total of sixty-nine years of service.

St. John's Church, Lexington County

This congregation was organized in 1832, but the first official mention of it is found in the minutes of 1833, when a petition was sent from St. John's Church, Calk's Road, requesting the pastoral services of Reverends Michael Rauch and George Haltiwanger, Sr. The request was granted.

At the convention of 1835, St. John's Church, Calk's Road, petitioned the synod to hold the convention of 1836 in that church. This request was likewise granted.

The early proceedings of the synod are so brief and disconnected that it is impossible at this late date to get any accurate information as to pastors and other details.

The old church was remodeled in 1913, and on July 19 of that year was dedicated, Rev. P. D. Risinger then being the pastor.

The names of pastors are as follows: Reverends Michael Rauch, George Haltiwanger, Sr., J. B. Lowman, J. H. Bailey, A. W. Lindler, Emanuel Caughman, J. N. Derrick, George A. Hough, C. P. Boozer, M. O. J. Kreps, J. G. Graichen, J. W. Nease, B. W. Cronk, P. D. Risinger, and O. B. Shearouse, the present pastor (since 1917).

The membership is 105, total Sunday School enrollment seventy-seven. The property value is $3,000.

St. Andrew's Church, Lexington County

This congregation was organized in 1835 under the ministry of Rev. Michael Rauch, and the church was dedicated in that year. The dedication is referred to in the minutes of November, 1835, at which time Levi Bedenbaugh, student for the ministry, had been elected pastor, "provided he be received by the synod and authorized to administer the ordinances of the Church." The pastors are named as follows: Reverends M. Rauch, Levi Bedenbaugh, J. F. W. Leppard, W. Berly, J. B. Anthony, Levi Bedenbaugh again, then William Berly again, W. A. Houck, J. E. Berly, W. A. Deaton, H. J. Mathias, S. L. Nease, V. C. Ridenhour, W. P. Cline, M. D. Huddle, R. R. Sowers, and the present pastor, J. W. Mangum (since 1922).

In 1917 a creditable new church was erected. The membership is 161, and the Sunday School has an enrollment of 161; property value $4,500.

St. Matthew's Church, Charleston

The charter name of this, the second Lutheran church to be organized in Charleston, is German Evangelical Lutheran Church of Charleston, S. C. As the German language is not used in any of the services now, the name is omitted and the congregation is called St. Matthew's.

The first meeting held for the purpose of organizing this German Lutheran congregation was on November 26, 1840. A week later, December 3, an organization was effected with an enrollment of 44, and Mr. J. A. Wagener was elected president of the congregation.

In 1841 Rev. F. Becker was engaged by the congregation to serve them for one year. During this year a lot on Hasell Street was purchased for $3,000 and a contract was made for the construction of a church building to cost $8,000. This building was completed in June, 1842, and dedicated June 22 of that year. On the same date Rev. F. Heemsoth was installed as pastor. He served the congregation until early in 1848. This first church building (years later) became the property of St. Johannes' Lutheran congregation.

Rev. Louis Mueller, D.D., became pastor April 1, 1848. He rounded out a full fifty years as pastor, death coming to him in April, 1898. Rev. W. A. C. Mueller, D.D., came to the congregation in January, 1892, as assistant to his father, serving in that capacity until his father's death, when he became full pastor. Dr. W. A. C. Mueller reckons that his father, while pastor of St. Matthew's, baptized 4,402 persons, confirmed 1,440, performed 1,503 marriage ceremonies, conducted funerals of 4,163 persons, and made 75,000 pastoral visits.

In 1856 the congregation established their own cemetery and called it Bethany Cemetery. This cemetery adjoins the city cemetery, Magnolia, and is the Lutheran burial ground for Charleston. Bethany Cemetery has an endowment of $40,000 for perpetual care.

The property on which the present church stands was purchased in January, 1867, and the cornerstone of the building was laid December 22, 1867. The church was dedicated

Maunday Thursday, March 28, 1872. Upon this occasion some 3,000 people marched in procession from the Hasell Street church to the new building. Mr. J. H. Devereux was the architect, and in turning over the building to the church authorities he presented the congregation with a silver key attached to a gold cross. The congregation presented to him a sterling silver tea service. The building measures 64 feet by 157 feet deep, capped by a tower and spire that extend 297 feet above the sea. The ceiling of the auditorium is 72 feet above the floor.

In 1901 a clock and chimes of ten bells were placed in the tower at a cost of about $7,000.

A Sunday School and parish building was constructed in 1909 at a cost of about $20,000. The present property is conservatively valued at $125,000.

Rev. W. A. C. Mueller, D.D., served as pastor until early in 1920, when he was made pastor emeritus, retiring altogether from the congregation in 1922. Rev. S. L. Blomgren was elected junior pastor in January, 1919. He later became full pastor, resigning in October, 1922.

In 1923, from Easter until October, Rev. T. G. Hartwig served the congregation as supply pastor.

In November, 1923, Rev. H. B. Schaeffer became pastor, being duly installed December 10 of the same year.

St. Matthew's congregation has the largest membership in the South Carolina Synod, numbering more than 800 confirmed members.

Good Hope Church, Saluda

This congregation was organized August 3, 1839, and was received into the synod in November, 1840. A house of worship was erected and dedicated April 19, 1840, prior to the congregation's reception into the synod. The first pastor was Rev. Robert Cloy. He was followed at intervals by Reverends Samuel Bouknight, A. W. Lindler, E. Caughman and David Shealy.

The record is not clear, but it is known that the following ministers served this congregation during a series of years:

Reverends S. R. Shepherd, J. H. Bailey, J. H. W. Wertz, S. T. Hallman (1869), L. E. Busby, H. P. Counts, James D. Kinard, P. D. Risinger, D. A. Sox, P. E. Monroe, M. L. Kester, and James D. Kinard (second term), the present pastor.

Two of Good Hope's sons entered the ministry, N. D. Bodie and George A. Stoudemayer.

The first building, dedicated by Rev. John P. Margart, was later replaced by a much better structure, although on another site. This building is now being remodeled. It will conform to modern ideals and will be more convenient and churchly.

St. James' Church, Jalapa

This church, now located in the town of Jalapa, seven miles west of Newberry, was organized in 1840, and dedicated in 1841, under the name of Liberty Hill.

The pastors have been as follows: Reverends Herman Aull, John C. Hope, G. H. Brown, William Berly, E. A. Bolles, W. H. Finck, J. B. Anthony, Stanmore R. Shepherd, R. J. Hungerpeler, Jacob Moser, Jacob Hawkins, James M. Schreckhise, J. D. Shirey, A. G. Voigt, A. J. Bowers, W. K. Sligh, J. D. Shealy, J. D. Kinard, P. E. Shealy, and L. P. Boland.

In 1869 a new building was erected on the old site. In 1890 the same building was removed from Liberty Hill to Jalapa through the efforts of Rev. W. C. Schaeffer, D.D., and dedicated December 21 in the same year, the name being changed as indicated.

In 1920, under the pastoral care of Rev. L. P. Boland, the church was rebuilt. It has been learned also that Rev. D. I. Dreher and Rev. J. H. Bailey once served this congregation. Rev. Z. W. Bedenbaugh was pastor in 1883 and 1884. From that date it was served by the pastors of Beth Eden and St. Matthew's. From 1843 to 1884—a period of forty-one years—this church was in a pastorate with Beth Eden, and therefore ministered to by the pastors of Beth Eden congregation.

The life of this congregation has been maintained through all the years of its existence under somewhat trying circumstances, but its life is brightening and the membership is now about 100 with 77 in the Sunday School. The church has a valuation of $6,000.

Bethlehem Church, Lexington County

(CALLED CHURCH OF SAND HILLS AND BLACK CREEK.)

The first mention of this church is in the minutes of the convention of synod in 1829.

The president, Rev. John Bachman, in his report, said: "We have received information of four new churches that either have been built or are in a great state of forwardness—a large and commodious church in Newberry (County, of course,), one at Edisto, one at the Sand Hills, in Lexington, and one in Columbia." Since Bethlehem was known in almost all of its history as "The Church in the Sand Hills", this reference is evidently to this Bethlehem Church, Lexington County. Another fact is that Rev. Godfrey Dreher, in 1831, reported as his charge seven churches, among which were two Bethlehems—one in Newberry District and this Bethlehem. Nazareth, not far away from Bethlehem, was one of the others. This shows that his pastorate covered that section of the county.

In 1831 the president of synod reported the dedication of this church "in the Sand Hills".[*]

Unquestionably the date of organization is therefore 1829, and Rev. Godfrey Dreher was the first pastor. The writer's father and mother were members of this congregation at a later date, and frequently spoke of Rev. Godfrey Dreher. As further proof of this fact, Rev. Mr. Dreher mentions Bethlehem as the name of a church in his charge in 1829; and then at the meeting of the synod in 1840, it was reported by the Secretary of Missions, Rev. John C. Hope, that "Rev. S. Bouknight takes charge of Bethlehem Church, Black Creek, Lexington County," thus showing conclusively that the date

*(Minutes of 1831, p. 20.)

of organization, 1841, as given in our present list of churches
in the minutes of synod, is not historically correct. The date
of organization is 1829, and that of dedication is 1831.

It is difficult at this time, after the lapse of ninety-five
years, to give in detail the list of pastors. The following,
however, have served this old congregation: Reverends Godfrey Dreher, 1829; S. Bouknight, 1840-48; J. H. Bailey,
1849-50; Emanuel Caughman, 1851-52; J. H. W. Wertz,
1852-56; E. Caughman, again, 1857-59; David Shealy,
1860-62; J. B. Lowman, 1866; David Shealy, again, 1867;
J. H. Bailey, 1872; A. D. L. Moser, 1880-82; Barney Kreps,
1883-87; D. Kyzer, 1889; L. E. Busby, 1891; J. D. Shealy,
1892-93; G. S. Bearden, 1894; S. P. Shumpert, 1895-97;
Jacob Austin, 1898-1900; A. R. Taylor, 1901-03; Jacob
Austin, again, 1904-06; A. R. Taylor, again, 1907-09; S. C.
Ballentine, 1911; J. D. Shealy, again, 1912; F. K. Roof,
1913; S. C. Ballentine, 1914; V. Y. Boozer, 1917-21; W.
D. Wise, since 1922.

A new church was dedicated October 6, 1912. The sermon was preached by Rev. S. P. Koon. Rev. J. D. Shealy,
the pastor, conducted the services and Rev. S. T. Hallman,
D.D., preached at the afternoon service.

The president of synod in reporting this service, said:
"The church is beautifully and substantially built and re-
flects credit on pastor and people."

Rev. S. T. Hallman, D.D., is a son of this congregation.
He was elected an elder in it when in his eighteenth year and
was chosen a lay reader at the same time.

The congregation has never been numerically strong, but
has been a blessing to many souls. The membership is now
eighty, with an enrollment of sixty-two in the Sunday School.
The property value is $1,500.

Corinth Church, Saluda County

The first reference to this organization is found in the
president's report at the convention of November 27 to December 1, 1841. He said: "Another church is about being
erected in Edgefield District under the care of the Rev. S.

R. Shepherd." At the meeting of the synod November 12-16, 1842, it was reported "On the fourth Sabbath in May a new Lutheran Church, by the name Corinth, in the District of Edgefield, was dedicated to the service of the Triune God."

Rev. G. Haltiwanger, Sr., preached the dedicatory sermon, and a sermon was also preached by Rev. William Berly on "The Doctrines, Government and Usages of the Lutheran Church in This Country". Reverends Herman Aull and S. R. Shepherd also took part in the services. The initial organization is officially reported at the meeting of synod in November, 1841, and the church was dedicated in May, 1842.

The list of pastors as furnished is as follows: S. R. Shepherd, 1842-52; Michael Rauch, 1852-54; J. H. W. Wertz, 1854-65; J. H. Bailey, 1865-66; Emanuel Caughman, 1866-68; S. T. Hallman, 1868-69; J. A. Sligh, 1869-70; Paul Derrick, 1870-75; C. P. Boozer, 1875-83; J. D. Bowles, 1883-88; C. P. Boozer, 1888-93; O. B. Shearouse, 1893-1902; J. H. Wyse, 1902-03; Z. W. Bedenbaugh, two months in 1903; D. B. Groseclose, April 1, 1903 to January 1, 1904; J. L. Buck, January 15, 1904, to December, 1904; J. B. Harman, January 1, 1906, to September 1, 1911; W. A. Dutton, January 15, 1912, to April 10, 1912; George S. Bearden, April 10, 1919, to December, 1919; C. K. Rhodes, December 1, 1919, to September 24, 1922. Supplied until June 1, 1924, by Rev. T. F. Suber, of Silver Street.

From this congregation the following have entered the ministry: Reverends Jacob Austin, J. H. Wilson and J. B. Harman.

Under the ministry of Rev. Paul Derrick on the fourth Lord's Day of October, 1871, the cornerstone of the new church was laid, and on the fourth Lord's Day of March, 1872, the church was dedicated, Reverends E. A. Bolles, Emanuel Caughman and the pastor, Paul Derrick, conducting the services.

Beth Eden Church, Newberry County

This congregation was organized in 1843 by Rev. G. H. Brown, who in 1842 was graduated from our Theological Seminary, then located at Lexington, and was received into the synod at the convention of that year. He was located at a place called "Liberty Hill Station", and was employed by the synod as a missionary in that section. The president of the synod reported, November, 1843, that a society had been fully organized at Liberty Hill, and at Beth Eden, with encouraging prospects. A church was built at a cost of $600, and dedicated September, 1843, Reverends G. H. Brown, John C. Hope and Herman Aull officiating. Pastor Brown served Beth Eden Church until 1845, at which time the synod sent him as a missionary to our Lutheran people in Mississippi.

The following pastors succeeded each other in the order here given: Reverends William Berly, E. A. Bolles, William Fink, J. B. Anthony, Stanmore R. Shepherd, R. J. Hungerpeler, Jacob Moser, Jacob Hawkins, James M. Schreckhise, J. D. Shirey, Z. W. Bedenbaugh, William A. Julian, W. K. Sligh, A. J. Bowers, Charles H. Armstrong, J. J. Long, R. E. Livingston, J. D. Shealy, J. D. Kinard, P. E. Shealy, and L. P. Boland, pastor now in charge.

Reverends J. A. Sligh, D.D., J. D. Bowles and Jefferson T. Bowles entered the ministry from this church, and the distinguished George B. Cromer is also a son of Beth Eden.

Rev. W. K. Sligh and Rev. A. J. Bowers, D.D., served two periods each as pastor. Rev. R. J. Hungerpeler died while pastor here, and his remains rest under a marble monument erected by members of Beth Eden and St. Matthew's congregations.

It is only just to say that Beth Eden congregation has not lived its eighty years in vain. It has contributed in men and money towards the building of other churches, has been a great helper in the cause of Christianity, and has been one of the prime factors in the building and maintenance of Newberry College. Strong men have occupied its pulpit and able laymen have there received their spiritual training. The older students of Newberry College knew the value of Beth Eden Church, and could never forget its sympathetic helpfulness to those who lived on the old campus.

The membership numbers 104, and the Sunday School 70. The church has property valuation of $3,000.

Church of the Resurrection, Cameron

In 1916 the cornerstone of this church was laid. In all respects it is a continuation of Mt. Lebanon Church on Four Holes Swamp, which was organized under the ministry of Rev. John P. Margart and dedicated March 25, 1843. The completed organization was not effected, however, until January 13, 1844.

It was during the ministry of Rev. J. W. Oxner that the Church of the Resurrection was built in the town of Cameron, two miles west of Mt. Lebanon, the members of which automatically became members of the Church of the Resurrection. The old church is still preserved, with its cemetery, and occasionally services are held there, but no organization exists under that name.

It is due to the history of Mt. Lebanon to state that, with St. Matthew's, it was a pastorate for many years and the two congregations were served by the same pastors and lived together in peace and harmony.

Mt. Lebanon contributed the following sons to the ministry: Rev. W. A. Houck, J. S. Hungerpeler (theological student), who died before completing his course in the Theological Seminary at Newberry, and Rev. J. B. Haigler.

The Church of the Resurrection has been served by Reverends J. W. Oxner, J. L. Yonce. Rev. Charles J. Shealy is the pastor now in charge.

This congregation possesses a beautiful house of worship and a comfortable parsonage, and is doing effective work in the Master's Kingdom.

The membership numbers 147 and the Sunday School 162. Church property is valued at $16,500.

St. David's Church, Lexington County

When Mr. J. F. Schirmer published sketches of the congregations in the synod, 1875, he was informed that this church was organized in 1840 with a membership of seven persons, under the ministry of Rev. J. F. W. Leppard; and this may be true; but the first reference to it is found in the minutes of 1845, page 14, in a petition from "St. David's

Church, Lexington, S. C.", asking to be received into the synod, which request was granted. Since it is hardly supposable that said congregation would have waited *five years* as an organized body before asking to be received into the synod, it is safe to accept the *documentary evidence* referred to, and fix the date at 1845.

We find no further reference to this church until the convention of November, 1846, and then Rev. Geo. Haltiwanger, Sr., was pastor. The next reference is in 1848, and the congregation was being served by Rev. J. F. W. Leppard. In 1849 Rev. J. B. Lowman was pastor, and continued up to 1864; but he again became pastor in 1867, and served until 1870. Then Rev. William Berly became pastor in 1871 and continued until 1873, the year of his death. The pastorate system, adopted in 1869, and the changed style of noting pastoral relations, renders it very difficult to trace further changes. This congregation has never been strong numerically and has suffered many periods of vacancies; but it still lives, and its future seems assured.

The membership is now about 100, with 175 on the roll of the Sunday School. The property value is $2,500.

Colony Church, Newberry County

This congregation was organized in 1845 under the ministry of Rev. William Berly, and was dedicated in August, 1846. The service was conducted chiefly by Rev. J. C. Hope, then president of synod.*

The original membership was composed of members of St. Paul's and St. Luke's Churches, which members lived in the vicinity of the new Colony Church. Rev. J. C. Hope said in his report: "They are indeed a church colony"—and hence the name.

The pastors in the order of service were as follows: Reverends William Berly, J. C. Hope, T. S. Boinest, J. P. Margart, J. H. Bailey, J. A. Sligh, Jacob Hawkins, H. S. Wingard, J. D. Bowles, George W. Holland, W. K. Sligh, Charles H. Armstrong, J. J. Long, R. E. Livingston, A. J. Bowers, J. D.

___
*(Minutes of 1846, p. 8.)

Kinard, P. E. Shealy, and L. P. Boland, the pastor now in charge. Rev. Jacob Hawkins served two terms as pastor, as also did Rev. J. A. Sligh. Rev. W. K. Sligh served three terms.

Many of the best people of Newberry County were included in the membership of this congregation, and although not now connected with Colony Church, several of the charter members are still living: Mrs. Jacob Aull, for instance, and, until recently, Mr. Aull and Mrs. Margaret McNeil McCullough.

Rev. H. A. McCullough, D.D., and Rev. I. E. Long are sons of this church. Rev. J. D. Bowles was buried in the cemetery near the church where he so faithfully preached the Gospel of Christ.

The members number 182 and the Sunday School 67. Church property is valued at $5,000.

Macedonia Church, Lexington County

Macedonia Church is situated on Calk's (formerly Lewie's) Road, near Saluda River, and is an offshoot of St. Peter's Church. Many years ago some differences among the members existed at St. Peter's Church, and about twenty-five members withdrew and formed Macedonia congregation. They worshiped during a short time in a building then called Lybrand's Church, situated about five miles east of the present church building. Then for about two years the congregation worshiped in a schoolhouse which stood on the present site of the church.

The congregation was organized November 18, 1847. The church was built in 1848 and dedicated in November, 1849, when the services were conducted by Rev. William Berly. Rev. George Haltiwanger, Sr., who served the congregation once a month as pastor, died before the church was completed.

The list of pastors follows: Revs. George Haltiwanger, Sr., 1848; William Berly, 1851-62; James H. Bailey, 1862-66; Samuel Bouknight, 1866-81; J. A. Sligh, 1881-84; C. P. Boozer, 1884-88; J. D. Bowles, 1888-89; A. J. Bowers (supply), 1889-90; J. A. Sligh, 1890-91; A. J. Bowers, again, 1891-92; W. A. Julian (January, 1892, until synod), 1892; J. A. Sligh, again, 1893; J. D. Bowles, again, 1893-94; J. H. Wyse, November-December, 1894; Jacob Hawkins (during early part), 1894; James D. Kinard (until synod), 1895; C. P. Boozer (until synod), 1896.

At this time Macedonia congregation became associated with Holy Trinity Church, Little Mountain, in a pastorate, with pastors as follows: Revs. H. P. Counts, 1896-99; S. L. Nease, 1899-1901; J. K. Efird, 1901-05; O. B. Shearouse, 1905-12; J. J. Long, 1912-22; J. B. Harman, present pastor, 1923.

The new church building was erected and completed in 1914, and was dedicated May 27, 1917, by Rev. J. W. Horine, D.D.

Sons of this congregation are: Revs. S. C. Ballentine and A. W. Ballentine, related as uncle and nephew, respectively.

Pine Grove Church, Orangeburg (now Calhoun) County

This congregation was organized September 27, 1847, under the ministry of Rev. John P. Margart. The original membership was about fifty-seven, most of whom were members of St. Matthew's Church in Amelia township. For several years before the formal organization they had occasional preaching in an old log building nearer Santee River than where the present church now stands. After two years of efficient service Rev. John P. Margart resigned, and Rev. Ephraim Dufford, a scholarly man, was elected pastor. He served the congregation for four years and taught a school in that locality part of the time. Rev. W. A. Houck, one of the best preachers of his day and a consecrated man of God, succeeded Rev. Ephraim Dufford, and for sixteen years served this church, together with Trinity Church, situated some twelve miles south of Pine Grove Church. No man was ever more highly esteemed by all classes of people in the entire community. At the close of his long ministry here, he recommended as his successor, Rev. S. T. Hallman, who entered upon his duties there in November, 1869, and remained pastor about six years.

The pastors in the order of their service were as follows: Reverends John P. Margart, Ephraim Dufford, W. A. Houck, S. T. Hallman, J. H. W. Wertz, J. Q. Wertz, M. O. J. Kreps, J. D. Bowles, B. W. Cronk, S. L. Nease, P. D. Risinger, W. B. Aull, L. P. Boland, E. W. Leslie, R. R. Sowers, and E. K. Bodie, the present pastor.

The present commodious building, the third in the history of the congregation, was erected under the ministry of Rev. J. D. Bowles, and the present parsonage is the third home for the pastor.

The South Carolina Synod met here in October, 1858, November, 1884, and November, 1911.

The bodies of Revs. E. Dufford and J. H. W. Wertz rest near the church where they had faithfully preached the everlasting Gospel.

The members number 152, and the Sunday School 163. Church property is valued at $14,000.

Trinity Church, Elloree

This congregation was organized August 19, 1849, under the ministry of Rev. John P. Margart. The first building was a log structure which was dedicated to God June 3, 1849, but the formal organization of the congregation did not take place until August of that year. The sermon at the dedication was preached by Rev. E. B. Hort, who also conducted the dedicatory service. The membership was made up of members of Pine Grove Church who lived south of what was known as "Half-way Swamp" and this explains the seemingly strange procedure of building and dedicating a church before the organization of the congregation. Pine Grove was providing a home for her people before dismissing those who were not located conveniently to the mother church.

The pastors have been as follows: Reverends John P. Margart, Ephraim Dufford, W. A. Houck, S. T. Hallman, J. H. W. Wertz, J. Q. Wertz, M. O. J. Kreps, J. S. Bowles, B. W. Cronk, S. L. Nease, P. D. Risinger, W. B. Aull, L. P. Boland, E. W. Leslie, R. R. Sowers, and H. S. Petrea, the pastor in charge.

The first building was constructed of cypress logs and stood on the Monck's Corner Road in a beautiful oak grove twelve miles south of Pine Grove Church and about twenty-five miles from Orangeburg.

Subsequently a very neat building was erected, which still stands, although not as a Lutheran church. In the course of events the Lutheran people of that immediate community drifted northward and the Methodists moved southward. Then, by an amicable arrangement, the two denominations exchanged buildings. This put the Lutheran congregation close to the town of Elloree, and in due time they erected a more desirable building in the town. This building was, however, destroyed by fire in June, 1913. On Palm Sunday, April 5, 1914, the cornerstone of another and far better house of worship was laid, the pastor, Rev. L. P. Boland, being assisted by Rev. R. C. Holland, D.D., who made the address. This edifice is built of blue granite and covered with green slate and it is in all respects a sanctuary well adapted to all the purposes of divine worship.

When the convention of synod met here in November, 1918, many expressions of approval and admiration were made in regard to the splendid work which the congregation had thus accomplished. Looking back on the old log church of 1849, and then on this splendid evidence of loyal devotion one might well exclaim, "Behold, what hath God wrought!"

Rev. William Stoudenmire was a son of this congregation.

The membership is 180, with an enrollment of 152 in the Sunday School. The church property value is $15,000.

St. Peter's Church, near Batesburg

The early history of this church can not be traced with any degree of certainty. It was built and dedicated in 1849, but by whom and when organized it has not been possible to determine. The first mention of it in the list of churches is in 1850, when it is in Rev. Samuel Bouknight's charge. He was evidently the first pastor, and must have been its organizer. He reported only eighty-three members in the three congregations served by him.

The pastors have been as follows: Reverends Samuel Bouknight, S. R. Shepherd, Jesse B. Lowman, D. Shealy, Emanuel Caughman, A. W. Lindler, A. D. L. Moser, J. H. Bailey, L. E. Busby, D.D., S. P. Shumpert, Jacob Austin, D. B. Groseclose, S. C. Ballentine, V. Y. Boozer, and J. D. Shealy, the present pastor, who took charge of this congregation in June, 1923.

The house of worship has been much improved. It has been rolled back from the cemetery and turned around, so as to face the public highway. It is now marked by new life and energy, and by increased attendance and numerical growth. The outlook is very encouraging.

Emanuel Church, near Lexington

This congregation was organized about 1852 by Rev. Adam Efird. A house of worship was built near the time of its organization. A second sanctuary was erected about 1888 and the third and present sanctuary in 1913. The congregation was connected with the Tennessee Synod until it went with that synod into the United Synod of North Carolina, and in the South Carolina Synod in 1922.

It has been served by Reverends Adam Efird, A. L. Crouse, Daniel Efird, assisted by Revs. J. A. Cromer and E. L. Lybrand while they were theological students, and by Rev. J. A. Cromer, upon his ordination. Rev. H. A. Kistler, the present pastor, took charge in 1922.

The lands on which the church was built were donated by Daniel Sox and O. Steele. Seven of its members have studied theology, of whom all but one are now in the active ministry.

Cedar Grove Church, Leesville

It appears that a portion of the members of the old Salem Church in 1853, on account of some dissatisfaction in the congregation, elected a delegate to the Tennessee Synod, sending a petition for connection with that body, after first organizing as a congregation to be known as Cedar Grove. It is probable that this organization worshiped in the old

church with the Salem congregation until about 1856, when
a house of worship was evidently built, forasmuch as the
first communion meeting of which any record can be found
was held in Cedar Grove Church in May, 1857. The house
of worship was dedicated in November, 1859, and burned in
1865. A communion service was held under an arbor in
1866, and the communion service for April, 1867, was held
in the new building which the congregation now occupies.

The pastors were: Reverends D. Efird, A. Efird, J. I.
Miller, A. L. Crouse, E. L. Lybrand, E. J. Sox, W. H. Roof,
B. D. Wessinger, B. L. Stroup, J. C. Wessinger. Rev. W.
D. Wise is the present pastor.

Reverends J. D. Shealy, P. D. Risinger, C. I. Morgan and
Enoch Hite entered the ministry from this congregation.

Church of the Redeemer (Originally Luther Chapel), Newberry

The first steps taken for the establishment of a Lutheran
church in the town of Newberry began in 1852, led by Rev.
T. S. Boinest, who was then pastor of Bethlehem Church, Pomaria. At that time the town had a population of about
400 and quite a number of Lutheran families had located
there and were without a convenient church home.

Sunday, July 10, 1853, after a service conducted in the
court house (the building still standing on the public square
of Newberry) by the Rev. Mr. Boinest, who preached to a
congregation which overflowed the court room, the organization was effected with the enrollment of twenty-one members, all of whom were regular communicants of various congregations in the Dutch Fork of Newberry and Lexington
Counties.

Wednesday, August 10, 1853, exactly one month after the
organization (so readily did the members respond in subscriptions and cash to build a house of worship), the cornerstone was laid in the presence of a large assemblage of persons at the site fronting on Boundary Street, midway between
the termini of Nance Street on the north and McKibben Street
on the south, the lot having been given by a citizen of the

town. Rev. John Bachman conducted the services on this interesting occasion.

At the convention in November, 1853, a petition was presented by the elders and members, asking to be received into the synod as a congregation which had been organized under the name of Luther Chapel. The president of synod said in his report: "The much needed Lutheran church in the thriving village of Newberry is rapidly progressing in construction. . . . Being surrounded by a dense Lutheran population, located in a growing village, populated by an intelligent, moral and pious people, with the blessing of God, success must crown the efforts which are there being made. The Christian enterprise had its origin and is still progressing principally from the efficient and well-directed efforts of Brother Boinest."

The congregation was chartered December 20, 1853, by an act of the General Assembly, as "the Evangelical Lutheran Church at Newberry, by the name of Luther Chapel." Rev. T. S. Boinest became the first pastor (a licentiate on the roll of the synod at the time), and provision was made at the convention of 1853 for his ordination to take place at the dedication of "his own church in Newberry village". Accordingly, the church having been completed December 1, 1854, it was dedicated Sunday, December 10, by Rev. John Bachman, D.D., assisted by the pastor and other Lutheran ministers.

The church was a frame structure, Gothic in style of architecture and of superior workmanship, the cost being $4,000, all of which, except $900, was provided in cash at the dedication. The latter amount was liquidated within less than three years almost entirely by the liberality of Matthias Barre, one of the charter members.

Rev. Mr. Boinest resigned as pastor of St. Luke's and Colony congregations after his ordination in order to devote more time to the Newberry church. This congregation is therefore a monument to this energetic and faithful man of God.

Rev. Mr. Boinest resigned as pastor of Luther Chapel in 1856 and was followed by Rev. William Berly, 1856-58,

when Rev. M. Whittle served temporarily in connection with
his professorship in Newberry College. Rev. Theophilus
Stork, D.D., was pastor in 1859 until a portion of 1860, in
connection with his duties as president of Newberry College,
and Rev. J. A. Brown, D.D., professor in the Theological
Seminary, assisted him, both returning, however, to the North
in 1861, Dr. Stork in February and Dr. Brown early in the
spring. Rev. J. P. Margart was then temporarily in charge
as pastor in 1860, in connection with Sandy Run Church,
until 1861.

Rev. J. P. Smeltzer took charge as pastor in May, 1861,
in connection with his duties as president of Newberry College, and served until the removal of the College to Walhalla
in November, 1868. A vacancy then existed for a year, the
congregation permitting the use of the church once a month by
the Episcopalians of the town until May 24, 1869, when the
church was struck by lightning during a terrific thunderstorm
and rendered unfit for services. The tall and stately steeple
was almost entirely demolished and the interior damaged
to a considerable extent. This disaster added materially to the
discouragement of the congregation which had been caused
by the removal of the College and the severance of the cordial relations which had existed between the congregation,
faculty and students. However, the members took fresh
courage, the church was repaired immediately after the disaster, the steeple being reduced in height and the interior
renovated.

The damage to the church by lightning occurred Wednesday
afternoon, and when the Episcopal rector, Rev. Mr. Trapier,
arrived from Walhalla on Saturday to fill his appointment
on the Lord's Day, he found the church unfit for use. The
Episcopal congregation, less than a score in number, put their
own church in as good condition as possible and held services there accordingly the next day. Their church had
fallen entirely into disuse during the Confederate War and
several years subsequently to that period. So May, 1869,
is the date when the Episcopal services were no longer conducted in Luther Chapel. Thus was allayed abundant fear
among leaders of our Church in the synod that the small band

of Lutherans at Newberry would be absorbed in like manner as history had recorded when other Lutherans in America had become associated somewhat similarly with Episcopalian strength. The editor of *The Lutheran Visitor* had referred facetiously to the conditions which thus existed in the Newberry church and he was agreeably disappointed by the final result.

Rev. Jacob Hawkins became pastor in September, 1869, in connection with his work at Beth Eden Church, but conducted services only each Sunday afternoon. He served less than a year after his installation January 9, 1870, by Revs. A. R. Rude and William Watkins Hicks. January 15, 1871, Rev. H. S. Wingard was installed as pastor by Rev. W. S. Bowman, D.D., and served until the fall of 1872, when the congregation was reported as vacant "but with some prospect of supply".

Rev. H. W. Kuhns, of Omaha, Nebraska, took charge in February, 1873, having accepted a call after he had visited the congregation in December, 1872. A new spirit was infused into the life of the congregation during his pastorship and the membership had grown from 54, in 1873, to 160 when he resigned in September, 1878. Supply services were secured until March, 1879, when Rev. S. P. Hughes was pastor until November, 1881. Then followed Rev. J. Steck, D.D., 1882-83; Rev. A. B. McMackin, 1885-87; Rev. W. C. Schaeffer, D.D., 1887-92; Rev. Junius B. Fox, Ph.D., 1893-99. Revs. George W. Holland and A. G. Voigt served as supply pastors during the series of vacancies (1884-95) while the former was president of the college and the latter seminary professor. Other clerical members of the faculty served likewise in subsequent periods, including Rev. W. K. Gotwald in 1921.

The movement to build a better house of worship originated during the pastorship of Rev. Dr. Schaeffer, when the nucleus of a building fund amounted to about $5,000 in subscriptions and two bequests, the latter provided by members of the congregation. The matter of changing the location of the church had also been considered during Dr. Schaeffer's term and it was finally decided in 1895 to secure an eligible lot bounded by Boundary, Wilson and Johnstone streets on the east, south, and west, respectively. Here the cornerstone of the present church was laid October 20, 1896, during the pastorship of Rev. Dr. Fox.

The congregation did not realize on the full value of the old church property by its sale by reason of the fact that in the gift of the lot the donor had not specified in the deed that it was made in perpetuity, and the heirs of his estate declined to relinquish their claims under the circumstances.

The handsome new church, including the lot, cost $14,500 and was occupied on the first Sunday in October, 1897. The beginning of the new century was signalized by the congregation with an offering at midnight, December 31, 1899, to cancel the debt of $5,000 on the new church. The amount of $4,000 was contributed. The remainder of $1,000 was paid in 1903 and the church was dedicated Sunday, February 28, 1904, during the celebration (February 25-27) of the semi-centennial anniversary of the congregation. The sermon was preached by Rev. M. G. G. Scherer, D.D., and the pastor, Rev. W. L. Seabrook, was installed at the evening service by Revs. Z. W. Bedenbaugh and S. C. Ballentine, president and secretary of synod, respectively. Addresses were delivered by Dr. George B. Cromer and Rev. W. K. Sligh during the celebration, which had been unavoidably postponed from July 10, 1903, the fiftieth anniversary date of the organization of the congregation. The membership at this time (1904) was 310. Dr. Scherer was a former pastor, having served from August 1, 1899 until 1901, when he was called to a professorship in the Theological Seminary, then located at Mt. Pleasant, S. C. Rev. W. L. Seabrook became pastor in the spring of 1902 and served until February 1, 1907. Under his ministry a fine large parsonage was erected at a cost of $4,000. Rev. Edward Fulenwider took charge March 9, 1908, and continued until October 24, 1920. It is a notable fact that under his ministry the accessions of 108 persons at the Easter celebration of 1909 numbered twice as many members as the congregation had included during the first twenty years (1853-73) of its history.

Rev. C. A. Freed, D.D., took charge April 18, 1921, and continues as the efficient pastor of this congregation, which has long since been acknowledged as one of the most influential churches in the synod. Its historic life of seventy-two years has not been lived in vain.

Three conventions of the southern general body have been entertained by the congregation—the General Synod in May, 1868, and May, 1878, and the United Synod in May, 1898, each convention having been signalized by important transactions in the progress of the Church, one at the former convention being the action which resulted in the establishment of *The Lutheran Visitor* as the southern church paper and another was provision for the publication of the Book of Worship. At the latter convention (1898) plans were instituted looking to the further endowment of the Theological Seminary, which resulted in securing $30,000 for this cause, having being designated as the "Century Memorial Endowment".

During 1923 substantial improvements were made to the church at a cost of $36,000, which included an addition in order to enlarge the seating capacity of the auditorium and provide modern and adequate equipment for the Sunday School, made necessary by the large increase in the membership of the congregation. This addition is 106 feet long, 55 feet wide and three stories in height, including the basement, which contains an up-to-date heating plant, a room for boys' work, kitchen and hall for social purposes. The primary department of the Sunday School is so arranged as to be separate from and yet accessible to the main auditorium. In the main section of the Sunday School department fifteen class rooms are so arranged that practically the entire space can be made available for seating a large congregation. It is therefore the largest auditorium of any church in the synod and compares in size with any other church in the state.

The membership is now 600, with an enrollment of 323 in the Sunday School. The amount contributed for benevolences in 1893 was $5,890.

Rev. J. J. Long, D.D., is a son of this congregation. One of the charter members is still living: Mrs. Mary L. Rawl (nee Barre), in Newberry, and is still a member of the congregation.

St. John's Church, Walhalla

The town of Walhalla, lying at the foot of the Blue Ridge Mountains, was settled in 1849 by a colony of Germans from Charleston. This colony was supplemented by other immigrants who came later. They were visited by Rev. C. F. Bansemer as a missionary from the South Carolina Synod. The congregation was not organized until 1859. At the meeting of synod in October, 1859, resolutions were adopted encouraging our Walhalla brethren in the laudable purpose to build a church, and Pastor Bansemer was authorized to bring their needs to the favorable consideration of all our churches. With some help our Lutheran people in Walhalla got out the timbers, provided the material and built a house of worship highly creditable to themselves. With some improvements that building still stands as a monument to the noble souls who projected and carried out that worthy enterprise.

At the meeting of synod in January, 1862, it was reported that the church was completed and had been dedicated in May, 1861. The synod expressed its pleasure at hearing this report.

Rev. C. F. Bansemer served the congregation from May, 1858, to April, 1860; then Rev. August Angerer, their first regular pastor, took charge in December, 1860, and remained until June 26, 1864. Rev. Louis Mueller served them at intervals from 1864 to 1867, during which time they also had lay services. Rev. Carl Weber was pastor from September, 1867, to August, 1869. Rev. J. H. C. Schierenbach was pastor from May 7, 1871, to February 21, 1875; Rev. J. F. Probst from May 23, 1875, to October, 1877; Rev. J. G. Bohm, 1878, during August; and then Rev. W. Pilz served the congregation some time in 1880, possibly to 1884. Rev. J. F. Probst again became pastor, serving 1884-85; Rev. J. C. Brodfuhrer, 1885-90; Rev. S. C. Zettner, 1890-92; Rev. G. J. Martz, 1893-94; Rev. J. G. Schaid, 1895-1903; Rev. H. C. Grossman, 1903-07; Rev. T. B. Epting, 1908-10; Rev.

J. B. Umberger, 1911-15; Rev. W. B. Aull, 1916-24. Rev. A. W. Ballentine is now (1924) the pastor.

From the founding of this church up to about 1869, probably much later, the services were conducted in the German language, but when Newberry College was located in Walhalla in November, 1868, it was found necessary to organize an English speaking congregation for the benefit of the student body, and the younger members of the German families who preferred the English language. This was done under Rev. J. P. Smeltzer, D.D., president of the college, with the consent of the officers of St. John's Church. This necessity passed when the college returned to Newberry in 1877; for a time the English organization ceased, but subsequently the English language became in use in all the services.

Union Church, Leesville

This congregation dates back to 1855. It was received into the synod at the convention of 1856 and was listed in Rev. M. Rauch's charge. The building was erected in 1855, the year of its organization, when there were sixteen members. The dedicatory services were conducted by Reverends M. Rauch and J. H. W. Wertz. The very meager records afford the information that Rev. M. Rauch was the first pastor. He was succeeded by Rev. J. H. W. Wertz and the following since that time: Reverends Barney Kreps, A. W. Lindler, L. E. Busby, C. A. Marks, J. D. Shealy, H. A. McCullough, Y. von A. Riser, E. C. Will, O. C. Petersen, and J. D. Shealy, the present pastor. It was under the ministry of Pastor J. D. Shealy that the new Union Church was built, and then dedicated August 13, 1905, the sermon being preached by Rev. M. O. J. Kreps, D.D., who was then president of synod.

The present membership is 179; Sunday School, 136. Property value, $2,600. One son in the ministry.

Orangeburg Lutheran Church, Orangeburg

The present church was organized in 1855, first through an interest developed by the visits of Reverends J. B. Anthony and John P. Margart, although there had been a church in Orangeburg in 1737-1749, ministered to by Rev. J. U. Geissendanner, referred to elsewhere in the early history of the synod. This old congregation was carried into the Episcopal Church by the younger Geissendanner, brought about by a very unjust law of the English authorities.

There is, then, no connection between the present church and that of 1737. There no doubt remained some of the descendants of those early Lutherans in whom there possibly survived a lingering Lutheran faith.

Soon after the organization of the church in 1855, a lot was purchased, and a house of worship was erected, which was dedicated in August, 1850. The congregation then numbered twenty-two members. At the meeting of Synod in 1856 the congregation was reported as giving "flattering prospects of success". The church had been completed and "a goodly number of communicants" had been gathered into the congregation, although regrets were expressed that they were to lose the services of their pastor, Rev. Jacob Hawkins, who was one of the first pastors. The church was vacant in 1857 and the synod appropriated $300 to aid the congregation in securing a suitable minister.

In 1858 the church was still vacant, but Rev. W. A. Houck served them regularly once each month during that year, the church being referred to as "Orange Chapel".

In 1859 "Orange Chapel" is referred to as in Rev. J. P. Margart's charge, and the prospects were encouraging; but very soon a dark and trying period came into the life of this mission, which lasted through the years of the War Between the States. About the close of the war the church was used as a temporary Federal Army hospital and later on was rented for a court house. It was thus used and abused for several years.

It was not until the synod met in 1872 that the president of synod in his report could say, "Our long neglected church in the town of Orangeburg has again been reorganized under the most encouraging auspices." Rev. G. A. Hough, then serving Pastorate No. 2, some fifteen miles from the town, had given them efficient help and encouragement. He resigned Pastorate No. 2 near the close of 1874 and accepted a call to the Orangeburg Church.   Through his labors the purpose to repair and refit the building was developed and some work was done to that end.

Early in 1876 Rev. G. A. Hough accepted work elsewhere. Rev. J. B. Haskell then became pastor, but on September 8, 1877, he too resigned and became the pastor of Christ Lutheran Church in Staunton, Va.   Rev. H. S. Wingard, then of Pomaria, supplied the church with preaching once each month in 1878.   Rev. J. F. Kiser was then called and entered upon the work early in 1879—and that was an important event in the life of this congregation.   He established a school and secured sufficient funds to enable them to carry out much of the work which had been previously projected. He resigned September 10, 1885, and thus rounded out about seven years of faithful service.

It will now be seen that our people here have been long-suffering, loyal and faithful to the trust committed to them, notwithstanding the many discouraging circumstances through which they have passed.

The following ministers are known to have served this congregation during the years since the organization in 1885: Reverends Jacob Hawkins, W. A. Houck (as a supply for one year), J. P. Margart, G. A. Hough, J. B. Haskell, H. S. Wingard (monthly supply for one year), J. F. Kiser, H. C. Grossman, S. L. Keller, J. Q. Wertz, N. D. Bodie, J. C. Dietz, J. P. Miller, R. C. Holland, J. H. Wilson, H. E. Beatty, P. E. Shealy, C. H. Ritchie, and Paul Cromer Sigmon, the present pastor.

Rev. W. H. Riser entered the ministry from this congregation.

The total valuation of its property is now $14,000, and its future is bright with promise.

Grace Church, Prosperity

This church was organized by Rev. William Berly early in 1850, and was dedicated on the fourth Sunday in August of that year under the name of Newville.   A neat and comfortable church had been erected.   The president of synod,

Rev. Samuel Bouknight, said in his report: "This was certainly a wise and timely effort for that place, as it is surrounded, more or less, by a population whose feelings have been identified with our Church." He adds: "This being a central point, affords facilities for access from every direction, and must always command a large congregation."

His words have been fully justified by the achievements of this congregation during all of its history. Rev. William Berly, although the organizer of this congregation, did not become its regular pastor; at that time he was pastor of St. Luke's and St. Andrew's Churches. Rev. J. L. Smithdeal

GRACE CHURCH, PROSPERITY

was called and accepted the Newville congregation and with it St. Luke's Church, Rev. Mr. Berly, who resided at Lexington, having given up the work. Rev. Mr. Smithdeal took charge of this congregation in 1860, the delegate being George Dominick. No meeting of the synod was held in 1861 but it convened January 16, 1862, and at that time Rev. Mr. Smithdeal had returned to North Carolina. At the convention in October, 1863, Rev. Webster Eichelberger is recorded as pastor of Newville Church. By midsummer of 1864, he had gone to Virginia as a missionary in the army, and Rev. J. A. Sligh's name appears in the record of synod as pastor of the Newville Church. The same record is also found in the minutes of October 12-14, 1865. When the synod convened on October 18, 1866, Newville, Colony and St. Paul's Churches are entered as constituting Rev. J. A. Sligh's charge—including also a "Newville colored congregation", which occupied a section in the church at the services. At the convention of October, 1868, the same churches still make up "Rev. J. A. Sligh's charge". At the convention of 1869 the churches are grouped into pastorates. The three churches constituting Pastorate No. 13 are St. Luke's, Newville and Colony. Thus Newville ceased to be under the ministry of Pastor Sligh.

In the adjustment of the new pastoral system, vacancies occurred and about that time Rev. J. P. Smeltzer, D.D., and H. S. Wingard, theological student, occasionally supplied Newville, but in 1871 Rev. Jacob Hawkins, D.D., served as pastor. From 1872 to 1876 Rev. H. S. Wingard was pastor. At the convention of October, 1877, the president said in his report: "In a letter dated November 6, 1876, Rev. Z. W. Bedenbaugh informed me that the Newville congregation at Prosperity, S. C., has engaged my services for the ensuing year as a supply." He was the supply pastor during 1877.

At the convention of November, 1878, in his annual report the president said: "The church in Prosperity has been regularly supplied during the synodical year by Rev. G. W. Holland, President of Newberry College." At the close of 1878, the president of the synod in his report said: "The congregation at Prosperity, S. C., has erected a new church in place of the old one, which was dedicated on the second of October, by the name of Grace Church."

It was therefore under the ministry of Rev. Geo. W. Holland, D.D., that the second church was built. The church at that time received the name of "Grace Church", which name it still bears.

December 27, 1878, Rev. Jacob Hawkins, D.D., notified the president of synod that he had accepted a call to Grace Church, and on that date had entered upon the work. He was pastor from 1879 to 1882, and was succeeded by Rev.

J. E. Bushnell, who took charge December, 1882, and continued to 1885. From 1886 to 1890 Rev. C. A. Marks was the pastor; 1890 to 1895, Rev. T. O. Keister; 1895 to 1900, Rev. S. T. Hallman; 1900 to 1902, Rev. W. H. Hiller; 1902 to 1905, Rev. W. A. Lutz; 1905 to 1911, Rev. M. O. J. Kreps, under whose ministry the present large and commodious church was erected; 1911 to 1916, Rev. E. W. Leslie; 1916 to 1922, Rev. C. J. Shealy. Rev. S. W. Hahn, the present pastor, took charge in 1922, and under his ministry the congregation is greatly prospering.

The congregation now has a property value of $21,500, and is active in all the work of the synod and in the general work of the Church.

The following sons of the congregation entered into the ministry of the Church: A. J. Bowers, E. H. Kohn, V. Y. Boozer, M. M. Kinard, and J. D. Kinard.

St. James' Church, Graniteville

This congregation was not fully organized until March 4, 1860, although it had been a preaching station as far back as 1850. Rev. Herbert C. Bell, in a historical sermon preached there some years ago, gives the following sketch of its early and subsequent history:

Graniteville was founded in 1845, and is one of the oldest cotton mill towns in the South. At that time the nearest Lutheran church was Mt. Calvary, where a church was built in 1828. The first Lutherans at Graniteville came from Mt. Calvary and from the older Lutheran communities of Saluda and Lexington Counties. Two Lutheran ministers resided here before a church was organized: Rev. Robert Cloy from 1850 until his death on May 4, 1853, and Rev. Nicholas Aldrich, 1854-56. The latter was state agent for the American Tract Society. He preached occasionally at Graniteville, found a number of Lutherans among his neighbors and in 1856 presented their cause to synod. The organization of this church may thus be said to have resulted indirectly from his residence here. In 1857 the Third Conference supplied the Lutherans of Graniteville with preaching, and since that date Lutheran services have been continued to the present time. Among those who preached here in 1857 was Rev. A. W. Lindler, who reported to synod that he has found nineteen persons at Graniteville who considered themselves members of the Lutheran Church.

In 1859 the Third Conference stationed Rev. J. N. Derrick at Graniteville as missionary and issued an appeal to all churches in the synod for financial assistance in building a church. An organization was effected, and the congregation adopted a constitution on March 4, 1860. The Synodical Missionary Society appropriated $300 for Graniteville in 1859 and $350 in 1860. The synod was unable to help its mission churches during the war, and thus the Graniteville church and its young pastor were thrown entirely upon their own resources. Mr. Derrick taught school and served as postmaster. The erection of a church building was begun and continued under many difficulties. It was dedicated (in an unfinished condition, however) on the third Sunday in November, 1863, by Rev. William Berly, president of synod, assisted by the pastor. It was finally completed in 1871, during the pastorate of Rev. Emanuel Caughman, and was rededicated in September of that year.

The location of this building was unfortunate. It was almost out of town, and the town never grew in that direction. Removal to a more eligible site finally became imperative and on May 28, 1905, the present location was selected by the council. The present church edifice is a frame structure, with corner tower and entrance, and was dedicated free from debt June 27, 1906, by Rev. Z. W. Bedenbaugh. The church lot, and also the lot upon which the old church stood, were donated by the Graniteville Manufacturing Company.

The succession of pastors has been as follows: Reverends J. N. Derrick, 1859-65; Barney Kreps, 1866-70; E. Caughman, 1871; Barney Kreps, 1872; E. Dufford, 1873; G. A. Hough, 1875; Barney Kreps, 1877-79; G. A. Hough, 1880; J. H. Wilson, 1881; A. W. Lindler, 1882-84; S. S. Rahn, 1885; E. E. Barclay, 1886; S. T. Hallman, 1888; S. L. Keller, 1890-91; J. W. Butler, 1892-93; C. P. Boozer, 1894; Clarence M. Fox, 1895; T. W. Shealy, 1897-1900;

Jacob Austin, 1900; J. D. Shealy, 1900-02; L. P. Boland, 1903-04; M. O. J. Kreps, 1905; J. W. Oxner, (supply) 1906-07; J. B. Derrick. 1907; J. I. Miller, D.D., 1908; J. B. Derrick, 1908-14; Herbert C. Bell, 1914-18; H. S. Petrea, 1918-24.

The membership numbers seventy-three, and the Sunday School seventy-eight. The church property is valued at $2,500.

St. Andrew's Church ("Wentworth Street Church"), Charleston

This congregation has a composite history which is worthy of special note.

In 1851 Rev. G. D. Bernheim, D.D., collected funds and purchased a lot on Morris Street, on which a house of worship was built, and dedicated January, 1853. It was named "Zion Evangelical Lutheran Church". The dedicatory services were conducted by Revs. John Bachman. D.D., Louis Mueller, D.D., E. A. Bolles, J. H. Bailey, E. B. Hort and G. D. Bernheim. The last named was chosen pastor and was installed February 6, 1853.

Rev. G. D. Bernheim came to the South from Pennsylvania. Originally he was from Germany. and his father was a converted Jew. The elder Bernheim became a Lutheran preacher, as did also his sons, G. D. and Charles H.; it was the latter who proposed the name, "United Synod of the Evangelical Lutheran Church in the South," upon the union of our southern synods at Roanoke, Va., June 25, 1886, which name our general body bore for many years.

In January, 1858, Rev. G. D. Bernheim resigned the pastorship and moved to North Carolina, although not without leaving behind him a zealous band of faithful workers. By death and removal, however, the membership was sadly depleted, and by May, 1859, only thirteen members remained.

As an evidence of their faith and loyalty, in that same year they extended a call to Rev. W. S. Bowman, then of Madison, Va., who entered upon the work May 22, 1859, and continued with that congregation and the later united congregation, called "Wentworth Street Lutheran Church", sixteen or more years.

In 1866 a Protestant Methodist Church, being also weak numerically, united with Zion Lutheran Church, and with great unanimity, under Rev. Mr. Bowman's ministry, combined with the fullest cooperation of Rev. John H. Honour, then a Protestant Methodist minister, a brighter day came for the united congregation. The Zion church property was sold and the Protestant Methodist church was repaired, the joint congregation becoming a Lutheran church. This was then known as "The Wentworth Street Lutheran Church", (now St. Andrew's Church), Rev. W. S. Bowman becoming pastor.

While the repairs were being made, the congregation worshiped in the chapel of the Charleston Orphan House until November 18, 1866, when the renovated church was opened for divine worship. The opening sermon was preached by Rev. J. P. Smeltzer, D.D.; and Reverends John Bachman, D.D., A. R. Rude, D.D., T. S. Boinest, J. H. Honour, D.D., Emanuel Caughman and Pastor Bowman took part in the services.*

From that period St. Andrew's Church has moved onward with unvarying degrees of success and for years has been a power in our Southern Church. It now has a membership of over 500, an enrollment of 253 in the Sunday School, a property value of $81,000, a splendid parish house and all the essentials of a well equipped sanctuary.

The following pastors have ministered here: Reverends G. D. Bernheim, D.D., W. S. Bowman, D.D., Luther K. Probst, D.D., R. C. Holland, D.D., J. A. B. Scherer, D.D., M. G. G. Scherer, D.D., and J. Howard Worth, the present pastor.

The South Carolina Synod has held several conventions in this church. Rev. Paul E. Scherer, D.D., now of New York City, entered the ministry as a son of this congregation. This church has contributed liberally to all the enterprises of the synod and the Church at large.

---

* (See Schirmer's Sketch, pp. 26-28.)

Providence Church, Lexington County

This congregation was organized in 1866 under the ministry of Rev. J. N. Derrick. In the parochial table of that year this church alone is named as constituting Rev. J. N. Derrick's charge, and the number of communicants is put down as sixty-five, with twenty-four confirmations.

This new congregation was composed chiefly of members of St. Stephen's Church, living three miles from the town. The church was built but was not dedicated until 1869, the service being conducted by Rev. T. S. Boinest, who was then president of the synod. In 1867 the congregation was served by Rev. J. N. Derrick (together with Bethel and St. Michael's Churches).

The original building remains, although having been remodeled.

The pastors have been the following: Reverends J. N. Derrick, 1866-70; J. H. Bailey, 1871-81; J. Q. Wertz, 1881-82; M. O. J. Kreps, 1883-88; S. S. Rahn, 1889; J. G. Graichen, 1889-95; C. P. Boozer, 1899-1900; George S. Bearden, 1901-04; J. W. Nease, 1905-06; B. W. Cronk, 1907-09; P. D. Risinger, 1912-16, and O. B. Shearouse, the present pastor (since 1917).

The present membership is 125; total Sunday School enrollment, 86. The property value is $4,000.

Bethany Church, Edmund, Lexington County

This congregation came into being in 1871, and, as Rev. J. B. Lowman is named as the first pastor, he must have been one of the organizers of the church. For two years services were held under a "brush arbor", somewhat after the custom of the wandering Jews of old in their "Feast of Weeks", or "Feast of Harvest". Then a very plain structure took the place of the arbor. This was later replaced by a better building which the congregation is still using, although feeling the need of a modern church, suited to its present condition. This church has been isolated as to its relation to other Lutheran congregations and this has rendered it difficult to form such pastoral relations as would be conducive to its rapid growth and development. A more desirable location and a new church are things now in the minds of the members, and with these a brighter day will come.

The following pastors have served this church: Reverends J. B. Lowman, Drewry Kyzer, David Shealy, J. H. Bailey, S. P. Shumpert, A. R. Taylor and C. J. Sox, the present pastor.

St. James' Church, Summit

This congregation was organized April 17, 1873. The number of members at the time of organization was thirty-one, and Rev. A. L. Crouse was elected pastor.

The cornerstone was laid July 17, 1873, the services being conducted by Reverends Daniel Efird and A. L. Crouse. A neat building was erected.

The following pastors have ministered to this congregation: Reverends A. L. Crouse, E. L. Lybrand, E. J. Sox, W. H. Roof, B. D. Wessinger, J. C. Wessinger, F. K. Roof. The present pastor is Rev. W. D. Wise.

There are now 150 members and a Sunday School enrollment of 131. The property value is $2,300.

Wittenberg Church, Leesville

This congregation was organized in 1870, the first pastor being Rev. Samuel Bouknight. Originally the name was Luther Chapel, which was changed to Wittenberg in 1917— the year of the four hundredth anniversary of the Reformation.

The first building, erected in 1874 under the ministry of Rev. Samuel Bouknight, was a frame structure; the second was erected in 1887 when Rev. L. E. Busby, D.D., was pastor. The present church was built in 1918, Rev. V. Y. Boozer, D.D., being pastor. This is constructed of red brick and is a large and churchly edifice, having a Sunday School department, the whole costing $26,000. This house of worship was dedicated March 3, 1919, the sermon being preached by Rev. H. J. Black, president of synod, the pastor and Rev. P. E. Monroe, D.D., conducting the service of consecration.

In the Spring of 1920 the congregation installed a two manual Estey pipe organ. The church in all of its appointments is highly creditable to pastor and people.

The pastors have been as follows: Revs. S. Bouknight, 1870-75; A. D. L. Moser, 1876-78; L. E. Busby, D.D., 1878-94; H. P. Counts, 1894-95; J. D. Kinard, 1895-1903; D. B. Groseclose, 1903-08; S. C. Ballentine, 1908-15; W. E. Schuette (supply), 1915-16; and V. Y. Boozer, D.D., 1916-23 (June 1), when he accepted a call to the church at Madison, Va.

Rev. J. W. Oxner is a son of this congregation.

The membership is now 219; the Sunday School has an enrollment of 145, and the property is valued at $34,700.

St. Thomas' Church, near Chapin

This church was organized in 1876, of members principally of St. Peter's Church (Piney Woods), together with a few others from the surrounding churches, under Rev. A. L. Crouse.

The congregation worshiped for several years in a dwelling-house which was built by Wesley Wessinger. A house of worship was built in 1899, practically at the same place as the dwelling house.

The following pastors served it: Reverends A. L. Crouse, J. S. Koiner, J. P. Smeltzer, W. L. Darr, Jacob Wike, J. F. Deal, Enoch Hite, O. B. Shearouse, W. J. Roof, J. C. Wessinger and R. M. Carpenter.

The congregation was first connected with the Tennessee Synod, afterward with the North Carolina Synod and later with the South Carolina Synod, the latter changes occurring in the process of the reunion of the Lutheran Synods in the South.

Reverends B. D. Wessinger, E. L. Wessinger, J. C. Wessinger and J. P. Derrick are sons of this congregation.

Mt. Pleasant Church, near Gilbert

The date of organization is 1875, but the records fail to indicate the building of the church. At the meeting of synod in 1877 the president of synod stated that Rev. H. W. Kuhns reported that he had dedicated Mt. Pleasant Church in Lexington County on June 24, 1877; it was, however, not until the convention of 1879 that this congregation, upon application, was received into the synod.

At the convention of 1880 it was reported that in December, 1879, Rev. A. W. Lindler had accepted a call to this church and had entered upon his work there as pastor.

This congregation has suffered much loss in membership by death and removals.

The following pastors are given as having served this church: Reverends A. W. Lindler, C. P. Boozer, J. D. Shealy, H. A. McCullough, O. C. Petersen, E. C. Witt, and J. D. Shealy, the present pastor.

The number of members is now 100, with a total Sunday School enrollment of 63. Property value $1,320.

St. Johannes' Church, Charleston

This congregation was organized in 1878 by Rev. Johannes Heckel, who was then a member of the Synod of Ohio. When St. Matthew's congregation built a new church up-town, they sold the old church on Hasell Street to other parties, which occupied the building up to about 1878. Then the German people who lived in the locality of the old church bought it back, and greatly improved and handsomely furnished it.

In October, 1878, the church was dedicated under the name of "St. Johannes' German Evangelical Lutheran Church". Pastor Heckel united with the South Carolina Synod at the convention held in November, 1878.

The following pastors have served this congregation: Rev. Johannes Heckel, 1878-90; Rev. Karl Bolt, 1890-94; Rev. A. Freyschmidt, 1894-97; Rev. Karl Bolt, 1897-1903, when he was called to his heavenly reward. Then Rev. Charles Koerner was pastor 1903-09; Rev. F. W. Hoppe, 1909-10; Rev. H. J. Black, 1910-20, when he was elected the first salaried president of the South Carolina Synod. Rev. I. E. Long then became pastor and is still serving the congregation.

In 1910 the use of the German language in the worship and in the instruction of the congregation was discontinued. In 1921 an adjoining lot was purchased, the church plant was enlarged and a modern parish house was erected. The church now has an enrolled membership of over 400, and a property value of considerably more than $50,000.

St. Andrew's Church, near Blythewood

This congregation was organized in 1878, presumably by Rev. E. L. Lybrand, as he was its first pastor. Reverends J. A. Cromer and J. W. Oxner were the next pastors.
These few facts alone were furnished.

Pisgah Church, Lexington County

This congregation was organized in 1879 and the church was erected in 1880. A lot given jointly by Messrs. M. L. Taylor, M. L. Kyser, John J. Taylor and J. J. Kyser, was used as the site, five acres in all, and on this lot a neat church stands.

The following pastors have ministered to this congregation: Reverends Barney Kreps, J. D. Shealy, Drewry Kyzer, J. G. Graichen, J. W. Nease, B. W. Cronk, P. D. Risinger, and the present pastor, O. B. Shearouse.

The membership is now 100, with a total Sunday School enrollment of 88. The property value is $1,100.

Mt. Tabor Church, Newberry County

This congregation was organized in 1880 under the ministry of Rev. J. A. Sligh, D.D., and was made up of members from other Lutheran churches living in that community. The people in that section have always been noted for industry, frugality, honesty and moral integrity; they have been noted also for church-going habits and for living the faith they confess.

In connection with St. Paul's Church, Rev. J. A. Sligh preached here for many years, but in the arrangement of pastorates Mt. Tabor was served successively by Reverends T. O. Keister, S. T. Hallman, W. H. Hiller, W. A. Lutz, M.

O. J. Kreps, E. W. Leslie, J. B. Harman, and Rev. J. L. Cromer, the present pastor.

We have no definite information as to the building of Mt. Tabor church, but in the minutes of the synod of 1880 we find that the church was dedicated on September 5, 1880, and its life has gone on quietly and successfully from that day to this. It now has a confirmed membership of upwards of 200, a Sunday School enrollment of over 150, a splendid parsonage, and is now planning for the erection of a more substantial church building. Its future is therefore full of promise for greater and better things.

Mt. Tabor Church, New Brookland

This congregation was organized in 1880 with twenty-two charter members, Rev. E. L. Lybrand, pastor. Pastor Lybrand served the congregation until 1918, when he became pastor emeritus. He died in 1918 and Rev. J. W. Oxner became pastor in that year and is the pastor at the present time.

The congregation has a membership of 270. The remains of Rev. E. L. Lybrand, for so long the beloved pastor of Mt. Tabor, rest in the church cemetery.

Rev. W. J. Roof is a son of the congregation.

This church belonged to the Tennessee Synod until 1921. After the merging of the Tennessee and North Carolina Synods, it was connected with the latter synod until 1922. Since that time it has been in the South Carolina Synod.

St. Philip's Church, Newberry County

St. Philip's Church was organized by Rev. H. S. Wingard in August, 1881, while he was pastor of Bethlehem charge. The organization was perfected in the home of Mr. Philip Sligh and the church building was erected in the same year. The building was dedicated November 5, 1882. The pastor was assisted in the dedicatory services by Rev. J. Steck, D.D. Rev. Mr. Wingard was succeeded as pastor by Rev. S. T. Hallman, December 2, 1883, and he was succeeded by H. F. Scheele, theological student, June 6, 1888, who served as pastor-supply. Rev. J. H. Wyse was called and became pastor February 2, 1890, and served the congregation two years. Rev. J. A. Sligh began work as supply pastor the first Sunday in December, 1892, for one year. Rev. Dr. Sligh was assisted in the work by his son, Rev. W. K. Sligh. Rev. J. D. Bowles succeeded Rev. J. A. Sligh, December 9, 1893, and served as pastor to October 2, 1898. Rev. J. J. Long was called as supply pastor and served until October, 1900. Rev. Dr. Hallman was again called and served St. Philip's, together with Mt. Olivet and Bachman Chapel as a pastorate, until January, 1901. Rev. H. P. Counts was called to become pastor of St. Philip's and Bachman Chapel and took charge February 3, 1901. He was succeeded by Rev. P. H. E. Derrick, March, 1902, and he served until 1905. Rev. Mr. Derrick was succeeded by Rev. J. C. Wessinger, November 26, 1905, and continued as pastor until March 28, 1909. Rev. J. J. Long served from April 11, 1909, to October 16, 1910.

At this time a new pastorate was formed, composed of St. Paul's, St. Philip's and Bachman Chapel. This pastorate called Rev. J. A. Sligh, as pastor and Rev. Y. von A. Riser as assistant. Dr. Sligh having retired from the active ministry, Rev. Mr. Riser became pastor. During his term as pastor the old church building was removed and the present one erected in 1914. Rev. Mr. Riser served until January, 1915, when he was succeeded by Rev. A. J. Bowers, D.D., whose services embraced a period of one year. Rev. S. P. Koon, the next pastor, entered upon the work December 10, 1916. Under his administration the debt on the new church has been paid off and additional improvements made in 1922. April 28, 1923, the church building was dedicated free of debt.

The congregation now numbers 240 members, with 109 in the Sunday School, and reports a church property value of $4,500.

St. Paul's Church, Columbia

This congregation was organized in 1886, a tentative organization being effected November 22 of that year. The congregation was served by several ministers of the synod the first year. The permanent organization was completed December 12, 1886, when it adopted the constitution for congregations recommended by the synod. Rev. E. A. Wingard, D.D., was called and became the first pastor. The congregation prior to the calling of Rev. Dr. Wingard had been served by different pastors of the synod, Reverends C. P. Boozer, J. A. Sligh, S. T. Hallman, Jacob Hawkins and others. The congregation was organized with twenty-nine charter members, fifty pupils being in the Sunday School. A lot was purchased at the corner of Bull and Blanding Streets and a neat chapel erected. The parsonage was located upon that part of the lot now occupied by the church.

An incident connected with St. Paul's Church stands without a parallel in the history of the congregations in the synod, or perhaps in that of our Church in this country, as an act of devotion and self-denial on the part of one of the charter members, when Mr. A. D. Haltiwanger mortgaged his home in order to secure the money to purchase the lot for the parsonage, his wife readily waiving her dower at the time, notwithstanding the demands upon them in the support of quite a large family and the suffering he endured periodically as the result of a severe wound which he had received as a soldier in the Confederate War, when he had been left on the battlefield as dead, covered by a blanket of snow. Both of these faithful Christians have gone to their heavenly reward. Their works do follow them.

So far as the records show this was the first congregation organized in the synod on a self-sustaining basis; yet the synod advanced $1,000 as a loan to the congregation in building the church. At the convention in 1902, the synod released this obligation in full, by request of the church council, which assured the synod that being relieved of this burden the members would prove their appreciation by an increase in contributions for the synodical treasury. The congregation has kept faith with the synod by its growth in liberality, as is shown by the contributions of $118.01 for benevolence in 1901; an increase of $400 in 1908; nearly four times as much, $1,981, in the next decade, which was more than trebled by the amount for benevolence, $4,353, in 1923.

During the summer of 1901, St. Paul's was supplied by theological student Edward Fulenwider. In September of that year Rev. W. H. Greever became regular pastor. At that time the membership of the congregation, a little less than one hundred, was burdened with a heavy debt. Many unidentified Lutherans were found in Columbia and suburbs and their interest was developed, so that the membership began to increase rapidly. Small improvements were undertaken on the property which led to the building of an addition to the church, to the installation of new pews, new chancel furniture and a pipe organ. Systematic efforts resulted also in the steady reduction of the church debt, the increase in pastor's salary and almost phenomenal increase of contributions to benevolences. The congregation furnished supporters for some of the most fruitful enterprises of the Church of that period, notably the publication interests and the Theological Seminary. It was about 1904 that the first vacation Bible school was held in St. Paul's Church, the pastor being assisted by Rev. J. L. Yonce, then a seminary student. That was the first school of its kind conducted in the country, and was but a feature of the emphasis placed by the pastor upon thorough religious instruction of its young. Pastor Greever resigned as pastor in 1908 in order to give his entire time to the publication work of the United Synod in the South, at which time the membership of the congregation was about 450, and St. Paul's was recognized as one of the leading congregations in the South.

A notable event in the history of St. Paul's Church was the cancellation of the entire debt, when Rev. Dr. Greever was supply pastor during a vacancy in 1911. Four years previously half of the debt of more than $5,000 had been paid, and in the spring of 1911 the officers of the church, in view of recent liberal contributions made by the congregation for missions, education and other causes of benevolence, including the amount of $2,000 for the location of the Theological Seminary in Columbia, decided to ask the congregation to cancel the remaining indebtedness by a voluntary cash offering at Easter. The announcement of the offering was made two weeks in advance of Easter Sunday, April 16, when, after a special service of song and prayer following the morning worship, the offering was taken. It amounted to $2,261.10, which was not sufficient to liquidate the debt of $2,545, but within a few minutes the balance was given readily and the entire debt extinguished. *The State* of Monday, April 17, in nearly a column account of the offering, said: "It is stated that this collection is perhaps the largest cash offering ever made by any congregation in the history of Columbia."

Under the ministry of Rev. Dr. McCullough a new granite church was erected in 1913 at a cost of $50,000. The original chapel has been converted into a modern Sunday School building and parish house. From the small beginning in 1886 the congregation has grown to 655 members in 1924, with an enrollment of 461 in the Sunday School and a church property of $125,000 in value.

Unity, harmony and a laudable aggressiveness have characterized the entire history of the congregation. Its work and finances have increased in like proportion and today St. Paul's is a power in the activities of its home city and the Southern Church.

The terms of service of the pastors of St. Paul's Church are as follows: Reverends E. A. Wingard, D.D., (died while pastor), 1887-1900; W. H. Greever, D.D., 1901-08; J. D. Mauney, 1909-11. Rev. H. A. McCullough, D.D., the present pastor, took charge in 1911. That the congregation has had only four pastors in thirty-seven years speaks volumes for the sound judgment, the spirit of unity, and the loyalty of St. Paul's people.

Rev. George S. Bearden is a son of this congregation.

Bachman Chapel Church, Newberry County

Bachman Chapel Church was organized with forty charter members by Rev. J. A. Sligh, D.D., April 17, 1887. At first he preached in the Ridge Road schoolhouse and the organization was called Ridge Road Church.

A nice church building was soon erected, which was dedicated free of debt October 13, 1889. This service was conducted by Revs. J. D. Bowles and J. A. Sligh, D.D. The name, Bachman Chapel Evangelical Lutheran Church, was at that time adopted and the congregation is still known by this name.

Dr. Sligh continued to serve the congregation until 1890. During that year he resigned and it seems that the congregation was vacant until 1891. Pastors after this time served as follows: Reverends W. A. Julian, 1891-92; C. P. Boozer, 1892-93; J. D. Bowles, 1893-94; J. A. Sligh, again, 1894-95; C. P. Boozer, again, 1896-99; H. P. Counts, 1899-1901; P. H. E. Derrick, 1901-05; J. C. Wessinger, 1905-08; P. H. E. Derrick, supply, 1908-09.

Bachman Chapel congregation in 1909 passed into the St. Paul's Pastorate, when Rev. J. A. Sligh, D.D., took charge a third time, but on account of his advanced age he was assisted by Rev. Y. von A. Riser. Dr. Sligh continued for one year, leaving the work in 1911. Rev. Mr. Riser then served alone and continued until 1915.

Rev. J. B. Harman took charge in 1915, and served for one year. He was succeeded in 1916 by Rev. S. P. Koon, who is still pastor.

The communicant membership is at present more than one hundred. The first church building is still used and is in good condition, but is too small for the congregation. Plans are now being made to enlarge the church. Its present value is $1,300. The membership numbers eighty-five and the Sunday School ninety-three.

Mt. Hermon, Peak

This congregation was organized under the ministry of Rev. J. B. Fox in 1889, and received into the synod in October, 1889. Mr. Brooks Swygert was enrolled as the first delegate from this congregation. The membership numbered forty, with a Sunday School enrollment of twenty-five.

The following pastors have served this congregation: Reverends J. B. Fox, A. J. Bowers, W. K. Sligh, A. G. Voigt,

J. D. Kinard, V. Y. Boozer, S. C. Ballentine, J. B. Haigler, V. L. Fulmer, H. S. Petrea, W. A. Dutton and J. B. Harman.

The property value of the church is listed at $2,800. From the location of the church near the river and not far from the historic old St. John's Church, its growth is naturally limited, notwithstanding the fact that it is made up of most excellent people.

St. James' Church, Sumter

The Lutherans of Sumter were organized into a congregation March 11, 1890, when six interested Lutherans were present and became charter members. A constitution and by-laws were adopted, and on the following day officers were elected and installed. It was due to the efforts of Rev. F. W. E. Peschau, D.D., pastor of St. Paul's Church, Wilmington, N. C., that the organization was effected, as he had become interested in the members of our Church who had located at Sumter, and he had visited the city and conducted services frequently. He thus directed the organization of the congregation and continued his pastoral oversight of Lutheran interests in this growing city.

It was not until June 13, 1893, that a lot was secured and plans adopted for a building and also not until the fall of 1896 that the church was erected. In the meantime services were held in some of the local churches and in a hall over a store.

Dr. Peschau served the congregation with services in connection with his pastorate at Wilmington from the date of the organization in 1896, with the exception of two months' service in the summer of 1894 by theological student, D. R. Sumstine, and also a few services held by Rev. B. W. Cronk, neighboring pastor, and Rev. J. C. Seegers.

Rev. J. C. Trauger became the first regular pastor in February, 1896, and his service extended to August, 1897. During his administration the church was erected and occupied and the congregation, together with St. Luke's, Florence, was constituted a pastorate. Following the resignation of Rev. Mr. Trauger, theological students Y. von A. Riser and Wilbur H. Riser acted as supply pastors until the former became regular pastor in February, 1908.

In October, 1900, the union with St. Luke's, Florence, was dissolved and the congregation became associated in a pastorate with Orangeburg Lutheran Church. This arrangement ceased early in the fall of 1902, while Rev. H. C. Grossman was pastor, and at the meeting of synod held the following month, St. James' was again placed with Florence; but it seems that the Florence congregation had disbanded and St. James' decided to become an individual pastorate, provided aid could be secured from the Executive Committee of synod. Rev. Mr. Grossman then resigned the Orangeburg Church to serve St. James' Church, but he served only a few months, resigning January 1, 1903.

A vacancy of five months then ensued, services being supplied by theological students from the Theological Seminary at Mt. Pleasant, Charleston. The services of regular pastors were resumed June 1, 1904, when Rev. Thaddeus B. Epting took charge. It was during his administration that at the Christmas festival of 1905 the church was freed from debt by a gift of $300 from Mrs. Maggie E. Laughrey, and also in 1907 that substantial improvements to the church were made.

Rev. Mr. Epting served four years, until June 1, 1908, when a vacancy of one year occurred. Then the congregation had the service of a regular pastor until October, 1912. A vacancy of two years ensued (services being supplied by theological students, as in all other similar periods), when Rev. J. H. Wilson, D.D., took charge in January, 1914. His death occurred July 11, 1919. The congregation had no regular pastor for a year, when Rev. J. P. Derrick took charge June 1, 1920.

Following is the record of service of all the regular pastors: Reverends J. C. Trauger, 1896-97; Y. von A. Riser, 1898-1900; H. C. Grossman, 1901-03; T. B. Epting, 1904-08; E. H. Kohn, 1909-11; W. H. Davidson (May-October), 1912; J. H. Wilson, 1914-19; J. P. Derrick, 1920-24.

The membership is 75, with 108 as the Sunday School enrollment, and the church property value is $7,500.

St. Matthew's Church, near Lexington

This church was organized in 1890, and since Rev. Drewry Kyzer was the first supply pastor the organization must have come about through his ministry. This congregation seems never to have had a regular pastor, but has been supplied by the following: Reverends D. Kyzer, S. P. Shumpert, A. R. Taylor, J. D. Shealy, W. H. Riser, and A. B. Obenschain.

The membership is 117, with a total Sunday School enrollment of 75. The property value is $1,200.

Mt. Horeb Church, Chapin

This congregation was organized in 1891, under the ministry of Rev. W. L. Darr, with about 25 members, and has now 260, which increase shows the wisdom of its founders and the need for its existence. The following pastors have ministered to the spiritual needs of the congregation: Reverends W. L. Darr, Jacob Wike, J. F. Deal, O. B. Shearouse, Enoch Hite, W. J. Roof, J. L. Cromer and J. M. Senter, the present pastor.

To the credit of the congregation and of its pastors stands the fact that four of its sons have entered the ministry: Reverends S. P. Koon, J. J. Bickley, B. J. Wessinger and J. E. Stockman.

The first church was erected in 1893, the second in 1917, a substantial and commodious brick building, churchly in all of its appointments.

Holy Trinity Church, Little Mountain

This congregation was organized January 1, 1891, with Rev. J. K. Efird as its first pastor, who was twice pastor. Rev. A. G. Voigt, D.D., was supply pastor, and then Rev. S. L. Nease was also twice the pastor, followed by Reverends H. P. Counts, O. B. Shearouse, John J. Long and J. B. Harman.

Reverends L. P. Boland and H. D. Chapman entered the ministry as sons of this congregation.

The present commodious, substantial and churchly brick house of worship was erected in 1917 at a cost of $14,000, under the ministry of Rev. John J. Long, D.D., and dedicated June 18, 1922. The sermon was preached by Rev. A. G. Voigt, D.D., LL.D. The president of synod, Rev. H. J. Black, and Reverends P. E. Monroe, D.D., J. C. Wessinger and Pastor Long took part in the services. The South Carolina Synod met in the old building in October, 1902, and the synod was convened in the new church, November 3-6, 1919. The Young People's Federation met here in 1921.

Holy Trinity is now recognized as one of the progressive and most efficient congregations in the synod. Its membership is 300, with 211 in the Sunday School. Its church property is valued at $16,000.

St. Luke's Church, Summerville

This congregation was organized August 13, 1892. The cornerstone was laid in January, 1893, and in May of that year the house of worship was dedicated, the sermon being preached by Rev. R. C. Holland, D.D.; Rev. Louis Mueller, D.D., and Rev. W. A. C. Mueller assisted in the service.

The original membership was composed chiefly of members of the Lutheran churches in Charleston and the city pastors took special interest in this organization and in its future progress, and often ministered to them in its early history.

The congregation is now under the pastoral care of Rev. G. W. Nelson, and is growing in numerical strength and efficiency. The membership is 106, and the Sunday School enrollment 108. The property value is $7,000.

Grace Church, Gilbert

This congregation was organized at Gilbert by Rev. J. A. Cromer, August 13, 1893. Rev. J. A. Cromer was elected pastor September 10, 1893, and the church was dedicated September 30, 1894. The following pastors have served the congregation: Reverends J. A. Cromer, B. D. Wessinger, J. L. Crouse, J. K. Efird, G. A. Stoudemayer, L. L. Lohr, Rev. Theo. C. Parker is the present pastor.

Mt. Vernon Church, White Rock

This church was organized in 1892, and was served by theological student H. A. McCullough. The church building was dedicated in 1897, the pastor, Rev. S. C. Ballentine, being assisted by Reverends W. A. Deaton and Jacob Wike. The present membership is 105.

The following have been the pastors of this church: Reverends S. C. Ballentine, 1894-05; J. B. Haigler, 1905-12; V. L. Fulmer, 1913-15; H. S. Petrea, 1915-18; W. A. Dutton, 1919-21; J. B. Harman, 1922-23.

St. John's Church, Steedman

Organized September 15, 1894. Rev. W. K. Roof was the first pastor, followed by Reverends B. D. Wessinger, J. L. Cromer, G. A. Stoudemayer and B. J. Wessinger.

This church has about thirty-five members and a property value of $1,000.

St. Mark's Church, near Fort Motte

This congregation was organized in 1896. The pastors have been the following: Reverends J. H. Wyse, S. L. Nease, P. D. Risinger, W. B. Aull, L. P. Boland and E. W. Leslie. This brings its history of pastoral services up to the synod of 1921. In 1922 Rev. R. R. Sowers supplied the congregation, but at the synod of 1923 it was reported vacant.

Mr. J. G. Maynard, the secretary and treasurer, writes: "Our little congregation has married off and moved away to such an extent that our band has been reduced to only four active members. We have no services now, but our little band continues to keep up our synodical assessments and other dues."

This church, being in a section in which are few Lutherans, has never been numerically strong, but our people there have been faithful and true. They deserve commendation for their devotion to the faith of their fathers and their helpfulness in the work of the synod.

St. Luke's Church, Florence

This church was organized in 1896 under the ministry of Rev. J. C. Trauger, with twenty members. The congregation was received into the synod under the care of its Executive Committee on Missions and placed in a pastorate with the Sumter congregation. Rev. J. C. Trauger was the first pastor. In 1897 he resigned and for a time the church was supplied by students from the Theological Seminary at Mt. Pleasant. Rev. Y. von A. Riser served the congregation, together with St. James' Church, Sumter, for some years, the pastorate being called Sumter and Florence mission. The Committee made annual appropriations to the pastor's support. Pastor Riser resigned the mission in October, 1900. For a short time President J. A. Morehead of the Theological Seminary made an earnest effort to supply Florence with the preached Word, but that service did not seem satisfactory to the congregation and it was discontinued.

A rather dark day had come in the life of the Florence congregation, but in 1902 the church was again placed in a pastorate with Sumter, and the church for part of the year had been supplied by students from our Theological Seminary. Rev. T. B. Epting was called to that mission, and in 1905 he reorganized the Florence congregation, and from that period dates its renewed life and growth. At the convention of synod held in November, 1906, the Executive Committee reports that "an earnest body of Lutherans has rallied around him, and a church building is now in process of construction". By November, 1907, a splendid artificial stone building was nearly completed, and the membership had grown to thirty-two faithful workers.

May 10, 1908, Rev. J. L. Yonce was installed pastor of St. Luke's, having taken charge December 1, 1907, and the mission was looking forward to a self-sustaining condition. By November, 1909, the membership had grown to forty-six, and become self-supporting. Pastor Yonce resigned, and June 1, 1910, Rev. H. J. Black became pastor, but he was called to St. Johannes' Church, Charleston, and soon after the Easter of 1911 assumed charge at that place. He was succeeded at Florence by Rev. W. E. Pugh, who was ordained by the synod in 1911. He resigned October 1, 1913, and was followed by Rev. J. L. Smith, who was installed July 12, 1914. He resigned November 1, 1917, and Rev. H. E. Beatty was installed May 19, 1918, remaining until March 15, 1922. Rev. T. S. Brown took charge June 1, 1922, and is the present pastor.

The membership is now 110. There are 60 on the Sunday School roll, and the property value is $16,500.

Mt. Hebron Church, Saluda County

This congregation was organized September 19, 1898, under the ministry of Rev. J. D. Shealy, and was received into the synod at the annual convention of that year.

The following ministers have served this congregation: Reverends J. D. Shealy, Jacob Austin, O. C. Petersen, E. C. Witt. Rev. J. D. Shealy is again the pastor.

The membership is not large but active and faithful. There are now 122 members enrolled and 85 in the Sunday School. The property value is $1,840.

Mayer Memorial Church, Newberry

This congregation was organized May 20, 1900, under the ministry of Rev. Charles H. Armstrong, Ph.D., and the first house of worship was built at a cost of $2,500, as an expression of the love of Dr. O. B. Mayer for his distinguished father, who in his day ranked as one of the ablest scholars, physicians and surgeons of South Carolina. He was also a life-long member and defender of the faith of the Lutheran Church. A professor in Newberry College once said, "Dr. Mayer told me more about Greek particles than I ever knew." His son, Dr. O. B. Mayer, was equally devoted to the Christian faith as confessed by our Lutheran Church, and worthily wore the mantle of his noble father.

The first house of worship was burned on January 12, 1919, but by October, 1919, a new church was ready for services. On the first Sunday in that month and year, it was occupied, and on January 1, 1921, it became independent of synodical aid.

The following pastors have served this congregation: Revs. Charles H. Armstrong, 1900-01; J. J. Long, 1902-03; R. E. Livingston, 1903-04; A. J. Bowers, D.D., 1905-06; J. D. Shealy, 1907-11; E. C. Witt, 1911-12; J. B. Harman, 1912-13; W. J. Roof, 1913-14; J. A. Shealy and A. J. Bowers, 1914; S. P. Koon, 1915; W. H. Dutton from 1917 to the present time.

The confirmed membership is now 161; the Sunday School enrollment is 187. The property value is $11,000.

Enon Church, near Leesville

This congregation was organized in 1901, presumably under the ministry of Rev. S. P. Shumpert, he being the first pastor. However, the name of the church does not appear until the convention of 1903, and then only in the parochial table, together with three other congregations constituting the charge of Rev. S. P. Shumpert. The church was dedicated May 8, 1904, and the membership was then thirty-seven, with an enrollment of fifty in the Sunday School.

The pastors have been as follows: Reverends S. P. Shumpert, A. R. Taylor, P. E. Monroe. Rev. J. D. Shealy is now supplying the church.

The roll shows seventy-four members and eighty-three officers and teachers in the Sunday School. The property value is $2,500.

Pomaria Church, Pomaria

This congregation was organized in 1910 to meet the needs of the growing town of Pomaria. The name of the town is from the Latin *Pomarius*, of or belonging to fruit; an orchard —because Mr. William Summer had established a prosperous fruit nursery near that station on the Columbia and Greenville Railroad.

The congregation was received into the synod at the convention of 1910, and the present pastor says, "The church was built some time during the following year."

It has been served by the following ministers: Reverends J. J. Long, I. E. Long, J. A. Linn, R. H. Anderson, S. C. Ballentine, Enoch Hite, H. A. Kistler, and J. B. Haigler, the present pastor. It now has seventy-five confirmed members and a Sunday School enrollment of eighty-one. The valuation of the church property is $4,000.

Mt. Pleasant Church, Saluda

This congregation was organized by Rev. D. B. Groseclose, June, 1903. The membership was numerically small but made up of excellent people. These have been joined by others, and from the beginning they have been making steady progress.

A lot was secured, a church was built and it was dedicated in the spring of 1914, the dedicatory sermon being preached by Rev. A. G. Voigt, D.D., LL.D. The pastor at that time was Rev. S. P. Koon. The following pastors have ministered to this congregation: Reverends J. L. Buck, Charles J. Sox, N. D. Bodie, S. P. Koon, Wade A. Dutton, George S. Bearden, and the present pastor, John J. Long, D.D. Pastor Long writes: "During the ministry of Rev. George S. Bearden the membership was greatly increased."

The congregation now numbers 140. On April 10, 1924, it began an effort to raise $10,000 to build a substantial brick edifice. In seven days nearly $9,000 was raised for this purpose and the new church is assured.

The total value of the present property is $4,500; so that the new church, when completed, will represent a property value of more than $15,000.

Beginning with about a dozen members, this is a highly commendable record.

Woman's Memorial Church, Spartanburg

This congregation was organized September 28, 1902, by Rev. S. T. Hallman, D.D., then missionary in the Piedmont section of the state. There were seventeen charter members, and Dr. Hallman has been the only pastor to this date.

The church was built on faith in God and paid for without resort to any money-raising devices. A pipe organ and art windows came in the same way of faith. About 200 Lutherans have come in and moved away to other sections since the church was built and occupied in October, 1907; and yet there is a baptized membership of 140, with 100 in the Sunday School. The church property is valued at $20,000.

St. Luke's Church, Olympia Avenue, Columbia

In 1902 the Olympia Mill district was referred to the Executive Committee by the Joint Conference made up of the South Carolina Conference of the Tennessee Synod and the Central Conference of the South Carolina Synod. The report of the Committee states that "by actual count, there are sixty confirmed members, forty ready for instruction and confirmation, and seven baptized children of the Lutheran Church in this district." But at the synod of 1903, held November 11-15, the Executive Committee and Advisory Board of Home Missions reported that, up to that time, "It has been impossible to effect an organization, and the work is yet in the experimental stage."

Then, in the minutes of 1904, the name of St. Luke's Church is given in the list of churches, and Rev. C. P. Boozer had been called by the Committee and had taken charge January 1, 1904. He was "preaching each Lord's Day for the Olympia Mill congregation and giving several days each week to pastoral visiting and other work connected with the mission."

Strangely enough, the exact date of organization does not appear in the synodical records, but the president's report states that the church was dedicated October 15, 1905, by Rev. C. P. Boozer, assisted by Reverends W. H. Greever, C. A. Freed and W. L. Seabrook, the latter preaching the dedicatory sermon.

The formal organization, then, must have been in 1904, under the ministry of Rev. C. P. Boozer, by authority of the Executive Committee on Missions.

The following ministers have served this congregation: Reverends H. C. Grossman, C. P. Boozer, C. E. Weltner, D.D., and M. O. J. Kreps, D.D., the present pastor, who has served this congregation since 1913.

A fact worthy of note is that Rev. C. E. Weltner took charge of this mission March 1, 1906, and in connection with his other duties conducted a school for the training of deaconesses, and two of our foreign missionaries received training in this Inner mission school, Miss Gertrude Simpson and Miss Mary Lou Bowers, now respectively Mrs. G. C. Leonard, Africa, and Mrs. L. G. Gray, Japan. Miss Lucy Copeland also received training under Pastor Weltner, and was employed by the proprietors of the several mill districts in which Rev. Dr. Weltner labored, to do welfare work.

Rev. B. M. Clark entered the ministry from this congregation. Together with the names of the several pastors of this church, the names of Mrs. C. E. Weltner and Mrs. M. O. J. Kreps will ever live in imperishable memory because of their efficient labors in this field.

Fairfax Church, Fairfax

This congregation was organized in April, 1902, under the pastoral care of Rev. P. E. Monroe; but preaching services had been conducted here as far back as 1893 by Rev. J. H. Wilson, D.D., and the church was erected during Dr. Wilson's ministry. No organization, however, was entered into until 1902.

The pastors have been as follows: Reverends P. E. Monroe, 1902-08; D. B. Groseclose, 1908-10; W. B. Aull, 1911-13; D. B. Groseclose, 1913 to the present. Candidates P. E. Shealy and I. E. Long supplied in 1909-10, following the division of the Mt. Pleasant pastorate, resulting in the formation of a new pastorate, which arrangement enlarged the interests and work of our Church in that section of the state.

The membership is now fifty-one, with thirty-two in the Sunday School, and property valued at $4,500.

Immanuel Church, Greenwood

This congregation was organized by Rev. S. T. Hallman, D.D., September 21, 1902, with twenty-two charter members. Until 1904 services were held twice each month, but the Executive Committee then authorized the mission pastor to give the Greenwood church one service each month. The Sunday School, however, was conducted regularly every Lord's Day. In 1907 a lot was purchased at a cost of $1,400, chiefly through the efforts and liberality of Mr. Kenneth Baker, and plans were submitted looking to the erection of a building to cost about $1,500. Later, however, it was deemed best to build a more expensive structure. Accordingly, the cornerstone was laid June 17, 1910, by the pastor and Rev. J. D. Bowles. The church was completed and plans were put in operation to secure a pastor who could give his entire time to this church. In 1912 Rev. J. D. Kinard, D.D., became pastor, and May 18, 1913, the church was dedicated, the sermon being preached by Rev. S. T. Hallman, D.D., and the pastor conducting the dedicatory services. Dr. Kinard closed his labors there June 1, 1918, and George S. Bowden, theological student, supplied the church for the four remaining months of the synodical year. Rev. A. J. Bowers, D.D., was then called and began his labors May 1, 1920. In July, 1920, under the leadership of Dr. Bowers a congregation was organized at Clinton, with twenty members, under the name of St. John's. For the time being, this pastorate is known as the Greenwood-Clinton mission. Because of impaired health Dr. Bowers relinquished the work and Rev. M. R. Wingard was called and began his labors January 1, 1924.

In addition to a neat, substantial brick church, the congregation has an excellent parsonage near the church. The membership is now nearly fifty; the Sunday school has twenty-eight scholars, and the property value is $12,500.

St. John's Church, Johnston

This congregation was organized July 28, 1903, under the ministry of Rev. James D. Kinard, D.D. He was succeeded by Rev. P. D. Risinger, who was instrumental in building the church. The congregation had seventeen charter members when organized, and now, 1923, has ninety-three members and church property valued at $7,450.

The pastors have followed each other in the following order: Reverends James D. Kinard, P. D. Risinger, D. A. Sox, P. E. Monroe, M. L. Kester and James D. Kinard (second term), who returned to this pastorate in 1918.

The church was dedicated during the pastorate of Rev. P. E. Monroe.

One young man entered the ministry from this congregation.

Ehrhardt Church, Ehrhardt

This church was built principally by Mr. Conrad Ehrhardt, the founder of the town of that name. He was a native of Germany. He set apart a lot of two acres of land in the town upon which he built a nice frame church. A few friends made small donations towards its erection. This building, completely furnished, without debt or incumbrance, was given to the congregation, which was organized April 10, 1904. The congregation was organized with thirty-eight charter members. Of these, twenty are still connected with the congregation. The first service in the church was held on the day of the organization of the congregation. The first pastor was Rev. P. E. Monroe, D.D., who was serving in the community at that time. Sunday, April 24, 1904, the church was dedicated. The sermon was preached by Rev. A. G. Voigt, D.D., Dean of the Lutheran Theological Seminary. The Southern Conference was being held in this church at the time of the dedication. Dr. Monroe resigned in November, 1908. Since then the congregation has been served by the following pastors: Reverends D. B. Groseclose, 1908-13; E. F. K. Roof, 1914-17; P. D. Risinger, 1917-22; Rev. A. W. Ballentine, 1922-24.

The congregation, (October 1, 1923) has a confirmed membership of sixty-two; Sunday School, teachers and scholars, fifty-six; property value $2,000.

St. Paul's Church, Aiken

This congregation was organized December 8, 1907, under the ministry of Rev. J. B. Derrick, with sixteen members. A lot was purchased in October, 1908, and the church was erected during the ensuing summer. The original cost was $2,500. The building was consecrated September 9 of that year, Reverends J. B. Derrick and W. J. Finck, D.D., of Augusta, Ga., officiating.

It is interesting to note that Rev. E. A. Bolles taught and preached in this town in 1848; Rev. N. Aldrich reported to synod in 1855 that he had found Lutherans there, and in 1857 this point was referred to the Executive Committee of the synod. It will therefore be seen that from 1848 up to 1907 the Lutherans of Aiken were without a church and for various reasons waited sixty years for a church of the faith of their fathers.*

The following pastors have served this congregation: Reverends J. B. Derrick, 1907-13; theological students, 1913-14; H. S. Petrea, summer of 1914; Herbert C. Bell, 1914-18; H. S. Petrea, 1918-1924.

Holy Trinity Church, New Brookland

This congregation was organized in 1908 under the ministry of Rev. D. A. Sox, who was the first pastor. It was associated with St. Luke's, Columbia, in a pastorate which was served by Rev. M. O. J. Kreps, D.D. Upon the dissolution of the pastorate Rev. D. A. Sox again became pastor and continued this relation until his death early in 1922. All other services have been under supply pastors until 1923, when Rev. J. C. Wessinger became the regular pastor.

The present membership is about sixty, with fifty-five enrolled in the Sunday School. The property value is $1,200, and the total benevolence for the year 1923 was nearly $600. Despite many struggles the congregation is growing, and the prospect is brightening.

*For an interesting history of the Aiken Lutheran Church see *Lutheran Church Visitor*, March 9, 1916.

Silver Street Church, Silver Street

This church was organized by Rev. S. P. Koon in 1908 with twenty-two members, and was received into the synod the same year. Pastor Koon served the congregation until 1916, when the church was reported vacant. This vacancy continued from 1916 to 1918; but in 1919 Rev. Thomas F. Suber became the pastor, and served the church until June, 1924, when he resigned to accept a call to the Church of the Incarnation, Columbia.

The membership is 194; the Sunday School totals an enrollment of 122. The church property value is $6,000, total benevolence $1,914.

Mr. Boyd Harman, now in Newberry College, is a student for the ministry from this congregation.

Trinity Church, Greenville

This congregation was organized August 29, 1909, by Rev. T. B. Epting, with twenty-seven members on the roll. Pastor Epting agreed to serve the congregation until December 1, 1910. Some time in 1911 this became a mission of the United Synod in the South, which early in that year assumed the general oversight of the mission. A lot was bought costing $10,000. Rev. C. Luther Miller took charge early in 1912. A pastor's home was secured and all necessary arrangements were made for the vigorous prosecution of the work. The church was then known as the First Lutheran Church of Greenville. The membership numbered sixty. The cornerstone of the church was laid March 1, 1914, by Reverends Edward Fulenwider and R. S. Patterson, D.D., who was then the Missionary Secretary of the United Synod, and the pastor C. L. Miller.

The convention of the synod in 1914 was held with this congregation.

Some time in 1920 the name of the church was changed from the First Church to Trinity Church, and it so appears in the minutes of the synod from that time.

Rev. C. L. Miller resigned in 1922. Rev. J. L. Smith received and accepted a call and entered on the work January, 1923.

The congregation now has a beautifully finished stone church, with all the essentials of churchly equipment. The membership is now 184, with 125 in the Sunday School. The property value is $60,000.

Mt. Hermon Church, near New Brookland

Mt. Hermon congregation was organized about 1910 by Rev. J. A. Cromer. Its membership was composed of members of Zion Church. It united with the Tennessee Synod upon its organization and remained there until 1921, when it joined the Tennessee Synod in forming the United Synod of North Carolina, and along with other congregations united with the South Carolina Synod in 1922.

The present house of worship was built in 1911 on land donated by T. J. Roof. Rev. J. A. Cromer served the congregation until his death in 1921. Rev. H. A. Kistler, the present pastor, took charge in 1922.

Summer Memorial Church, Newberry

This church was organized July 24, 1910, by Rev. J. D. Shealy. Like Mayer-Memorial Church, it, too, is the evidence of filial love, having been established by Messrs. Charles E., J. H., and George W. Summer as a memorial to their father and mother, George W. and Martha D. Summer.

The following pastors have ministered to this congregation: Revs. J. D. Shealy, 1910-11; E. C. Witt, 1911-12; J. B. Harman, 1912-13; W. J. Roof, 1913-14; J. A. Shealy, A. J. Bowers, D.D., 1914-15; S. P. Koon, 1915-16; W. H. Dutton, the present pastor, since 1917. This church also became independent of synodical aid on January 1, 1921.

The confirmed membership is now 100; there are 150 in the Sunday School. The property value is $3,000.

Good Shepherd, Swansea

This church was organized in 1912 under the ministry of Rev. W. B. Aull. The cornerstone was laid March 2, 1913, by the pastor, the sermon being preached by the president of synod, Rev. W. H. Greever, D.D. The property value is given as $2,000, and the membership is increasing.

The following pastors have served this congregation: Reverends W. B. Aull, D. B. Groseclose and B. D. Wessinger.

Epiphany Church, St. Matthews

This congregation was organized May 26, 1912, under the ministry of Rev. W. H. Greever, D.D., and has been supplied by the following ministers: Reverends W. H. Greever, D.D., J. L. Yonce and C. J. Shealy.

A desirable lot was donated by two generous-hearted members and a building committee was appointed. Any information beyond this brief statement has not been vouchsafed.

St. Barnabas' Church, Charleston

This congregation was organized August 18, 1912, although this had been a Sunday School for a number of years, under the auspices of other Lutheran churches in the city.

At the convention of 1911, Hon. John D. Cappelmann, in behalf of St. Barnabas' Sunday School, asked that, if possible, this work, together with Mt. Pleasant and Summerville, be constituted a mission pastorate. At the convention of 1912, the president of synod reported that this had been done, and that Rev. A. G. Voigt, D.D., was supplying these churches. June 14, 1913, Rev. Bernard Repass accepted a call to St. Barnabas' Church, the congregation then worshiping in what was called St. Barnabas' Chapel.

It was, however, not until the convention of 1920 that the president of synod reported that the congregation had plans well under way for relocating and erecting a new church edifice. A desirable lot had been purchased in a rapidly growing section of the city. The cornerstone of the new church was laid March 27, 1921, the following ministers taking part in the service: Reverends George S. Bowden, pastor; H. J. Black, president of synod; A. D. R. Hancher, Superintendent of Home Missions for the Southern District; I. E. Long, J. H. Worth, S. L. Blomgren, and George J. Gongaware, D.D.

This new church was dedicated March 5, 1922, with services conducted by Rev. George S. Bowden, pastor. The sermon was preached by the president of synod. Revs. George J. Gongaware, D.D., W. A. C. Mueller, D.D., S. L. Blomgren, I. E. Long, J. Howard Worth and O. C. Petersen took part in the services.

The following pastors have ministered to this congregation: Reverends Bernard Repass, Arthur M. Huffman, George S. Bowden, and W. J. Roof, the present pastor.

The membership is now 155. There are 251 in the Sunday School and the property value is $32,000.

Church of the Ascension, Eau Claire, Columbia

This congregation was organized through the zealous efforts of Rev. W. H. Greever, D.D., in 1912, with a membership of about 35. It has been self-sustaining from its organization, and has been a proportionate supporter of the general work of the Church.

It has an attractive, churchly structure, neat and inviting in all of its arrangements, and filling an important mission in that beautiful and growing suburb of Columbia. Being near the Theological Seminary, it forms an important adjunct in the training of our young men, and at the same time it is exerting a most wholesome and helpful influence in the general community. It now has a membership of 200, a Sunday School enrollment of 172, with a property value of $25,000.

In 1922 the congregation received a gift of a pipe organ costing more than $5,000. The gift was made by Mr. and Mrs. P. C. Price in memory of their son George Edward, who died in infancy.

Holy Trinity Church, Pelion

This congregation was organized September 21, 1913, but by whom and with what numerical strength has not been ascertained. It now has a membership of twenty-five, with thirty in the Sunday School. The property value is $1,500.

The following pastors have had charge of this congregation: Reverends B. D. Wessinger, J. L. Cromer, J. K. Efird, G. A. Stoudemayer and B. J. Wessinger.

St. John's Church, near Irmo

This church was organized in 1914, presumably under the ministry of Rev. J. W. Horine, D.D., since he is named as the first pastor.

About six years before the formal organization, a Sunday School was conducted in a school building. The attendance was so large that a chapel was erected, but this, too, was inadequate, and in 1922 the congregation decided to build a better house of worship. They now have a very neat and substantial church which meets the needs of the congregation.

Rev. W. P. Cline, D.D., followed Dr. Horine, and students from the Theological Seminary at Columbia have rendered valuable service to this small but faithful flock. Rev. J. M. Senter is the present supply-pastor.

St. John's Church, Clinton

This church was organized by Rev. A. J. Bowers, D.D., July 11, 1920, with twenty members. Under the able ministry of Dr. Bowers this young congregation began life with enthusiastic devotion, and a bright future is predicted for the Lutheran congregation in Clinton.

In 1923 Rev. Dr. Bowers resigned the Greenwood Pastorate, of which St. John's, Clinton, is a part, and was succeeded by Rev. M. R. Wingard, who is the present pastor of the congregation at Clinton, having begun his ministry there January 1, 1924.

The membership is 33. The Sunday School has an enrollment of 25. The valuation of church property is $1,300. Plans are in preparation for building a house of worship.

Church of the Incarnation, Shandon, Columbia

This church was organized under the ministry of Rev. J. A. Shealy January 2, 1921. It is located in the section of Columbia called Shandon, and began its life on a self-sustaining basis, with twenty-eight charter members. Rev. J. W. Horine, D.D., rendered valuable assistance in the organization of this church.

The lot on which the church stands is 140 by 218 feet in size. On this an attractive chapel was erected in three working days by the members themselves to serve as the temporary abode of the congregation, but a brick or stone structure is being planned as the future home of this young congregation. Pastor J. A. Shealy resigned the church Easter, 1924, and was succeeded on June 1, 1924, by Rev. Thomas F. Suber.

The number of members is seventy-seven and the Sunday School numbers seventy-six. The property value is $7,000.

Immanuel Church, Ridge Spring

This congregation was organized on March 20, 1921, under the ministry of Rev. James D. Kinard, D.D., with thirty-four charter members. Although one of the youngest congregations in the synod, its life and energy are shown in the devotion of its members to a progressive church life.

In October, 1921, a lot was purchased and a building was begun. In August, 1922, the cornerstone was laid and by April, 1923, the building was completed, the whole costing $5,000.

Faith and works have gone together and the results have followed. There is a bright future for this band of loyal Lutherans.

St. James' Church, Saxe-Gotha, near Lexington

This congregation was organized in October, 1921, after Rev. C. J. Sox had preached two years at this place in a "union" church building, and without compensation, looking forward to the organization of a Lutheran church.

As early as 1737 there were Lutherans in Saxe-Gotha township, Lexington County, S. C., forty years before American Independence, and some of their descendants are found in this new congregation—a fact worthy of note. The church has been built, and although having only about thirty members when organized, the congregation is growing and conditions are favorable to the establishment of a large membership in a few years—a fitting monument to a worthy ancestry, a devoted pastor and a loyal people.

Record should be made of the fact that a mission called Red Bank Church existed in the Saxe-Gotha community in the latter part of the Nineteenth century, but the congregation disintegrated and some of the members were lost to the Lutheran Church.

Grace Church, Rock Hill

Grace Church, Rock Hill, was organized April 15, 1923, with 15 charter members. Rev. H. A. Schroder has been pastor since June 1, 1923. The congregation now (August, 1924) has a confirmed membership of 32 and a total enrollment of 37 in the Sunday School, exclusive of Winthrop College students. For three years our Lutherans in Rock Hill have been given the privilege of worshipping in the hall of the Chamber of Commerce. A centrally located lot has been purchased at the corner of Oakland Avenue and Aiken Street for a church and parsonage. The Woman's Missionary Society of the South Carolina Synod has assumed the task of financing the erection of the church and parsonage. Our Lutheran students at Winthrop College take advantage of the presence of Grace Church, and are faithful attendants at the services while the school is in session.

Chapter IX

ROLL OF MINISTERS

AULL, WILLIAM BOWMAN.—Born March 19, 1870, in Newberry County, South Carolina. Educated in Newberry College, receiving the A.B. degree; graduated from the Southern Lutheran Theological Seminary in 1901, then located at Mt. Pleasant, S. C. Ordained in 1901 by the Virginia Synod at Jadwyn, Va. Received into the South Carolina Synod in 1904. In this same year he took his B.D. degree at the Chicago Lutheran Seminary. He served the following pastorates: Pine Grove, Lone Star. S. C., 1904-07; China Grove, N. C., 1907-10; Fairfax, S. C., 1910-13; St. John's, Walhalla, S. C., 1915-23. He is now postmaster in the town of Walhalla, S. C.

BALLENTINE, ARTHUR WILLINGTON.—Born at Chapin, S. C., March 17. 1885. Educated at Newberry College and the Southern Lutheran Theological Seminary. Ordained by the Mississippi Synod, July 2, 1911. Admitted into the South Carolina Synod, November, 1922. Pastorates served: Lingle, Miss., 1911-16; Graham. Va., 1917-18; Senoia, Ga., 1918-22; Ehrhardt, S. C., 1922-23; called to St. John's Church, Walhalla, early in 1924, where he is now located.

BLACK, HENRY J.—Born December 7, 1879, at Leesville, S. C. Educated at Newberry College and the Southern Lutheran Theological Seminary. Ordained by the South Carolina Synod November 13, 1910. Pastorates served: St. Luke's, Florence, S. C.. January 1, 1910 to April 18, 1911; St. Johannes', Charleston, S. C., April 18, 1911 to January 1, 1920. In the meantime he was secretary of the Southern Conference, later becoming its president; vice-president of the South Carolina Synod, 1917-18, and elected president, 1918. In 1920 he was elected the first salaried president of the synod. At the expiration of his first four year term of office he was reelected. Newberry College conferred upon him the degree of Doctor of Divinity in 1924.

BLOMGREN, SIGFRID LUTHER.—Born in Bridgeport, Conn., April 8, 1892. Educated at Augustana College, graduating in 1912: graduate of the Augustana Seminary in 1915. Ordained June 13, 1915. by the Augustana Synod. Admitted into the South Carolina Synod in 1919. Pastorates served: Springfield, Mass., 1916-19: St. Matthew's. Charleston, S. C., 1919-22. He has received both the A.B. and B.D. degrees.

BODIE, EARL KENNAN.—Born November 8, 1895, at Orangeburg, S. C. Educated at Collegiate Institute, Newberry College and Southern Lutheran Seminary, with post-graduate work at the Philadelphia Seminary. Ordained in 1921 by the North Carolina Synod. Pastorates: St. Stephen's, Cabarrus County, North Carolina, 1921-24; Pine Grove, Lone Star, since May 1, 1924, becoming a member of the South Carolina Synod shortly thereafter. He received the degree of A.B. from Newberry College, and that of B.D. from the Philadelphia Theological Seminary.

BOLAND, LAWSON PETTUS.—Born at Little Mountain, S. C., February 12, 1875. Educated at Newberry College and the Southern Lutheran Theological Seminary. Ordained by the Mississippi Synod October 14, 1901; first received into the South Carolina Synod February 4, 1903, and the second time on February 8, 1908, on returning from the North Carolina Synod. Pastorates served: Graniteville, S. C., and Orange Chapel, S. C., February 4, 1903 to November 1, 1904; Pine Grove Pastorate, S. C., February 12, 1908 to January 1, 1916; Betheden Pastorate, S. C., February 1, 1916 to this date. He served the Lebanon Pastorate, North Carolina Synod, November 15, 1904 to February 1, 1908. In connection with other pastoral work, he supplied Mt. Calvary, S. C., February 4, 1903 to November 1, 1903. He served as secretary, vice-president, and then president of the Southern Conference; later secretary of the Newberry Conference, and then president. He has been a member of the Board of Trustees of Summerland College since the fall of 1913.

BOWERS, ANDREW JACKSON.—Born October 1, 1860, in Newberry, S. C. Educated at Newberry College and the Southern Lutheran Theological Seminary. Ordained by the South Carolina Synod in 1883. He served Ebenezer Church, Columbia, S. C., the Church of the Ascension, Savannah, Ga.; Floyd Charge, Va., Greenwood and Clinton, S. C., and for many years was teacher of Ancient Languages in Newberry College, and at the same time supplied churches adjacent to the town of Newberry. Erskine College, Due-West, S. C., conferred on him the degree of Doctor of Divinity.

BROWN, PLEASANT DAVID.—Born November 26, 1886, at Salisbury, N. C. Educated at Roanoke College and the Philadelphia Theological Seminary. Ordained by the North Carolina Synod, May 11, 1913. Admitted into South Carolina Synod, July 20, 1921. Pastorates served: Emmanuel Church, High Point,

N. C., May 15, 1913, to July 20, 1921: Ebenezer Church, Columbia, S. C., July 20, 1921, to this date. He served on the Board of Trustees of Mt. Pleasant Collegiate Institute, N. C., 1918-21; was secretary of the Board two years, and president of the Eastern Conference of the North Carolina Synod in 1921. His A.B. degree was conferred by Roanoke College in 1900, and the degree of M.A. in 1910 by the same college.

BROWN, Thomas Shannon.—Born in Wythe County, Va., November 24, 1857; graduated from Roanoke College and from the Lutheran Seminary at Gettysburg, Pa.; ordained by the Southwest Virginia Synod, 1882, and admitted into the South Carolina Synod, November, 1923. Pastorates served: St. Mark's, Charlotte, N. C., Mt. Zion, Pittsburgh, Pa.; St. Stephen's, Lexington, S. C., Macedonia Church, Burlington, N. C., and St. Luke's Church, Florence, S. C., of which he is the present pastor. The degree of M.A. was conferred on him by Roanoke College.

CLINE, William Pinckney.—Born near Newton, N. C., March 21, 1853. Graduate of the University of North Carolina, 1878. Instructed in theology by Rev. Dr. A. J. Fox and ordained to the Gospel ministry in 1881. In 1884 Rev. Mr. Cline accepted a call to a pastorate of four churches in Davidson County, North Carolina, where he was instrumental in building a parsonage. Seeing the general neglect of education he at once opened a school and in 1885 built and opened an academy under the name Holly Grove Academy. Here he taught with great success until the close of 1891. Rev. Mr. Cline was largely instrumental in founding and building Lenoir College, in which he served for nine years as professor of Latin and History, being also financial agent of the college. In 1901 he resigned his chair and was elected chairman of the Board of Trustees, in which capacity he served for five years. In 1907 he accepted a call to St. Michael's Pastorate, Lexington County, South Carolina, and in the same year was appointed a member of the Board of Publication of the United Synod. He soon became its president, which position he held for many years. At the close of 1911 he resigned as pastor of the St. Michael's charge and became superintendent of the Lowman Home for the aged and helpless at White Rock, S. C., serving this institution until December, 1922, when he tendered his resignation on account of physical disability. The resignation was accepted by the Board with regret and expressions of appreciation of Dr. Cline's many years of faithful service. During his ministry he organized the following congregations and aided in building their houses of worship: Holly Grove. Davidson County. North Carolina; Mt. Hermon, Iredell County, North Carolina: St. Martin's. Maiden. N. C.; Emanuel. Lincolnton, N. C.; Bethlehem, Catawba County, North Carolina; and St. Andrew's. Hickory, N. C. In 1913 Lenoir College conferred upon him the degree of Doctor of Divinity.

CROMER, JOSEPH LEE.—Born in Lexington County, S. C., September 7. 1874. Educated in Concordia and Lenoir Colleges, and the Theological Departments of Concordia and Lenoir Colleges. Ordained by the Tennessee Synod September 1, 1895, and admitted into the South Carolina Synod November, 1922. Pastorates served: Newton. Gastonia. N. C.; Rhodhiss and Maiden. N. C.; St. Paul's and Chapin pastorates. S. C. He has been president and secretary of the North Conference of the Tennessee Synod, president of the Joint Conference, and of the South Carolina Conference of the Tennessee Synod; and was at one time business manager of Lenoir College and a member of the Board of Trustees. He was also a member of the Publication Board of the United Synod. He received his A.B. and A.M. degrees from Lenoir College. He now has charge of the Mt. Tabor pastorate, Prosperity. He has been instrumental in building five new churches, three parsonages, and in making improvements on other churches and pastors' homes.

DERRICK, JOHN PERRY.—Born July 3, 1890, at Chapin, S. C. Educated at Newberry College and the Southern Lutheran Theological Seminary. Ordained November 12, 1920, by the South Carolina Synod. He has been president of the Southern Conference and was pastor of St. James' Church, Sumter, his first charge, 1920-24.

DUTTON, WILLIAM ADDISON.—Born April 16, 1859, near Rural Retreat, Va. His father having died in the service of the Southern Army, and owing to the prostration and impoverishment following the war, he was denied a collegiate education. In 1895 he became a licentiate of the Southwestern Virginia Synod and in 1897 was ordained by that synod at Blue Ridge Springs, Va. He served the following pastorates: Price's Fork, Va.. 3 years; Gold Hill. N. C.. 7 years: Bethel pastorate, Richfield. N. C.. 5 years: St. Mark's and Corinth Churches, Leesville. S. C.. 7 years: Bethel pastorate. White Rock. 2½ years, until compelled to relinquish his work on account of physical disability.

DUTTON, WADE HAMPTON.—Born February 24, 1890, at Rural
Retreat, Va. Educated at Newberry College and the Southern
Lutheran Theological Seminary. Ordained by the South Caro-
lina Synod, November 15, 1917. He became pastor of Mayer-
Summer Memorial Churches, Newberry, and is still in charge
of that pastorate. He received his A.B. degree from Newberry
College at the time of his graduation.

FREED, CHARLES ABRAM.—Born August 23, 1868, near Waynes-
boro, Va. Graduate of Roanoke College (1890) and Philadelphia Theological Seminary (1893). Ordained by the Ministerium of Pennsylvania in Philadelphia in 1893. Served pastorates as follows: Middlebrook Pastorate, Virginia, 1893-
1903; Ebenezer Church, Columbia, 1903-21; Church of the Redeemer, Newberry, 1921-   . Received the degrees of A.B. and
M.A. from Roanoke College and the degree of Doctor of Divinity from Newberry College in 1911. Admitted to the South
Carolina Synod in 1903. President of the Virginia Synod,
1902; president of the South Carolina Synod, 1908-10; member of Merger Committee, U. L. C.; vice-president West Indies Mission Board, U. L. C.; member National Lutheran Council, 1920-   . Chaplain State Senate of South Carolina General Assembly for nine years. At present president of Board
of Trustees of Lutheran Theological Southern Seminary at
Columbia.

GONGAWARE, GEORGE J.—Born December 17, 1866, at Frees-
burg, Pa. Educated at Thiel College and Philadelphia Theological Seminary. Ordained by the Pittsburgh Synod in 1896,
and entered the South Carolina Synod in 1913. Pastorates
served: St. Paul's, Uniontown, Pa.; First Lutheran Church,
Pittsburgh, Pa. On March 1, 1913, he accepted a call to St.
John's Church, Charleston, S. C., and is still pastor. He was
president of the Pittsburgh Synod, 1910-13; president of the
General Council Board of Education, 1909-12; and elected
member of the Board of Education of the United Lutheran
Church in 1918, on which he still serves. He received the
degrees of A.B., M.A. and D.D. from Thiel College.

GOODMAN, REUBEN ALONZO.—Born July 23, 1881, at Amity,
N. C. Educated at Roanoke College and the Southern Lutheran Theological Seminary. Ordained by the North Carolina Synod in 1909, and entered the South Carolina Synod
July 22, 1921. Pastorates served: Christ and Calvary Churches,
Spencer, N. C.; and Holy Trinity, Mt. Pleasant, N. C. He is
now Professor of Bible and Christian Ethics in Newberry Col-

lege, and his ministerial record covers twelve years as pastor, two years as instructor in Mt. Pleasant Collegiate Institute, and eight years as the principal of Mont Amoena Seminary, Mt. Pleasant, N. C.

GREEVER, WALTON HARLOWE.—Born in Burkes Garden, Va., December 18, 1870. Educated at Roanoke College, and at the Philadelphia Theological Seminary. Ordained by the Southwestern Virginia Synod. He was received into the South Carolina Synod in 1901. Pastorates served: Immanuel Church, Bluefield, W. Va.; St. Paul's, Columbia, S. C.; Church of the Ascension, Eau Claire, Columbia, S. C. He has been manager of the Board of Publication, Columbia, S. C., editor of the *Lutheran Church Visitor*, editor and manager of the *American Lutheran Survey*, and field secretary and professor in the Southern Theological Seminary. He received the degrees of A.B. and M.A. from Roanoke College, and the degree of D.D. from Newberry College. He is now pastor of the Church of the Ascension, Eau Claire, Columbia, editor and manager of the *American Lutheran Survey*, and professor in the Southern Theological Seminary.

GROSECLOSE. DAVID BITTLE.—Born October 20. 1855, at Ceres, Va. Educated at Roanoke College. After being instructed by Drs. L. A. Fox, J. J. Scherer and J. B. Greiner, he was ordained in August, 1892, by the Southwestern Virginia Synod, although he had served as a licentiate, 1888-92. He was received into the South Carolina Synod, March, 1903. and has served pastorates as follows: New River. 1890-97: Prices Fork, Va., 1897-1903, Blacksburg Southwestern Virginia Synod; St. Mark's, Saluda. S. C.. 1903; Leesville, S. C., 1904-08; Ehrhardt, S. C., 1908-13; Fairfax, S. C.. 1913. The pastorate was divided in 1910, and he remained at Ehrhardt until 1913, when he removed to Fairfax. where he is located at present. The charge is composed of Fairfax, St. Nicholas' and Early Branch. He organized the church at Saluda, built the parsonage at Leesville, added three new rooms to the pastor's home at Fairfax, built the parsonage at Ehrhardt, enlarged St. Nicholas' Church, and built two new churches and parsonages in Virginia.

HAHN, SAMUEL WAICHTSTILL. --Born May 23, 1895, at Hickory, N. C. Educated at Lenoir College and the Southern Lutheran Theological Seminary. Ordained September 5, 1919, by the Southwestern Virginia Synod. Admitted to the South Carolina Synod November 20, 1922. Pastorates served: Burkes Garden, Tazewell charge, 1919-22. and Grace Lutheran Church,

Prosperity, S. C., from 1922 to this time. He received his A.B. degree from Lenoir College.

HAIGLER, JAMES BOWMAN.—Born in Cameron, S. C., December 3, 1863. Educated at Newberry College and Philadelphia Theological Seminary. Ordained by the Ministerium of Pennsylvania in 1892. Received into the South Carolina Synod in 1905, and again in 1922. Pastorates served: Zion, Spring City, Pa.; Midville Parish, Wentzel's Lake, Nova Scotia; Bethel Pastorate, White Rock, S. C.; Ebenezer, Rincon, Ga.; Roanoke Pastorate, Salem, Va.; Union Pastorate, Salisbury, N. C.; Bethlehem Pastorate, Pomaria, S. C., his present work.

HALLMAN, SAMUEL THOMAS.—Born in Lexington County, South Carolina, September 3, 1844. His classical training was received at Newberry College, 1866-68, and he was graduated from the Southern Lutheran Theological Seminary, together with the late Rev. H. S. Wingard, D.D., in 1868, and was inducted into the office of the holy ministry by the South Carolina Synod October 19, 1868. He has served the following churches: Corinth and Good Hope, Saluda, S. C., 1868-69; Pine Grove and Trinity Churches, Orangeburg County, South Carolina, 1869-75; St. Matthew's and Mt. Lebanon Churches, Orangeburg County, South Carolina, 1875-80; St. James', Cold Water and Mt. Hermon Churches, Concord, N. C., 1880-83; Bethlehem, St. Philip's and St. John's, Pomaria, S. C., 1883-88; Holy Trinity, Augusta, Ga.; 1888-95; Grace and Mt. Tabor, Prosperity, S. C., 1895-1900; and then he supplied St. Philip's, Mt. Olivet and the Church of the Redeemer, Newberry, S. C., for a short while. November 8, 1900, he was elected Piedmont missionary, and organized Immanuel Church, Greenwood, S. C., September 21, 1902, and Woman's Memorial Church, Spartanburg, S. C., September 28, 1902. These he served jointly for a while, and then confined his labors to Spartanburg, S. C., in which city he has labored continually for twenty-four years, being pastor of the Woman's Memorial Church from its organization September, 1902, to this time. He received the degrees of M.A. and D.D. from Newberry College. He served two years as president of the North Carolina Synod; served on the Board of Trustees of North Carolina College; was eight years secretary of the South Carolina Synod, three years its president; was secretary of the Board of Trustees of Newberry College about ten years; has been a member of the College Board over forty years; was twenty years secretary of the United Synod in the South, and was editor of the *Lutheran Visitor* about ten years, 1895-1904. He has been instrumental in building five churches, in remodeling three others, and in improving several preachers' homes. With the exception of about three years, his entire ministry of fifty-six years has been in the South Carolina Synod, and he has been an active participant in our church work in the most important formative period of our Church in the South. He was a contributor to *The Lutheran Visitor* from his early ministry, long before he became its editor; he published a monthly in 1890, called *Gospel Echoes*, which in 1891 became *The Mission News*, and was issued under the direction of the Board of Missions of the United Synod in the South. About March, 1894, this suspended publication, and a department taking its place was carried in *The Lutheran Visitor*. He also edited for several years the Sunday School paper called *The Southern Lutheran* (changed to *Tidings* when purchased by the United Synod Publishing Company in 1904), then published by Col. E. H. Aull, Newberry; and still later he published *The Piedmont Missionary*, which monthly contributed to the building of the Lutheran churches in Spartanburg and Greenwood.

HARMAN, JULIAN BACHMAN.—Born in Lexington County, South Carolina, October 28, 1874. Educated at Newberry College and the Southern Lutheran Theological Seminary. Ordained by the South Carolina Synod November 11, 1906, and received into the synod at that time. He has served the following churches: St. Mark's and Corinth, Saluda County, South Carolina; Mayer Memorial and Summer Memorial, Newberry, S. C.; Mt. Pilgrim and St. Philip's Churches, Senoia, Ga.; Mt. Tabor Pastorate, Newberry County, South Carolina; Bethel Pastorate, White Rock, S. C., and Holy Trinity Pastorate, Little Mountain, S. C. He has served as secretary, vice-president and president of Newberry Conference, and on the Executive Committee of Missions for two years, and served as secretary of the Joint Conference.

HORINE, JOHN WINEBRENNER.—Born May 23, 1869, in Smithsburg, Md. Educated at Muhlenberg College, graduating in 1889, and at the Philadelphia Theological Seminary, graduating in 1892. Ordained by the Ministerium of Pennsylvania, 1892. Received into the South Carolina Synod in 1897, and again in 1914. Pastorates served: Church of the Incarnation, Philadelphia, Pa., 1892-97; St. John's Church, Charleston, S. C., 1897-1907; St. Luke's Church, Philadelphia, Pa., 1907-14; editor of *Lutheran Church Visitor* 1914-19; professor of Old Testament and New Testament Exegesis in the Southern Lutheran Theological Seminary since 1919. The degree of D.D. was conferred upon him by both Newberry and Roanoke Colleges, in 1914. Since 1919 he has been associated with

The Lutheran as special reporter for the Lutheran Church South, and since 1922 has been editor of *The Lutheran Messenger*, the monthly bulletin of the South Carolina Synod.

KINARD, JAMES DAVID.—Born July 1, 1866, near Prosperity, S. C. Educated at Newberry College and the Southern Lutheran Theological Seminary. Ordained October 27, 1895, becoming a member of the synod. Pastorates served: Leesville Pastorate, 1895-1903; St. Matthew's Pastorate, Orangeburg (now Calhoun) County, South Carolina, 1903-10; Newberry Pastorate, 1910-12; Immanuel, Greenwood, S. C., 1912-18; Johnston Pastorate, since 1918. Has served as secretary, and president of the South Carolina Synod; as a member of the Board of Trustees of Newberry College and its secretary over fifteen years, and as a member of the Board of Trustees of the Southern Lutheran Theological Seminary. The degree of D.D. was conferred on him by Newberry College in 1917. His entire ministry has been in this synod (until October, 1924). His record of service is remarkable, having missed not more than six services during twenty-nine years' pastoral service, except when on vacation.

KISTLER, HENRY ALFRED.—Born December 30, 1879, near Lincolnton, N. C. Graduated from Lenoir College in 1902, with degree of A.B., and from the Southern Seminary in 1903. Studied for three months at Chicago Seminary in 1910. Ordained in 1905 by the Tennessee Synod at Stanley, N. C. Pastorates: Watauga, Watauga County, North Carolina, 1905-10; Sullivan County, Tennessee, 1911-20; Bethlehem Pastorate, Pomaria, 1920-22; Zion Pastorate, Lexington County, 1922- . Admitted into the South Carolina Synod, 1920. Vice-president of Holston Synod; member of Board of Directors Southern Seminary, 1919-20; member of Board of Trustees Summerland College since 1922.

KOON, SAMUEL PATRICK.—Born November 8, 1877, at Chapin, S. C. Graduate of Newberry College and Southern Seminary. Ordained in 1902 by the Southwestern Virginia Synod in St. Paul's Church, Wythe County, Virginia. Received into the South Carolina Synod in 1903. Pastorates served: Immanuel Church, Bluefield, W. Va., 1902-03; St. Luke's Church, Prosperity, 1903-12; Silver Street Church, 1913-15, and with the Mayer Memorial Charge, 1915-16; St. Paul's Pastorate, Pomaria, 1916- . President of Summerland College, 1912-13. The degrees of A.B. and M.A. received from Newberry College in 1899 and 1906, respectively. Member of Executive Committee of Synod, 1906-11, and Chairman of same, 1912-13; Secretary of Synod, 1908-10; Vice-president of Synod, 1910-

12. Secretary of Committee on Ministerial Education at present date. Supply pastor at various times at the following churches: Bethlehem (Black Creek), Leesville; Saluda pastorate, Saluda; Mt. Pilgrim Church. Prosperity; Mt. Olivet Church, Prosperity. It was during Rev. Mr. Koon's pastorate that St. Luke's parsonage, Silver Street church and parsonage, and St. Paul's parsonage were built.

KREPS, MULLER O. J.—Born in Lexington County, South Carolina, December 29, 1857. Received his classical and theological training at Newberry College and the Southern Seminary. Ordained by the South Carolina Synod in 1883. Began his ministry of the Word in the county of his birth, being cordially received by the people who had known his father, Rev. Barney Kreps, than whom a better and more devout Christian could not be found. In Lexington County his father spent his ministerial life from 1862-1887; and it was therefore fitting that the son should follow in the father's footsteps. He was then called to the Pine Grove and Trinity pastorate, Lone Star, S. C., where he remained a number of years, and then to St. Paul's, Newport, Va.; then to Luther Memorial, Blacksburg, Va.; then to Holy Trinity, Augusta, Ga.; then to Grace Church, Prosperity, S. C., where he was instrumental in the erection of the elegant and well equipped house of worship, which is highly creditable to that congregation and the projector of it. His next move was to St. Luke's, Columbia, where he remains the spiritual adviser and able counsellor of that congregation. He served two terms as president of this synod, has been a member of the Board of Trustees of Newberry College for a number of years, and is also a member of the Southern Seminary Board. For three years he was the Financial Secretary of our Southern Theological Seminary, during which term he visited nearly every parish within the bounds of the United Synod in the South, soliciting funds for the erection of the present administration building of the Seminary. He received his A.B., M.A. and Doctor's degrees from Newberry College.

LONG, IRVING ERNEST.—Born June 19, 1882, at Prosperity, S. C. Graduate of Newberry College in 1907 and Southern Seminary in 1910. Ordained in St. Andrew's Church, Charleston, by the South Carolina Synod in 1910 and received into the synod at that time. Pastorates served: Pomaria Pastorate, Pomaria, 1910-11; St. Mark's Church. Mooresville. N. C.. 1911-16; Augsburg Church, Winston-Salem, N. C., 1916-20; St. Johannes' Church, Charleston, 1920-   . Treasurer of the Northern Conference of the North Carolina Synod, 1913-20. Member of Board of Trustees of Mt. Pleasant Collegiate Institute, 1914-20.

LONG, John Jacob.— Born November 5, 1871, in Newberry County, South Carolina. Educated at Newberry College and Southern Theological Seminary. Ordained by the South Carolina Synod in 1898, and received into synod the same year. Has served the following pastorates: Bethlehem, Newberry, Bethlehem (second time), Little Mountain, Saluda. He is serving the Saluda Pastorate at the present time. Received the degrees of A.B. and D.D. from Newberry College.

MANGUM, John W.—Born June 26, 1888, at Wicker, Miss. Educated at Newberry College, Normal College of Mississippi and Southern Theological Seminary. Ordained in 1910 by the Mississippi Synod. Received into the South Carolina Synod in 1923. Pastorates served: Scott County Pastorate, Homewood, Miss.; Newhope and St. Mark's Pastorate, Sallis, Miss.; St. Michael's Pastorate, Irmo, 1923- .

McCULLOUGH, Henry Antine.—Born December 18, 1865, in Newberry County, South Carolina. Educated at Newberry College and Southern Seminary. Ordained in 1895 by the South Carolina Synod in St. Michael's Church, Lexington County, and received into the synod the same year. Pastorates served and positions held: Concord, N. C.; Cameron, S. C.; Mt. Pleasant, N. C.; Albemarle, N. C.; St. Paul's, Columbia. For four years principal of Collegiate Institute, Mt. Pleasant, N. C. Received the title of A.B. from Newberry College, B.D. from Chicago Seminary, D.D. from Newberry College. At this time is pastor of St. Paul's Church, Columbia.

MILLER, David Leander.—Born December 30, 1875, at Hickory, N. C. Educated at Lenoir College and Chicago Theological Seminary. Ordained in 1907 by the Tennessee Synod. Received into the South Carolina Synod in 1924. Pastorates served: Stony Man and Forestville in Virginia; Donegal in Pennsylvania; Trinity, Cabarrus, and Iredell in North Carolina. At present pastor of St. Peter's Pastorate, near Chapin.

MONROE, Pleasant Edgar.—Born December 18, 1875, in Salisbury, N. C. Educated at North Carolina College and Chicago Theological Seminary. Ordained in 1901 by the Southwest Virginia Synod. Received into the South Carolina Synod in 1902. Pastorates served and positions held: Pulaski, Va., 1901-02; Ehrhardt, 1902-08; Johnston, 1908-13; President of Summerland College, 1913-24. Received the degrees of A.B. and M.A. from North Carolina College and the title of D.D. from Newberry College. President of the South Carolina Synod, 1914-15, 1915-16.

MORGAN. FRANCIS GROVER.—Born November 19, 1889, at Delmar, near Leesville, S. C. Graduate Lenoir College. A.B.; University of South Carolina, A.M. Graduate the Lutheran Theological Southern Seminary. Ordained by the Tennessee Synod, 1913. Service: Taught Latin and Education. Lenoir College, 1913-1918, 1922-24; Lutheran Camp Pastor, Marine Barracks, Parris Island, S. C., 1918-1921; Pastor. Madison, Virginia, 1921-1922; Director of Extension Work, Lenoir-Rhyne College, 1923; Instructor, University of North Carolina, Summer of 1924; President, Summerland College, Leesville, S. C., since September 1, 1924. Admitted into Synod of South Carolina, 1924.

NELSON. GEORGE W.—Born April 21, 1894, in Brooklyn, N. Y. Educated at Muhlenberg College, Allentown, Pa.; and the Southern Theological Seminary. Ordained in 1921 by the Synod of North Carolina. Received into the South Carolina Synod the same year. Pastor of St. Luke's Church. Summerville, from 1921 to date.

OBENSCHAIN, ARTHUR BITTLE.—Born March 15, 1883, in Vinton, Roanoke County, Virginia. Educated at Roanoke College and Philadelphia Theological Seminary. Ordained in 1910 by the Synod of New York and New England. Received into the South Carolina Synod in 1920. Pastorates served: College Point, New York City, 1910-12; Albany, New York, 1912-20; St. Stephen's Church, Lexington, 1920 to date. Received the degree of A.B. from Roanoke College in 1907; also certificate in Philosophy at Washington and Lee University.

OXNER. JOHN WITHERSPOON.—Born of Lutheran ancestry in Edgefield County, South Carolina. September 23, 1882. Graduate of Leesville College (1903). Newberry College (1905), Southern Lutheran Theological Seminary (1908), with post-graduate work at Chicago Seminary in 1912 and at the University of South Carolina in 1918. Ordained in 1908 by the Synod of Georgia and Adjacent States. Received into the South Carolina Synod in 1910, into the Tennessee Synod in 1920, and again into the South Carolina Synod in 1923. Has served the following pastorates: Mt. Pilgrim, Haralson. Ga.. 1908-10; St. Matthew's Parish, Cameron. 1910-18; Mt. Tabor, New Brookland. 1918 to the present time, also supplying the Sandy Run Pastorate. Since 1921 Rev. Mr. Oxner has been Chaplain of the 118th Infantry, South Carolina National Guard, and since 1922 Chaplain of the Officers' Reserve Corps. He is president of the Lutheran Ministers' Association of Columbia, a member of the Board of Trustees of Summerland College, and secretary of the South Carolina National Guard Association. Among other positions formerly held he was editor of *Our Church Messenger*, 1919-22, president of the Orangeburg Conference, vice-president of two other Conferences and secretary-treasurer of three ministerial associations.

PARKER, Theodore Calvin.—Born November 18, 1866, in Rowan County, North Carolina. Educated at North Carolina College and Gettysburg Theological Seminary. Ordained in 1899 by the Southwestern Virginia Synod. Received into the South Carolina Synod in 1924. Pastorates served: Roanoke County Pastorate, Va.; Floyd Pastorate, Va.; St. John's, Concord, N. C.; St. Luke's, Mt. Ulla, N. C.; Lebanon, Barber, N. C.; St. Michael's, Troutman, N. C.; Pembroke, Pembroke, Va.; New River, Blacksburg, Va.; St. Paul's, Gilbert, at the present date. Degrees received, A.B. and M.A. President of Roanoke Conference of the Virginia Synod, and secretary of the North Carolina Synod for about four years.

PETREA, Henry Smith.— Born November 1, 1888, at Concord, N. C. Educated at Newberry College and Southern Seminary. Ordained in 1915 by the Synod of North Carolina. Received into the South Carolina Synod in 1915. Pastorates served: White Rock, 1915-18; Graniteville-Aiken Mission, 1918-24; Trinity Church, Elloree, his present charge. Statistical Secretary of the synod since 1920.

PETERSEN, Otto Carl.—Born May 10, 1870, in Charleston, S. C. Graduated in 1899 from Newberry College with degree of A.B. and from the Southern Seminary in 1910. Ordained in 1902 by the Synod of Southwestern Virginia in St. Paul's Church, Wythe County, Va. Home Missionary, Holston Synod, 1903-08, serving at Morristown and Sinking Springs, Tenn.; Union Pastorate, Delmar, S. C., 1908-10; Bethlehem Church, Florida, 1910-13. Colporteur of South Carolina Synod (mainly in Charleston), 1920-24.

RISER, Marion Claude.—Born in 1878 near Leesville, S. C. Educated at Newberry College and Southern Seminary. Ordained in 1909 by the Holston Synod. Received into the South Carolina Synod in 1912. Has served the Monroe County Pastorate, Tennessee, and supplied the Birmingham, Ala., Mission, summer of 1911, and Springfield (S. C.) Church, summer of 1915. Received the title of A.B. from Newberry College. At present is engaged in teaching at Brunson, S. C.

ROOF. FRANCIS KEITH.—Born October 17. 1868, in Lexington County, South Carolina. Educated at Newberry College and Southern Seminary. Ordained in 1900 by the Tennessee Synod. Received into the South Carolina Synod in 1924. Pastorates: St. Timothy's Pastorate, N. C., 13 years; Cedar Grove Pastorate, S. C., 8 years; Morganton, N. C., 3½ years; St. David's Pastorate, Lexington County, South Carolina since May 15, 1924. Received from Newberry College the title of A.B. at time of graduation.

ROOF, WALTER JAMES.—Born February 17, 1880, in Lexington County, South Carolina. Educated at Lenoir College and Southern Seminary, with a half year's postgraduate work in the Southern Seminary and University of South Carolina. Ordained in 1910 by the Tennessee Synod. Received into the South Carolina Synod in 1923. Pastorates served: Chapin Pastorate, 1910-15; Mayer Memorial, Newberry, 1915-16; Lenoir (N. C.) Pastorate, 1916-19; Lincolnton (N. C.) Pastorate, 1919-23; St. Barnabas' Church. Charleston, 1923- . Received M.A. degree from Newberry College in 1915. Secretary of North Carolina Conference of Tennessee Synod for four years, and Chairman of Synodical Home Mission Board for four years.

SCHAEFFER, HARRY BRENT.—Born August 30, 1891, at Newberry, S. C. Educated at Newberry College and Southern Seminary. Ordained in 1915 by the Holston Synod. Received into the South Carolina Synod in 1923. Pastor at Chattanooga, Tenn., and Kings Mountain. N. C. Camp Pastor during the World War. Secretary of the Tennessee Synod. 1920. and of the United Synod of North Carolina, 1921-23. North Carolina Chairman World Service Campaign. 1921. Received the degrees of A.B. and M.A. from Newberry College. Present pastor of St. Matthew's Church, Charleston.

SCHERER, MELANCHTHON GIDEON GROSECLOSE.—Born March 16, 1861, in Catawba County, North Carolina. Educated at Roanoke College and Southern Lutheran Seminary. Ordained in 1883 by the Synod of Virginia. Received into the South Carolina Synod in 1899. Pastorates served and positions held: Church of the Redeemer, 1899-1901; Professor in the Theological Seminary at Mt. Pleasant, S. C., 1901-04; St. Andrew's Church, Charleston, 1904-19. Received the degrees of M.A. and D.D. from Roanoke College. For many years a member of the Board of Directors of the Southern Lutheran Theological Seminary. Since 1919 Secretary of The United Lutheran Church in America, with residence in New York City. A member of the Board of Trustees of Newberry College and influential in securing contributions from the General Education Board (the Rockefeller Foundation) through several visits to the headquarters of that Board in New York City.

SCHRODER, HENRY ANDREW.—Born August 7, 1896, in Charleston, S. C. Educated at College of Charleston and Southern Lutheran Seminary. Ordained in 1923 by the South Carolina Synod and received into the synod at that time. Student supply at Danville, Va. Pastor of Grace Church, Rock Hill, 1923-   .

SECKINGER, EDWIN HUGHES.—Born December 31, 1886. at Springfield, Ga. Graduate of Newberry College and Southern Seminary. Ordained in 1922 by the South Carolina Synod and thereupon received into the synod. Pastor of St. Luke's Pastorate, Prosperity, from 1922 to date.

SENTER, JONAS MICHAEL.—Born November 11, 1863, in Gaston County, North Carolina. Educated at Gaston College, Dallas, N. C. (one year), St. Paul's Practical Seminary, Hickory, N. C. Ordained in 1890 by the Joint Synod of Ohio. Received into the South Carolina Synod in 1922. Has served St. Matthew's Pastorate, Masonville, W. Va., 1890-1902; Hardin Pastorate, 1902-12; Holly Grove Pastorate, 1912-18, Iredell Pastorate, 1918-20; Chapin Pastorate, 1920 to the present time. Received the degree of Doctor of Divinity from Newberry College in 1924. He has held the following positions: In Joint Synod of Ohio, Vice-President of Concordia English District; Secretary Board of Directors of St. Paul's Practical Seminary. In Tennessee Synod, Vice-President (two terms). In South Carolina Synod, member of Executive Committee; member of Board of Trustees of Newberry College.

SHEALY, CHARLES JACKSON.—Born September 27, 1889, near Leesville, S. C. Educated at Newberry College and Southern Lutheran Seminary. Ordained in 1915 at Plains. Ga.. by the Synod of Georgia and Adjacent States. Received into the South Carolina Synod in 1916. Has served pastorates as follows: Oglethorpe, Ga., 1915-16; Grace Church, Prosperity, 1916-22; St. Matthew's Pastorate, Calhoun County. 1922 to the present time. Received the degrees of A.B. and M.A. from Newberry College.

SHEALY, JEFFERSON DAVIS.—Born in 1862 near Leesville, S. C. Educated at Newberry College and Southern Seminary. Ordained in 1891 by the South Carolina Synod and thereupon received into the synod. Has served the following pastorates: Union Pastorate; Graniteville Mission; Bethlehem Pastorate, Pomaria; Newberry Pastorate, Mayer Memorial and Summer Memorial (Mission), Newberry; St. Andrew's Church, Concord, N. C. For 24 years pastor of the Union Pastorate, near Leesville. In this period two new houses of worship were built and other church property was improved. While pastor of Summer Memorial, the church was built; also Bethlehem (Black Creek). President of the Joint Conference for two years.

SHEAROUSE. Oswell Benjamin.—Born August 31, 1861, at Springfield, Ga. Graduate of Newberry College and Southern Seminary. Ordained in 1892 by the Synod of Georgia and Adjacent States. Received into the South Carolina Synod in 1892. Pastorates: St. Mark's. Edgefield County (afterward Saluda County), 1892-1902; St. Jacob's. Lexington County, 1902-05; Holy Trinity and Macedonia, Little Mountain, 1905-12; St. Enoch's, Kannapolis. N. C., 1912-17; Lexington Pastorate. Lexington, S. C., 1917 to the present time. While serving the St. Mark's Pastorate, the Joint Council purchased six and a half lots at Saluda Court House for church purposes. The present church building and parsonage stand on a part of this property. In the St. Jacob's Pastorate. a new church was built.

SIGMON. Paul Cromer.—Born May 17, 1896. at Newton. N. C. Educated at Lenoir College and Southern Lutheran Seminary. Ordained in 1921 by the Synod of Georgia and Adjacent States. Received into the South Carolina Synod in 1922. Pastor of the Church of the Reformation. Savannah. Ga., 1921-22. Since February 15, 1923, pastor of the Orangeburg Church. Orangeburg, S. C. Received the degree of M.A. from the University of South Carolina.

SMITH, John Lewis.—Born March 13. 1879, in Rowan County, North Carolina. Educated at Lenoir College and Southern Lutheran Seminary. Ordained in 1911 by the Synod of North Carolina. Received into the South Carolina Synod in 1922. Pastorates: Florence. 1913-17: Harrisonburg. Va., 1917-20; Bristol. Tenn.. 1917-22 (all three pastorates were home mission work); Trinity Church. Greenville. 1922 to the present time. The degree of A.B. was received from Lenoir College in 1908.

SOX. Charles Jason.—Born September 27. 1873, in Lexington County, South Carolina. Educated at Lenoir College and

Southern Seminary. Ordained in 1905 by the Southwestern Virginia Synod. Received into the South Carolina Synod in 1906. Pastorates: Saluda Pastorate; Bethany and St. James' in Lexington County at the present time. The degree of A.B. received from Lenoir College.

SUBER, THOMAS FRANK.—Born March 24, 1890, at Pomaria, S. C. Educated at Newberry College and Southern Seminary. Ordained in 1919 by the South Carolina Synod and received into the synod at that time. Pastor of Silver Street Church, 1919-24; Church of the Incarnation, Shandon, Columbia, 1924- .

WESSINGER, JOHN CALVIN.—Born April 5, 1868, near Chapin, S. C. Educated at Lenoir College and Southern Lutheran Seminary. Ordained in 1893 by the Tennessee Synod. Received into the South Carolina Synod in 1921. Pastorates: Manassas Mission, 1893; Trinity Pastorate, N. C., 1894-1903; Knox County Pastorate, Tenn., 1904; Lower Davidson, N. C., 1905; St. Philip's Pastorate, 1906-09; Cedar Grove Pastorate, 1909-12; St. Jacob's Pastorate, 1912-16. Received the degrees of A.B. and M.A. Pastor of Holy Trinity Church, New Brookland, since 1923.

WINGARD, MULLER BAWI.—Born November 18, 1893, in Effingham County, Georgia, son of the late Rev. Henry S. Wingard, formerly a member of the South Carolina Synod. Educated at Newberry College and Southern Lutheran Seminary. Ordained in 1919 by the Synod of Georgia and Adjacent States. Received into the South Carolina Synod in 1924. Pastorates: Plains Pastorate, Plains, Ga., 1919-23; since January 1. 1924, pastor of the Greenwood-Clinton Mission. Received A.B. from Newberry College, and M.A. from the University of South Carolina. Secretary of the Georgia Synod, 1920-1923.

WISE. WALTER DANIEL.—Born May 12, 1880, in Penola County, Sardis, Mississippi. Educated at Lenoir College and Southern Seminary. Ordained in 1903 by the Tennessee Synod. Received into the South Carolina Synod in 1922. Pastorates: St. James', Newton, N. C.; Claremont. Claremont. N. C.; Maiden, Maiden, N. C.. Cedar Grove Pastorate, near Leesville at the present time. President for two years and secretary for two years of the North Carolina Conference of the Tennessee Synod.

WORTH, JOHN HOWARD.— Born October 22. 1880. at Lancaster, Pa. Educated at Muhlenberg College and Philadelphia Seminary. Ordained in 1905 by the Ministerium of Pennsylvania. Received into the South Carolina Synod in 1919. Pastorates: St. Andrew's Church, Atlantic City, N. J., Mt. Zion's Church. Pittsburgh, Pa., Messiah Church, Brooklyn, N. Y., St. Andrew's Church, Charleston, since 1919. Received the degrees of A.B. and M.A. from Muhlenberg College. Studied at University of Pennsylvania, 1901-02, and at University of Leipzig, 1907-08.

Chapter X

LEADING PERSONALITIES*

DREHER, GODFREY.—Was one of the prime factors in the organization of this synod in 1824, and conducted the opening services. He it was who explained in detail as recorded in the minutes of the first convention of synod in 1824, the "rites and titles which were established by our ancestors in the year 1788, and sanctioned by the government of this state, for the benefit of the Evangelical Lutheran Churches within the limits of its jurisdiction".

This reference is to the Corpus Evangelicum of 1788; and when the six ministers and five laymen present decided to organize the synod Godfrey Dreher was elected the president. At the second convention, held in St. John's Church, Lexington County, November, 1824, he was chosen treasurer, which office he filled successfully for about fourteen years, an evidence of his high integrity and sound business judgment.

He was recognized as a preacher of marked pulpit ability, a church organizer and one of the most influential men in the synod.

BACHMAN, JOHN, D.D., LL.D.—Came to this state from Rhinebeck, N. Y., in January, 1815, under a call from St. John's Church, Charleston, of which he remained the recognized pastor for nearly fifty-seven years, then passed on to glory February 24, 1874.

He was elected as the second president of this synod, November, 1824, and held that office ten consecutive years. Then, expressing in feeling terms his gratitude for the confidence reposed in him, he insisted on being allowed to retire from that office.

He was prominent in the synod for forty-six years, and was the chief mover in the establishment of our Southern Seminary and Newberry College.

When the "General Synod of the Evangelical Lutheran Church of the Confederate States" was organized in 1863, he was elected president and took an active part in all proceedings of that body.

As indicative of the soul of the man, we cite the fact that during an epidemic of yellow fever in Charleston, his congregation could not persuade him to leave the city and he

---

*NOTE.—Among the personalities that have helped largely in making the history of the synod are to be included not a few of the ministers at present on the roll of synod, whose biographical sketches form Chapter IX of this book.

therefore remained and ministered to all classes of people, nor did the scourge ever touch his person.

Being a naturalist of great fame, he said he could go from the sea to the mountains, carry no textbook with him, and give the names and habits of every plant, bird, animal and reptile to which his attention would be called.

He and John James Audubon were the joint authors of "Quadrupeds, Birds and Reptiles of North America", one of the greatest works of its kind ever published in this country.

As he had lived so he died—a true soldier of the cross.

BOINEST, THADDEUS STREET.—During twenty years he was one of the outstanding figures in this synod, and few, if any, of our preachers ever touched life at as many points as he did.

He was brought up in Charleston under the direction of the sainted Dr. John Bachman, and was thoroughly trained in the doctrines and principles of our evangelical faith.

Impressed with the desire and duty of preaching the Gospel, all of his energies moved in that direction. Under the tutelage of Dr. Hazelius and Rev. William Berly he developed traits and abilities which made him the equal of the strongest pulpit men of his day; and the records of the synod show that he was always in demand. In the affairs of Newberry College he was in the front rank; and as secretary, and later as president of the Board of Trustees, he had no superior; in fact, he was a power in the synod. During four years consecutively he was president of the synod—the longest term of any presiding officer up to that time, except Dr. Bachman,—and from the second convention of the General Synod, South, he was a member of all our delegations until his death. As preacher, pastor, companion, adviser and helper in every good work he met every standard of excellence, and justly deserves a place in the gallery of Christian fame.

HAZELIUS, ERNEST LEWIS, D.D.—Came into the life of this synod in 1833, having accepted a professorship in the Theological Seminary of the Evangelical Lutheran Synod of South Carolina and Georgia, filling the vacancy made by the death of Rev. J. G. Schwartz, and continued in that capacity until 1853.

So highly was he esteemed by the King and Queen of Prussia, whence he originally came, that in 1842, on a visit to his Fatherland, they plead with him to return and spend the remaining days with them, offering a lucrative position. However, he chose to remain with our Seminary and train the ministry of our Church in this part of the South. This he did, finishing out a great life work February 20, 1853, at Lexington, where his ashes await the day of resurrection.

His career with us is more fully sketched in the main part of the history of this synod. A history of his life, from 1808 to 1853, will be found in Annals of the American Lutheran Pulpit, published in 1869, by Carter & Brothers, New York.

REV. A. R. RUDE, D.D.

RUDE, ANTON R., D.D.—In some respects, a more remarkable man never lived among us than Rev. Dr. Anton R. Rude. He was born in Denmark, October 25, 1813, educated first in his homeland, then at Andover and Gettysburg, where he studied theology. He was ordained to the office of the ministry in 1842. He located later on a rich farm in the fertile Shenandoah Valley of Virginia, near New Market, where he preached and gave himself to reading. Here, following his bent of mind, he read on every subject and imbibed a vast knowledge of the literature of the world. In the wide range of literature, science and theology he exhibited the most extensive familiarity and never lacked for a ready answer to every question. He told the writer that he read the whole of Shakespeare in English three times before he left Denmark; and he spoke German so fluently that he was frequently taken for a native German.

Strong, evangelical, devoted to God and the Church and full of deep sympathy, he was at once a preacher and writer of acknowledged ability. He was the devoted pastor of Ebenezer Church, Columbia, for many years and was greatly loved by his people.

It was during this period that he kept our Theological Seminary in his home in one of the trying transition periods in its history. Newberry College had been removed to Walhalla; the Seminary was without a home and he cared for the two young men: G. A. Hough and C. P. Boozer, who were students in the Seminary.

Dr. Rude was the first editor of *The Southern Lutheran* (1862-66) and *The Lutheran Visitor* (1868-78). His ability as editor was as marked as was his scholarship in the pulpit.

At the close of his active ministry with us a touching scene was witnessed in St. Matthew's Church, Charleston, in 1882. The synod had just adopted a series of tenderly worded resolutions of regret and sympathy because of his failing health and retirement. With deep feeling he responded, gave to each member a parting hand shake, pasesd out, and they "saw him no more". He went to the home of an only son, living in Texas, and within two weeks he went home to God, May 21, 1883.

HAWKINS, JACOB, D.D.—Born in Newberry County, South Carolina, September 4, 1828, and on July 16, 1895, called to his heavenly reward. He was confirmed at the age of 15 years, entered the Classical and Theological Seminary at Lexington, S. C., in his twenty-first year, and at the completion of a five years' course he was licensed in 1855, and spent forty years in the active ministry of the Lutheran Church. He was a writer possessed of rare gifts; a contributor to magazines and other periodicals: the author of a series of Catechisms, and was editor of *The Lutheran Visitor* nearly twenty years.

He served at different times both as secretary and president of this synod; was for many years on the Board of Trustees of Newberry College, and was an influential member also of the General Synod South. He was always in demand as one of our most popular preachers.

BERLY, WILLIAM.—A native of Newberry County. He was one of the brightest early graduates of our Classical and Theological School located at Lexington, having completed his course in November, 1836. Soon thereafter he became principal of the classical department and also taught in the theological department. He was not only a preacher of splendid ability,

but a highly successful teacher as well, and was employed as
an instructor of youth for thirty years.

When the Theological Seminary was removed to Newberry,
he at once established a female academy in the vicinity of Lexington, of which he remained principal until a short time before his death. He was an active participant in all affairs of
the Church, was a successful organizer, and in all respects one
of the thoroughly efficient and useful men in the synod, passing away in 1873 in his sixty-third year.

REV. J. HAWKINS, D.D.

SLIGH, J. A., D.D.—Born in Newberry County, South Carolina,
December 12. 1835, and died August 6, 1917, in his eighty-sec-
ond year. In his early youth he became a member of Beth
Eden Lutheran Church, and soon developed a strong tendency
towards the ministry. All his studies tended in that direction.
In due time he entered the Classical and Theological School
at Lexington. S. C., spent two years there. and went with that
institution when it removed to Newberry and became a regularly constituted college. In 1858 he was employed as the assistant of Mr. Whittle in the Preparatory Department of the College and in 1863 he was licensed to preach the Gospel. He was

ordained in St. Mark's Church, October 22, 1866. Until a few years before his death he was active in all the work of the ministry and filled positions of honor and trust in almost every department of life. He was continuously the pastor of St. Paul's Church, Newberry County, S. C., from the beginning of his ministry, covering forty-six years, in the meantime serving other congregations in the synod.

As president of this synod; as chairman of the Board of Trustees of Newberry College; and as church builder, he was one of our strongest and most influential preachers of the Gospel. Newberry College never had a better advocate and supporter than he; but his noblest monument was reared in the hearts of the thousands to whom he preached Christ crucified, the hope of the world.

WINGARD, EMANUEL A., D.D.—A native of Lexington County, South Carolina, which county has furnished fifty or more men to the Lutheran ministry. He was born July 29, 1849, and died November 26, 1900, rounding out 52 years of a noble Christian life, twenty-five of which were devoted to the ministry of the Word in the Lutheran Church. He was designated "a born poet", and published a volume of verse before he died.

A devout child of God from his earliest years and possessed of a brilliant intellect, he graduated from Newberry College in his twenty-third year, bearing off the highest honors of his class and then taking the course in the Theological Seminary with the same ease and brilliancy. A fine scholar, a preacher of rare ability, a pastor in the truest sense and a man of the highest ideals, he has left an undying impress on the Church in the South. The original St. Paul's Church, Columbia, S. C., where he spent a half of his ministerial life, will always be remembered as one of the jewels in his crown of pastoral devotion.

HOLLAND, GEO. W., PH.D., D.D.— Came into the life of this synod in 1873 as the pastor of the Bethlehem charge, Pomaria, S. C., which he served with marked success. His ability as a teacher, however, was too well known for him to be long kept out of college work. Accordingly in 1874 he was elected to the Professorship of the Greek and Latin languages and literature in Newberry College and began a brilliant career in that institution, which lasted to the hour of his death, September 30, 1895. In 1877 he was elected vice-president of Newberry College, and in 1878 became its honored president; and throughout his life in the synod and the College he held the high esteem and love of all our people.

His fine personality, his deep piety, persuasive force in the pulpit and in the College, and his noble traits of character, won all hearts to Him. His whole life and bearing placed him at once in the front rank as a leader of men; and he embodied in himself the highest type of the Christian scholar and perfect gentleman. Faithful unto death, his last words were, "God bless Newberry College."

BOOZER, CORNELIUS PRIOLEAU.—Born in Newberry County, South Carolina, in 1846, and died January 25, 1921. When a young man, like many others, he left Newberry College and enlisted in the Confederate Army, losing an arm in battle. In 1866 he resumed his studies in Newberry College, graduating with the class of 1870. Subsequently he studied theology under Rev. A. R. Rude, D.D., while the Southern Seminary was temporarily located in Columbia. He was a faithful, painstaking student, a sermonizer of excellent ability, and was sound and evangelical as a teacher of the Word.

In 1885 he was elected on the Board of Trustees of Newberry College, and served faithfully and efficiently up to very near the close of his life. He was, moreover, the first chairman of the Board of Summerland College. Two years he was the president of this synod, and held other official positions in this body; but perhaps his services as treasurer of the Bachman Endowment Fund, which office he filled from 1892 to near the close of his life, more than anything else illustrated his fine ability, sound business judgment and high integrity. His loyalty and devotion to the interests of Newberry College were marked features of his life; and in the exercise of his splendid gifts he was a power in the affairs of the Church.

HORN, EDWARD TRAILL, D.D., LL.D.—Son of Col. Melchior Hay and Matilda Heller Horn. He was born at Easton, Pa., June 10, 1850, and died March 4, 1915, being in his 65th year.

Dr. Horn graduated from Pennsylvania College, Gettysburg, Pa., in 1869. He studied theology in the Philadelphia Theological Seminary, graduating in 1872. He was ordained by the Ministerium of Pennsylvania and served Christ Church, Chestnut Hill, Philadelphia, as his first parish, 1872-1876. He was then called to historic St. John's Church, Charleston, S. C., which church he served from 1876-1897. During this time he figured actively and prominently in the founding of the United Synod of the South. He was called to Trinity Church, Reading, Pa., in 1897, serving this large and important parish until he followed the call of the Church to the professorship of Ethics and the Theory and Practice of Missions in the Phila-

delphia Theological Seminary in 1911. This chair he filled
with marked success until his death in 1915.

Dr. Horn was a recognized power in the Church, a man of
strong personality and a natural leader. He was twice honored with the title of D.D., and later received the title of LL.D.
Although serving in important and strenuous parishes, he maintained the most studious habits and attained eminence as a
scholar and an authority especially on questions of liturgics.
He was the author of the following books: The Christian Year,

REV. E. T. HORN, D.D., LL.D.

1876; Old Matin and Vesper Services of the Lutheran Church,
1882; The Evangelical Pastor, 1887; Outlines of Liturgics,
1890; Lutheran Sources of the Common Service, 1890; English Translation of Loehe's Catechism, 1893; Commentary on
Philippians, I and II Thessalonians and Philemon, 1896; The
Application of Lutheran Principles to the Church Building,
1905; Summer Sermons, 1908; Translation of Loehe's Three
Books on the Church, 1908, and also a number of contributions to *The Lutheran Church Review*, *The Lutheran Cyclo-
pedia* and various church papers.

SMELTZER, JOSIAH PIERCE, D.D.—Came into the life of this synod in 1862, under the call of the Board of Trustees of Newberry College. The War Between the States was on; Rev. Dr. J. A. Brown had gone back to York. Pa., early in January of that year, and a crisis had come into the life of the College. The Board met in extra session, and on February 5, 1862, extended a call to that quiet but heroic man of God.

He was elected president *pro tem* of the College, and professor of theology in the Theological Seminary. Later he was made president of the College.

At the same time he accepted the pastorate of the Newberry Lutheran Church, which he filled with great satisfaction. Early in May of that year a contagious disease broke out in the town, and the college exercises were suspended about the first of June and were not fully resumed until September, with about fifty pupils, including all departments. President Smeltzer then faced trials which have never confronted any other president of the College; but he faced them unflinchingly, stood firm when Federal soldiers occupied the building, and established a bakery in his home that he might support his family and keep the College going.

Faithfully he discharged the duties of his high office up to the closing of the session of 1876-1877, and then laid down a position which he had held sixteen years, leaving a memory which will live down to the end of time. His name is worthy to be carved in marble and brass, painted in letters of gold, and thus handed down to the generations yet unborn.

BERLY, JOHN EUSEBIUS, M.D.—A son of Dr. Joel A. Berly of Pomaria. S. C., who was a physician held in high esteem by all who knew him. He was a nephew of Rev. William Berly, at one time professor in our Southern Seminary. Coming, as he did, from a family distinguished for intellectual ability and high moral and religious character, he was distinguished by the same traits of nobility and excellence.

Educated in the best academic schools of his section, graduated from Newberry College, trained in our Southern Seminary, and then graduate from the Philadelphia Seminary. perhaps no other young man ever entered the ministry in our Church in the South more thoroughly educated and equipped for his chosen calling than he. He had previously graduated in medicine and practiced for a year and a half, but felt the call of God to preach the Gospel of Christ to men. Accordingly he was ordained in 1886, and in September was installed over Pastorate No. 9, Selwood, S. C., which he served up to July 19, 1890, when he passed to his home in glory. In 1887 he

was elected secretary of this synod, and served efficiently to
the close of his life. His remains rest under the shadow of
the church in which this synod was organized in 1824, and of
which he was the pastor when called to his reward.

An unwritten page in his modest, though brilliant life, deserves to be recorded in this sketch. When in the Charleston
Medical College some prominent members of the old, historic
Congregational church of that city learned to know and love
him. Later on, when he entered the ministry, he was asked
to become its pastor. He declined that remarkable offer, pre-
ferring to remain with his present pastorate.

WILSON. JAMES HERBERT. D.D.—Born at Williamston, South
Carolina, April 16, 1854, and died at Sumter. South Carolina, July 11, 1919. His father and mother died when
he was three years old and he was left to the care
of foster-parents. He entered the Freshman class of Newberry College in 1873, and was graduated in 1877. He completed the course in our Theological Seminary. at Salem, in
1880, and he was ordained by the South Carolina Synod in
November of that year. During his ministry of thirty-nine
years, he served pastorates at Early Branch, Cameron, Ehrhardt, Orangeburg, Salisbury, Savannah, and Sumter.

In 1880 Newberry College conferred upon him the degree
of Master of Arts, and in 1905, the degree of Doctor of Divinity. As financial agent, in 1907-08, he canvassed the Southern
Lutheran Church for our Orphan Home and raised the money
to pay a debt of $17,000. He loved and attracted children,
and by disposition. as well as by bitter experience, he was
inclined to help the orphans. He also did valuable work as
financial agent of Marion College.

For years he was a member of the Board of Trustees of
Newberry College and a member of the Board of Directors
of the Theological Seminary. His loyalty to this synod and
its institutions was absolute and unfaltering. His familiarity
with the history of the synod and with its procedure, together
with his sound judgment and saving common sense, made his
services invaluable. He was a wise leader, an able preacher.
a strong debater. He served several terms as president of
synod, and was often a delegate to the United Synod.

His grasp of the underlying principles of our faith was firm
and sincere. He preached the simple Gospel. At the time of
his passing he was president of the Ministerial Association of
Sumter, and one of the surviving members paid him the fine
and well merited tribute of declaring that he was loved and
admired by the entire community, without regard to creed, and

that his simple faith in Christ had made a profound impression upon the entire community.

MULLER, HENRY.—The name of Henry Muller is first found in the proceedings of this synod in 1827, representing the following congregations under the care of Rev. Godfrey Dreher: Zion's, St. Peter's, St. Michael's, Bethlehem, Nazareth, and Sandy Run. From that date on his name frequently occurs on committees, the Board of Trustees of the Classical and Theological Institute, founded later on at Lexington, S. C., and when that school was located there in 1832 he was one of the prime factors in its establishment, he and Rev. Godfrey Dreher being on a special committee to make estimates of the properties offered by Sandy Run (where Mr. Muller resided) and Lexington village. Mr. Muller himself gave $4,000 for the establishment of that institution. It was the largest individual gift to the cause of Lutheran education which had been made in South Carolina until that time. Subsequently Rev. Godfrey Dreher and Mr. Henry Muller were appointed a committee to solicit donations and subscriptions for our Theological Seminary.

It will, then, be readily seen that the subject of this sketch was a real benefactor, and worthy of being held in grateful memory.

SUMMER, HENRY.—Was born in Lexington District (now Newberry County) on April 11, 1809. He was the son of John Summer and wife (Mary Margaret Houseal Summer), his father being the only son of Capt. Nicholas Summer, who was killed at Granby during the Revolutionary War. He was thus the grandson of the pioneer John Adam Summer (the father of Nicholas Summer), who came from Odenwald, Germany, in 1741, and after landing at Philadelphia proceeded to South Carolina and became one of the first settlers in the Dutch Fork of Broad and Saluda Rivers. A large body of immigrants accompanied him, having crossed the Broad River at Cohoes Falls (now the site of the Parr Shoals Power Company).

Henry Summer was graduated from South Carolina College (now the University) in 1831, with the A.B. degree, and began immediately the study of law in the office of his brother, Nicholas Summer, at Newberry. He located in Talladega, Ala., to practice his profession, but his brother Nicholas dying in the Seminole War, he returned to Newberry within about a year and assumed his brother's law practice, and thus made his home in that town for the remainder of his life, becoming eminent in his profession and a most useful citizen. He was quiet in disposition and studious in habit, with a deep and abiding passion for the best books. He possessed the largest and most select law library of the time, it being his custom to purchase new and rare books on trips to New York and Boston at least every two years. His library embraced also many valuable volumes of history, philosophy, and even theology. He was an earnest student of theology, having been occupied at the time of his death (in 1869) in writing a book on "Relation of History and Religion", several essays on this and similar subjects from his able pen having been published in *Star of the West*, a Cincinnati paper.

The state never had a more public-spirited citizen. As a member of the General Assembly and later registrar in bankruptcy for the district in which he resided (having been appointed after the Confederate War to this office by the Federal Government) he performed conspicuous service and at the same time was instrumental in the upbuilding of his own town. He was not only a patron of learning himself but he exerted his splendid influence among young men to persuade them to secure a liberal education. With this end in view, and to advance the cause of the Lutheran Church, to whose faith he was earnestly devoted, he was deeply interested in the movement to establish a college at Newberry. He was a member of the committee which formulated the charter for Newberry College and was ever after a staunch supporter of the institution. He held the office of secretary of the Board of Trustees of the College from its organization, January 13, 1857, until his death in 1869. His term in this office embraced the most trying period in the history of the College, yet he never wavered in unselfish and loyal service, and even when many of the supporters of the institution were losing hope, his official reports to the synod, while relating in the most candid manner the difficulties of the situation, voiced a clear and optimistic note.

An incident showing his devotion to the interest of the College is the following. On one occasion while in Charleston on his way to Florida to inspect his large planting interests, he met Rev. John Bachman, president of the Board of Trustees, who informed him that he was planning to call a important meeting of the Board and expressed regret that Mr. Summer would be absent from the meeting. Mr. Summer at once canceled his visit to Florida at that time and returned to Newberry for the meeting.

A thrilling incident during the closing days of the Confederate War transpired to shorten his life. His health had become greatly impaired by the exigencies of the period of 1861-65, and he sought rest and recuperation at his plantation at

Cross Roads. While in this enfeebled condition a portion of the Federal army under General Sherman overran his farm, and his home was burned by the soldiers because of his inability to comply with their demands for money, which they charged he had concealed on his premises. He was carried to the barn by the soldiers, who placed a rope around his neck and threatened to hang him if he did not reveal the hiding place. Mr. Summer calmly explained that he had no money and begged permission to offer a prayer. Kneeling in the barn he fervently offered a petition to God, at the same time asking forgiveness for the soldiers, his tormentors. The firm Christian attitude of Mr. Summer confused the soldiers, who, alarmed at this unusual proceeding, and hesitating, a superior officer came upon the scene and ordered the captive set free. His health, impaired by this hardship, continued to decline and he passed away in his sixtieth year, January 3, 1869, mourned throughout the state. His grave is very near the place of his birth in the family burying ground near the old Pomaria Nurseries.

HOUSEAL, WILLIAM WALTER.—Born in Newberry County, South Carolina, August 15, 1818. His father, John Houseal, was descended from Capt. William Frederick Houseal of Revolutionary fame, who was one of the original German settlers of the Dutch Fork. He died when William Walter was six years old, thus leaving him the last male member of his line. When seventeen years of age he was confirmed in the old historic church, St. John's, Broad River, and in the truest sense he lived up to the sacred vows then taken. When called home, November 1, 1889, his death was lamented by thousands of faithful friends.

He was educated at the Classical Institute, Lexington, S. C., finishing his course about 1840, after which he taught school several years, and also engaged in farming. Removing from Pomaria, S. C., he located in the northwestern section of Newberry County, and was one of the founders of Beth Eden Church. In January, 1853, he located at Newberry and was one of the charter members of "Luther Chapel", now the Church of the Redeemer, and aided liberally in building that house of worship. When that congregation was organized in 1853, he was elected on the church council, and served continuously until his death. His labors, however, were not confined to the local church, but were widely distributed. He was treasurer of this synod 1862-1865, and served as delegate to both the district and the General Synod a number of terms. He was also a member of the Board of Trustees of Newberry College and the

Theological Seminary. He aided materially in the erection of the first college building, and also in its relocation in Newberry, when the institution came back from Walhalla in 1877.

He was honored by the people of the county first by being elected sheriff in 1855, and again in 1863. He was then elected county assessor, 1866-1868, and served nearly three terms as county auditor, his death occuring when completing his third term in this office. He was one of the most highly esteemed merchants of Newberry, from 1853-1884. In all the relations of his useful life he maintained a high sense of honor and of Christian manhood. True to his fellowmen, his Church and his God, he was deserving of the honors conferred upon him.

JACOB S. SCHIRMER

SCHIRMER, Jacob F.—The name of this devout and faithful servant of God appears first in the records of this synod at the convention of 1830; and from that time to the date of his death, October 12, 1880, his life was closely linked with our synod as delegate to or officer of this body. In 1852 he was elected president of the Synodical Missionary Society, which position he held continuously up to 1870; and in the meantime he was also elected the treasurer of the Seminary Fund; and, while

a great majority of institutions lost all their funds during the
existence of the Southern Confederacy, such was his business
tact, judgment and care that he preserved almost intact our
Seminary Fund. This office he held 1857-1879. His interest
in the synod was shown by the fact that he was perhaps the
only man at that time who had preserved a complete file of
the minutes of the synod; and this enabled him, at the request
of this body, to collect and publish a sketch of the Lutheran
congregations of South Carolina; which sketch was approved
by the Synod, October, 1873.

His blameless life, his devotion to God and all the interests
of the Church he loved so well, and his more than forty years
of faithful service in this synod, bespeak for him the undying
gratitude of our whole Church in the South.

MAJOR P. E. WISE

WISE, Patrick E.—Born in Newberry County, S. C., October
6, 1830, and on May 18, 1895, passed from a life of great usefulness to the rest and glory of heaven. In his fifteenth year
he was confirmed at St. Mark's Lutheran Church; when only
eighteen he was elected to office and throughout life he adorned
"the doctrine of God our Savior in all things". He was prom-

inent in the councils of the Church, an active participant in the
work of the synod, and in the truest sense the abiding friend
of the pastor.

For thirty years he was the honored treasurer of this synod,
and not a single discrepancy was ever found in his accounts.
Nor did Newberry College ever have a truer friend, nor a more
faithful member of her Board of Trustees. He stood by the old
college when its life was seriously threatened and rejoiced in
its every success. In the words of Doctor Geo. B. Cromer:
"In business he was just and honest; in his intercourse with
others gentle, courteous and unassuming; in his official capacity punctual, regular, and faithful. His devotion to the Church
was strong and unwavering, and he bore in his life the peace-
able fruits of righteousness."

O. B. MAYER, M.D.

MAYER, ORLANDO BENEDICT, SR., M.D., A.M.—This distinguished
scholar and man of God was a graduate of the old South Carolina College in its palmiest days. Later on he finished his medical education at Paris. He was recognized throughout his pro-
fessional career as one of the finest physicians and surgeons

in the South, and he was in the truest sense "The friend of man". No sufferer ever appealed to him in vain; nor did he ever forget his allegiance to God and the Church. When he passed away, July 16, 1891, in his seventy-fourth year, this synod felt that it had lost one of the most distinguished laymen in the southern Lutheran Church. Not only was he a classical scholar of rare attainments, but also a talented musician, being an authority on vocal music, and himself a composer of no small ability.

For many years his life was linked with that of Newberry College. He served on its Board of Trustees, and for a series of years he was Professor of Chemistry, Geology, Botany, and Lecturer on Physiology and Hygiene. He was an outstanding figure in this synod, and the fruit of his labors endures.

BACHMAN, WILLIAM KUNHARDT.—The subject of this sketch was a son of Rev. John Bachman, D.D., LL.D. He was born November 23, 1830, in Charleston, S. C., and died October 29, 1901, in Columbia, S. C., in which city he practiced law from 1856 throughout the remainder of his life. He was educated at the College of Charleston, and after three years' study at the University of Goettingen, Germany, entered fully upon his legal career.

He was Assistant Attorney General of this state eleven years, 1877-1888, having thus given the commonwealth the benefit of his wise counsel in the restoration of the state from the misrule of reconstruction times in the initial period of Governor Wade Hampton's administration. He was no less distinguished during the War Between the States. He trained an infantry company in military tactics, and this unit became famous under his command, as Captain, as part of the renowned "Hampton Legion"; and as "Bachman's Battery" his command did valiant service throughout the war.

When he located in Columbia, S. C., he identified himself with Ebenezer Church, and served forty years on the Church Council, 1861-1901.

In the establishment of our College in Newberry, S. C., he was an efficient helper and rendered invaluable service as one of its Board of Trustees. He was at one time president of the Foreign Missionary Society of the synod, and served in a similar capacity for the Relief of Disabled Ministers.

High-toned, fair, honorable, and just as a legal counsellor, and true to the principles of right, he was never found wanting. When a tribute to his memory was written, after his death, the writer closed with these words: "His life was one of devotion to his family, his state, his people, and, above all else, to God and his Church. Generous, brave, loyal to his friends, many that he leaves behind will sincerely mourn his death."

CHISOLM, ROBERT GEORGE.—Few men have contributed to the good of their neighbors in loving service and in the true spirit of Christian fellowship, proportionately as much and as generously as did Robert George Chisolm. He was born in Charleston, S. C., on November 30, 1831, and died in that city on December 22, 1907. His father, Robert Trail Chisolm, was one of Charleston's prominent citizens, and with a brother was the owner of the widely-known Chisolm's Rice Mill, which in its day was one of the most prosperous institutions of its kind in South Carolina. The mill was a solid brick structure and still stands with its top story razed, as a monument of departed prosperity.

In later years he became interested in the profitable and extensive business of mining and manufacturing phosphate rock, and at the time of his death he held an important, and responsible position in the Charleston Mining and Manufacturing Company.

At times Mr. Chisolm was also engaged in other enterprises connected with or growing out of his chief undertakings. Thus he was ever diligent in the prosecution of some useful avocation, and yet he always found ample opportunity for gratuitous and useful service in the great fields of charity, of benevolence and of religion.

On April 23, 1859, he was united in marriage to Miss Mary Gregg of Mars Bluff, S. C., by whom he had two sons and two daughters who survived him. His elder daughter became the wife of Rev. Dr. Edward T. Horn, of blessed memory. In his later life, upon the death of Mrs. Chisolm, he was united in marriage to Miss Maria L. Horlbeck of Charleston, S. C.

In his young manhood he became deeply interested in the Sunday School of St. John's Lutheran Church of Charleston, and was later chosen as its superintendent, which important position he continued to fill with marked success to the end of his life, nearly a half century of service!

He was also elected to the responsible office of president of the corporation of St. John's Church, and of its vestry and church council, which offices he held to the day of his death, nearly a score of years.

He was frequently sent in his earlier life as a delegate to the Synod of the Evangelical Lutheran Church in South Carolina and Adjacent States, and his practical business capacity made him a useful member of that body.

He was a life-member of the Charleston Bible Society, which, it may be remarked, is even older in point of years than the American Bible Society, and he served most acceptably as its president one or more terms.

Always mindful of the poor and needy he was from its foundation an active member of the Associated Charities Society of Charleston, S. C. He was elected as president of this useful organization and served as such for several successive terms.

As a thank-offering the congregation of St. John's on one of its anniversaries resolved to build St. Barnabas' Church on America Street in Charleston. The necessary funds were provided almost wholly but not altogether by the people of St. John's. One member deeded the lot of land on which the building was erected, Mr. Chisolm contributed more than half the lumber needed, (the structure was entirely of wood) and the late John H. Steinmeyer of Charleston contributed the balance of the lumber. There were of course also contributions of cash. Mr. Chisolm took a very deep interest in the project, and its successful completion caused him to rejoice with a thankful heart.

As a citizen he always took a keen interest in civic affairs. His ballot was cast only after careful investigation of the men and the methods proposed. Without any seeking on his part he was elected an alderman of the City of Charleston and as such rendered useful service during the noteworthy administration of Mayor Courtenay.

Thus the useful life of this exemplary citizen was spent in unending service. To him service was not only a bounden duty but a continuing source of unmixed happiness. He fully experienced the truth that in promoting the happiness of his neighbor he was enhancing his own.

The liberality of Mr. Chisolm was proverbial. He regularly set aside a specific fraction of his income for charity and benevolence, and he was thus always in funds to respond when the call came. The fund so set apart was a sacred appropriation for the Lord's treasury and could not be otherwise used.

BOOZER, DAVID LUTHER.—Youngest son of Mr. David Boozer and Mrs. Katherine Rawl Boozer. Born on his father's farm near Lexington, S. C., September 11, 1833. When he came to years of maturity he chose dentistry as a profession, locating in Columbia, S. C. He was deeply interested in the Theological Seminary, then located at Lexington, and was always a great friend of the students. Soon after locating in Columbia the War Between the States began and he volunteered for service, remaining in the war to the close. After the war he moved his membership to Ebenezer Church, Columbia, where for many years he was active in both the local and the general church work, often being a delegate to synod.

When in the minds of some of the members it was considered wise to begin another church in Columbia, which culminated in organizing St. Paul's, Dr. Boozer became a charter member of this church, which was organized in his home, 1320 Blanding Street. He was elected an elder of St. Paul's and faithfully served in that capacity till his death, June 26, 1902.

Dr. Boozer's interest in the Lutheran Church was broader than the boundary lines of the local church. He kept well posted as to her work and needs, and actively linked his life with the welfare of the whole Church. Moreover, although loyal to the Church of his fathers, he was not unmindful of the worth and work of other denominations, among whom he had many faithful friends.

The Theological Seminary was ever near and dear to his soul, nor did he fail to use his means and influence in its behalf. Largely through his solicitation two of his nephews, who enjoyed the means to do so, became liberal helpers in the building up of this important institution. Devoted to his family, his Church and his God, his influence abides.

EPTING, JACOB.—Eldest child of Adam and Eve (Koon) Epting. Born in Newberry County, South Carolina, October 18, 1823. He was brought up on the farm. At the age of twenty-three he was married, January 28, 1847, to Elizabeth Vina Kinard, daughter of William and Christena (Werts) Kinard, and granddaughter of Capt. John Werts, an officer in the American Army during the Revolutionary War, and his wife Anna Catherine (Hair). To this union ten children were born.

After a few years spent on a farm near his parental home, Jacob Epting located near St. Paul's Church, Newberry County, and became actively identified with that congregation, which activity he maintained throughout the remainder of his life. For about fifty years he served as an elder and also as superintendent of the Sunday School. Endowed with talents for vocal music above the average in his day, especially where opportunity for training in music was lacking, he acquired by persistent study and application a fair knowledge of the elementary principles of music and led the singing (without organ) in the Sunday School and church services, at prayer meetings and conferences and other religious assemblages. He was foremost in conducting prayer meetings in the church and in the homes of aged and sick members. In the absence of his pastor he frequently conducted lay service. Often he was called, day and night, to the homes of the sick and dying to pray with them and point them to the Savior. He was a man of positive conviction, fearless and unyielding when principle was involved, of deep piety, strong faith, and mighty in prayer.

For more than thirty years he served as treasurer of the Newberry Conference and seldom missed a meeting. When his life-work had ended the Newberry Conference adopted the following tribute: "Major Jacob Epting, who departed this life April 15, 1893, was from early manhood a consistent and zealous member of St. Paul's Evangelical Lutheran Church, Newberry County, S. C., and for forty years was the honored superintendent of its Sunday School. From the organization of the Newberry Conference—excepting the interval of two years, owing to change of boundary lines of the Conference by the South Carolina Synod, when he was in another Conference—he was its faithful and efficient treasurer. In the domestic circle, in recognized leadership in the Church, in civil and official position, it may truthfully be said of him, 'he was found worthy'."

The sphere wherein he exerted the greatest influence and made the most lasting religious impressions was, perhaps, the Sunday School. He was a lover of children and young people, and they loved him. He realized that in them was the hope of the Church and the State in the years to come. He unfailingly held up before them the high Christian ideals of life and strongly urged upon young men the claims of the Church and the ministry of the Gospel. Knowing of the need for recruits to the ranks of the ministry he was an ardent advocate of beneficiary education and encouraged and supported in every way any movement to help promising and worthy and needy young men during their college and theological seminary training. Due in no small measure to his influence as superintendent of the Sunday School the following young men entered the Gospel ministry in the Lutheran Church: J. E. Berley, M. M. Kinard, S. T. Riser, Monroe J. Epting (son), H. F. Counts, J. D. Kinard, Geo. A. Riser, Thaddeus B. Epting (grandson), R. E. Livingston, E. H. Kohn, and G. A. Hough.

Major Epting's war record is not without interest. Soon after the beginning of the War Between the States he volunteered and reported for duty at Lightwood Knot Springs, near Columbia, S. C. Having risen to the position of Major of militia in his district and being an efficient tactician and drillmaster, he was detailed by the Governor for home military duty under special orders to train men for service. Subsequently he resigned as Major and reported for duty at the front as a private, but was ordered by the Governor to return to his home for designated service until further orders. In May,

1861. he reported to the military authorities for duty. was assigned to Company H. Thirteenth South Carolina Infantry, and served until the end of the war. While serving his state and the cause of the Confederacy during the conflict of war as occasion permitted he conducted prayer meetings for his comrades and knelt in prayer by the side of the sick, the wounded and the dying.

Returning from the war he faced ruin, poverty and oppression. He took up the broken thread of life with unfaltering courage and gave his service toward the restoration of his state and community and the welfare of his Church, leading a life of unobtrusive simplicity and untiring industry until failing health bade him cease from labor. After long and painful, but submissive suffering he fell on sleep at the home of his daughter in the town of Prosperity. S. C., and was gathered to his fathers. passing from the Church militant to the Church triumphant April 15. 1893, and thus entering into the rest that remaineth to the people of God.

CAPT. J. C. SEEGERS

SEEGERS. JOHN C., CAPT.—For many years one of the most successful, progressive and highly esteemed men of Columbia,

S. C. Thoroughly frank, honest, just and fair in his dealings
with men he naturally became prominent in business affairs
and occupied important positions in the city of his adoption.
But the brightest jewel in his crown was that of his devotion to the Church of God and the splendid service which he
rendered to his fellowmen.

For half a century or more he was identified with Ebenezer
Church, the friend of every pastor, and liberal in all the enterprises of the Church, local and general. In our synodical sessions he stood in the front rank of an aggressive and yet conservative leadership; fearless and honest in the expression of
his views on all important issues he was recognized as a safe
counsellor.

No mistake was made when he was elected on the Board of
Trustees of Newberry College in 1886, for he proved faithful
and efficient to the end of his goodly life, which closed in 1912,
he having served on the College Board twenty-six years.

A life of noble deeds has ended, but that life is enshrined in
imperishable memory.

HALTIWANGER, ABNER DANIEL.—A son of Rev. George Haltiwanger, Jr., and wife, Elizabeth Dreher. He was born March
29, 1841, and was confirmed in the historic Salzburger Church,
Effingham County, Ga., of which his father was pastor. He
was called home May 31, 1916, when nearing the close of his
75th year.

In the year when he was to have graduated from Springfield College, Ga., and when he intended to enter upon the
study of theology, his country was called into war, and he became a soldier in the Confederate army. Twice he was left
for dead on the field of battle; but his life was spared for
service to the Church, in which he spent all the remaining years
of his life. He served as Sunday School superintendent and
as elder for many years. He often represented the local church
as delegate to synod, and was largely instrumental in the organization of St. Paul's Church, Columbia, in whose interests he
at one time mortgaged his home, willing to risk all for the
Church of God.

It is not surprising, then, that he occupies a place in this
synodical history, as he does in the grateful memory and af-
fectionate esteem of those left behind him.

RAST, GEORGE D., CAPT.—Born, reared and spent his long and useful life in Orangeburg County, S. C. He was descended
from loyal Lutheran stock whose name goes far back into
the early Nineteenth century. His paternal ancestor was Cap-

tain George Rast, of Santee, S. C., whose name appears as a delegate from that section in the minutes of this synod, November 18, 1824; again from St. Matthew's Church, Orangeburg County, November 25, 1825.

The subject of the present sketch therefore has a background of which any one might be proud. He was unsurpassed in his faithfulness to the Church, to Newberry College, and to all the interests of our Lutheran Zion. For many years he served as a delegate to the synod, and in 1884 was elected on the Board of Trustees of Newberry College, which office he held for seventeen years, 1884-1901. Several of his sons and nephews were educated in Newberry College; and he remained throughout life a warm friend and supporter of that institution.

He had been an elder in his home church for many years, and has left for his posterity the priceless legacy of a well-spent life.

FICKEN, JOHN F., ESQ.—The subject of this sketch was born in Charleston, S. C., June 16, 1843. His earlier education was received in private schools in that city and he was later graduated from the College of the City of Charleston with the degree of B.A., and subsequently his alma mater conferred upon him the degree of Master of Arts.

During the War Between the States he served in the Confederate army, and at the close of this civil strife he went abroad and matriculated as a student at the University of Berlin. Returning to America he entered the legal profession and for upwards of forty-five years he enjoyed a large and lucrative practice in the courts of South Carolina. At the end of this period he partially retired and assumed the presidency of the South Carolina Loan and Trust Company.

Colonel Ficken has always held and exemplified the finest ideals of Christian citizenship and has given of his splendid talent to civic affairs and to the service of his state and of his political party.

In 1877 he was elected a member of the legislature of South Carolina in which office he served with distinction for ten successive years.

In 1891 he was elected mayor of Charleston, S. C., and gave the city his time and strength for the full term of four years— an administration which is still remembered for its reform measures and for the unquestioned integrity of the city officials.

During a period of ten years Colonel Ficken served as president of the Charleston Library Society within which period the present splendid library building on King Street was erected. He has also served for a number of years as president of the Carolina Art Association, and in the South Carolina militia as Judge Advocate General with the rank of Lieutenant Colonel on the staff of the Major General of the division.

For many years he has served as president of the Board of Trustees of the College of Charleston and has also served as a trustee of Newberry College and of the Southern Lutheran Theological Seminary.

For more than a score of years he has been president of the Corporation and of the Church Council of St. John's Lutheran Church of Charleston, S. C., in which office he has consistently fostered the fine traditions of this historic congregation and where his judgment is eagerly sought by his fellow officers.

Colonel Ficken has frequently served as a delegate to the meetings of the Synod of South Carolina and was honored by an election as delegate to the Washington Convention of the United Lutheran Church. He also served as a member of a Joint Committee on Constitution for the United Lutheran Church which met in Harrisburg, Pa., in which gathering his wise counsel was gratefully received and freely acknowledged, and he is now a member of the Board of Ministerial Relief of the United Lutheran Church.

Colonel Ficken's life has been a busy, useful and successful one not only in his chosen profession and in the department of civic affairs and large business interests but preeminently so in the service of the Church, and in this respect he is eminently worthy of the recognition which synod hereby accords him in giving him place in its official history.

JENNY, J. W., CAPT.—Born February 24, 1842, in Barnwell County, South Carolina. He was baptized in St. Nicholas' Church in March, 1842, confirmed in July, 1869, and has spent his life from that time to this as a faithful member of that congregation. On March 17, 1879, he was installed elder, and this office he still holds. In 1892 he was elected on the Board of Trustees of Newberry College, and has faithfully served in that capacity to this time—32 years—and has given time, money and service to the College, so dear to his heart.

CAPPELMANN, JOHN D., ESQ.— Born on July 21, 1857, near Walhalla, S. C. He was a son of Eimer and Dorothea Cappelmann, who were pioneer settlers in Oconee County in 1850, then a part of the old Pickens District. The first school he attended was conducted in the town of Walhalla as a Lutheran Parish School. From his infancy he was taught the use of the German language. His course at Newberry College was interrupted by sickness. He moved to Charleston in 1879, where he has been active in church work. He is now a member of St. Barnabas' Church, which he helped to organize, and superintendent of its Sunday School. He has been a member of the Board of Trustees of Newberry College for years, from which he received the degree of Master of Arts. He was an active member of the Board of Directors of the Lutheran Theological Seminary located at Mt. Pleasant, Charleston. He was a delegate to the convention which organized the United Synod of the Lutheran Church in the South at Roanoke, Virginia, where he served on a special committee with the late Dr. Socrates Henkel of the old Tennessee Synod. Mr. Cappelmann is fond of quoting Dr. Henkel's remark as the report of this committee was agreed upon; in speaking of his co-committeemen, he exclaimed: "You are better Lutherans than I thought you were."

The United Lutheran Church has signally honored the subject of this sketch by appointment to important work of the Church. At present he is serving as a member of the Board of Deaconess Work and also as a member of the Executive Committee of the Brotherhood, for both of which causes he is frequently called upon to speak at conventions and synods.

Mr. Cappelmann has always been a devoted and loyal son of the Church, and has on all occasions rendered every possible service in her upbuilding. As treasurer of the Board of Home Missions and Church Extension of the United Synod, he was a faithful and painstaking officer, affable, courteous, and a real friend of the missionaries on the field. Those who happened to be home missionaries could never forget his cheering and helpful letters.

KOHN, ARTHUR HAYNE.—Born at the old homestead, near St. Paul's Church in Newberry County, September 1, 1858. While a small boy he was confirmed in this church. His father was killed in the War Between the States and he was denied the privilege of a college education. Before coming to Prosperity to engage in the mercantile business he taught school several terms. He married Mary Birge and they have had five children. Mr. Kohn was an active citizen of this town until he moved to Columbia. He served Grace Sunday School as superintendent for twenty years. In 1895, on the death of Major P. E. Wise, he was appointed treasurer of synod, which position he held until his health forced him to resign after twenty-two years of faithful and efficient service. Mr. Kohn moved to Columbia in 1910 as secretary and treasurer of the Carolina Life Insurance Company, which position he still holds. Here he has identified himself closely with St. Paul's Church and its many activities, acting first as superintendent and at present as teacher of a flourishing Men's Bible Class. He was a member of the Merger Convention of the United Lutheran Church in America in 1918 and has ever since been a member of the Publication Board. For thirty-seven years he was a member of the Executive Committee, and he also serves on the Newberry College Board and the Theological Seminary Board of Trustees. He is the only living South Carolina Synod representative present at the Diet at Salisbury in 1884, out of which grew the United Lutheran Synod in the South, which convention, with two exceptions, he attended until the merger. Mr. Kohn's American ancestor was Capt. William Frederick Houseal, one among the first German settlers of Dutch Fork.

EFIRD, C. M., Esq.—A grandson of Rev. Godfrey Dreher, who was the first president of this synod and whose name appears again and again in its organization and in the development of its early history. Coming as he does from a noble ancestry and possessed of a fine intellect, he has been a prominent figure in the Church from early life. He was born December 18, 1856, in Lexington County, South Carolina, and graduated from Newberry College with the A.B. degree in 1877. The Master's degree was conferred upon him by the same institution.

After he was admitted to the Bar he was soon associated with some of the ablest lawyers of his native county and state. He was very soon recognized as one of the rising jurists of the state and was elected a member of the Senate, in which capacity he proved himself to be one of the strong and useful men in that body. He also serves as one of the special Judges, and is characterized by ability, fairness and a strong judicial insight.

But it is his character as a churchman which is here of special interest. In his district synod and in the general body, his advice and counsel have been invaluable. Always willing to advise on all legal questions in synodical sessions, or elsewhere, he has been a most efficient helper.

Naturally he has served on our important boards of direction, has been constantly elected delegate to the meetings of both district and general synods. He was a member of the Ways and Means Committee to organize the United Lutheran Church in America, and since its organization has served continuously as a member of the Executive Board. He was for many years the treasurer of the Theological Seminary Fund, resigning only because of increasing work and cares. Faithful in all the relations of life, devoted to God and the Church, he is in all respects a man whom good men delight to honor.

HOUSEAL, WILLIAM PRESTON.—Born in Newberry, S. C., July 30, 1856. He received his educational training in the schools of his native town, including the Preparatory Department of Newberry College (1866-68), embracing a period altogether of less than five years. With this foundation he entered, as an apprentice, the printing business in 1873. In due time he became one of the founders of *The Newberry News* in 1878.

Such was his progress that in April, 1881, he took charge of *The Lutheran Visitor* as printer and publisher. He became its owner from 1882 to 1888; and then a stockholder for six years, under a somewhat changed management; and then again its owner until it was sold to and remodeled by "The Lutheran Visitor Company," Columbia, S. C., in 1904. He was connected with the paper, editorially, from 1881 to 1904, and then was the associate editor until April 21, 1920, when that paper was consolidated with *The Lutheran;* thus rounding out a period of 39 years of continuous service with the paper.

He was also one of the founders of *The Newberry Observer* in 1883, its editor 1898-1901, and was one of the owners of *The Newberry Herald and News*, 1887 to 1894.

In these years and under the influence of that training and experience, he acquired an education of no mean proportions. Recognizing this fact Newberry College conferred on him the deserved degree of Master of Arts in 1910.

His church life has not been less distinguished. He was a faithful and efficient member of the Lutheran Church of the Redeemer, Newberry, S. C., from 1870 until moving to Columbia, in 1907, when he transferred his membership to St. Paul's Church, Columbia. While living in Newberry he was a teacher in the Sunday School; and was assistant superintendent later on. He also served as superintendent of St. Paul's Sunday School for several terms. These activities covered 50 years as pupil, teacher, officer, Sunday School worker, and church worker. He was chairman of the first convention, held in Columbia, 1908, of the Laymen's Interdenominational Missionary Movement, and served on important committees of the convention of 1916. He was also secretary of the first Lutheran Laymen's Convention of the South held in Columbia in December, 1907.

As a fitting conclusion to this sketch it will be of real historic interest to make mention of the ancestral line from which he comes. One of his ancestors, Dr. Bernard Houseal, was professor in the Theological Seminary at Heilbronn. Germany, in 1727: and the family has been Lutheran since the Reformation of 1517. His American ancestor was Capt. Wm. Frederick Houseal, brother of Rev. Bernard Michael Houseal, pastor of Trinity Church, Reading, Pa. The literary cast of W. P. Houseal's mind is traceable to that worthy ancestry. This finds expression in newspaper work, in which he is still engaged, being connected with *The State*, Columbia, S. C.

He was the first publisher in Newberry to use steam and gasoline power presses in the printing business, and other appliances for folding and mailing. He has spent 51 years in newspaper work.

CROMER, GEORGE B., ESQ., LL.D.—Born in Newberry County, South Carolina, October 3, 1857, and graduated from Newberry College in 1877, with the highest honors of his class. Immediately after his graduation he was elected assistant in the Preparatory Department, and Adjunct Professor in Ancient Languages, an honor rarely conferred on any young man so soon after graduation. His advancement in the college faculty to the professorship of Latin, History and Political Science soon followed; but in 1881 he resigned, and soon thereafter entered upon the practice of law, in which profession he has won signal success and is recognized as one of the ablest lawyers and public speakers in the South.

Newberry College, however, could never relinquish her hold on one of such scholarly attainments and strength of character; and so, when Dr. Geo. W. Holland was translated to his heavenly rest, September 30, 1895, the eyes of the Church in this State refused to see any man but Geo. B. Cromer, Esq., as his successor; nor could his great soul refuse this urgent call of the Church. He therefore became president of Newberry College in 1895, but he had been secretary of the Board of Trustees for some years previously, his interest in his alma mater never having wavered.

He held the presidency of the College with great satisfaction and success up to 1904; and the president of this synod expressed the feeling of the whole Church in the South when, in his report, he said: "It is with feelings of profound regret that I record the resignation of the most worthy president of the College, Dr. George B. Cromer, and of his retirement from this work." But Dr. Cromer did not give up the College absolutely. Very soon he was made president of the Board of Trustees, and has been ever since one of the most efficient and valuable officers in the entire history of the College. As a churchman he has had few equals, with the fullest cooperation helping laity and clergy in promoting the interests of the Church of God. He has served on all the important boards of the synod, district and general; as president of the Board of Publication of the United Synod; as chairman of the Layman's Missionary Movement; as chairman of the South Carolina Board of Charities and Corrections; as secretary of the State Board of National Red Cross; as a member of the Board of Education of the United Synod; and for many years on the Board of Directors of the Theological Seminary of the South.

In all the relations of life he has shown himself a Christian gentleman without reproach; a scholar of splendid ability; a devout and humble child of God, and a man deserving the highest esteem and love of all our people.

DERRICK, SIDNEY J., A.M., LL.D.—Born in Lexington County, S. C., November 10, 1867. His birthplace is near Little Mountain, S. C., among a people noted for industry, honesty and religious devotion.

In due time he bore off one of the honors of his class at Newberry College, won the Essay medal, and was one of the debaters of acknowledged ability. After graduation he took work at Cornell and Columbia University. In 1896 he was elected as head of the Preparatory Department of Newberry College, which he held with signal success up to 1904, when he was elected Professor of History in connection with his duties as the principal of the Preparatory Department. In 1906 to his chair was added Civics; in the next session was added assistant to the chair of Philosophy; and in 1918 he was elected president of the College, which position he has filled to the present date with entire satisfaction.

In recognition of his splendid ability some years ago Lenoir College, Hickory, N. C., conferred on him the degree of Doctor of Laws.

Not the least important fact to his credit is that he has always been devoted to the Church and to all of its activities. He has been honored with membership on the State Board of Education; the Lutheran Board of Publication; the Home Mission Board of the United Lutheran Church; and during the world war he was chairman of the Newberry County Exemption Board; and is now a member of the South Carolina Colonization Commission.

Modest, unassuming, conscientious, and faithful to every trust, he is held in high esteem, and is deservedly popular with all classes.

COUNTS, R. C.—Manager of the Southern Branch of the United Lutheran Publication House, located in Columbia, S. C. One of the prominent laymen of our Church in the South. He was born July 18, 1875, at Prosperity, S. C., and graduated from Newberry College in 1895. He then took a special course at Vanderbilt University. He followed the profession of teaching for a number of years, and subsequently became associated with our Publication House in Columbia. He served as treasurer of what was called, "The One Day's Income," a synodical organization for raising funds for Home and Foreign Missions; was made treasurer of "The Lutheran Brotherhood Fund", a synodical fund brought into use for taking care of our soldiers during the World War; and then he was chosen treasurer of the $300,000 Newberry-Summerland College Education Fund—all these offices evidencing his strong business integrity, his acknowledged ability in matters of business and his devotion to all the interests of the Church. Prominent in the counsels of the local church and in the synod, district and general, he is recognized as one of our leading laymen. Faithful, courteous, and helpful to preachers and congregations alike, he is at once popular and highly esteemed as the Manager of our Publication House.

BAKER, KENNETH.—Born in Adairville, Kentucky, October 3, 1869, son of Leander Baker, a Kentuckian, and Martha Eply Baker, from Augusta, Ga. Early in life the family moved to Gaffney, S. C., where parents still reside. Was educated in the High School of Gaffney, Wofford College (one year) and University of South Carolina (two years). Taught school for two years and then went into the cotton business, and has remained a cotton broker ever since. Was a member of the Baptist Church early in life but soon after marriage with Miss Beulah Barre of Prosperity, S. C., in 1893, became a member of Grace Lutheran Church of that place. For a number of years was a teacher in Grace Sunday School. In 1902 moved to Greenwood and, in the absence of a Lutheran organization, taught in the Presbyterian Sunday School for a number of years. Became superintendent of the Sunday School when Dr. S. T. Hallman, Piedmont missionary, organized a Lutheran congregation in Greenwood. Since the Immanuel Lutheran Church was built in 1910, has been superintendent of the Sunday School, a member of the church council, and secretary and treasurer of the congregation. Was treasurer of the Laymen's Missionary Movement of the United Synod in the South. Has been president (also district president) of the Greenwood County Interdenominational Sunday School Association. Has been a trustee of Newberry College for a number of years. Was mayor of Greenwood for 6 years and president of the Chamber of Commerce 4 years. Was a delegate to the Democratic convention in 1908; also a presidential elector from South Carolina. Served as chairman of the County Board of Exemption during the World War. Is a member of the State Highway Commission, and is president of the Commercial Trust Company and the Greenwood Building and Loan Association.

RAWL, Mrs. M. C.—Born September 15, 1840, and died March 6, 1895. She was chosen president of the Woman's Home and Foreign Missionary Society of the Evangelical Lutheran Synod of South Carolina at its fifth annual convention, which met at Newberry, S. C., and continued to fill that office until the ninth convention, when on account of ill health she was compelled to resign. She was very deeply interested in mission work.

In this term of service, extending from October 24, 1890, to March 6, 1894, she greatly endeared herself to the whole Church not only in South Carolina but also beyond the borders of the state.

Being a poetess of no mean ability, she wrote many gems of devotional verse and inspired her readers to noble deeds. A beautiful art window in the Woman's Memorial Church, Spartanburg, S. C., evinces the high esteem in which she was held, and the love of those who sorrowed when she left them for the home in glory.

KREPS, Mrs. M. O. J.—This devoted servant of God, who has given twenty-five years of continuous and highly efficient missionary service in this synod and to the Church at large, is easily one of the most prominent and thoroughly useful women in the Lutheran Church. Gifted as speaker, writer, poetess and organizer, she is widely sought after and is always heard with keen pleasure and special profit.

In 1899 she was made recording secretary of the Woman's Synodical Missionary Society of the Lutheran Church in South Carolina, and was made its president in 1908, which office she still fills with entire satisfaction. She edited the Woman's Missionary Department in the *Lutheran Church Visitor* for twenty years; is now the editor of a well conducted industrial magazine, called *The Spinner*, at the Pacific Mills, Columbia, and is also president of the King's Daughters of South Carolina.

With all these various agencies of service, she has never failed in fully measuring up to all the demands made on a faithful pastor's wife. A remarkable woman, and in the highest degree a King's Daughter—a child of the Christ!

Born in Fincastle, Va., September 27, 1861, a daughter of Mr. and Mrs. E. H. Carper, and located in Salem, Va., she became the wife of Rev. M. O. J. Kreps, D.D., in 1883; and her

life has been a benediction to her family, to the Church, and
to all who have had the pleasure of being associated with her.

EARGLE, MRS. KATE (nee Sarah Kate Smeltzer), daughter of that
godly man the history of whose life will long live in the history
of Newberry College and our Southern Theological Seminary,
was born in Newberry, S. C., May 16, 1865, soon after the close
of the War Between the States. Carefully reared in that Christian home and educated under godly teachers, her life has ever
been a ray of sunshine, a star of hope to others. She has been
a dutiful child of God from infancy and noted for devotion to
her Lord, to His Church, and all the interests of His Kingdom.
It is not surprising, then, that she has always been prominent in
missionary work. In 1895 she was elected vice-president of the
Synodical Society, became corresponding secretary in 1896,
recording secretary in 1908, and honorary secretary in 1919,
and this at her own instance, slightly reducing her labors, but
by no means lessening her interest in the great cause of missions.

In 1911 she organized the Woman's Missionary Society in
the Greenville Lutheran Mission, and in 1922, by her instru-
mentality, led to the organization of the Woman's Piedmont
Mission Conference, of which she remains the president.

WISE, MRS. J. L.—Fills the important position of Cradle Roll Superintendent of the Woman's Missionary Society of this synod.
She has now been before the Church in this capacity for about
17 years, and is recognized as a thoroughly efficient officer.
Before the convention of 1907 the women had given attention
to the children's societies, but at the convention held in Spartanburg, S. C., November 3-5, 1907, it was determined to take
up in an organized capacity the Cradle-Roll Department, and
Mrs. J. L. Wise was elected secretary and treasurer of this
Department. She is one of our most highly esteemed workers; and no one has a deeper interest in the babes of the
Church than this faithful servant of God.

HABENICHT, MRS. MARGARET SOPHIA.—The daughter of Capt. and
Mrs. Jno. C. Seegers, and sister of Rev. J. C. Seegers, D.D., a
professor in the Philadelphia Theological Seminary. In 1906
she was elected vice-president of the Synodical Missionary Society, and served up to 1912, when she resigned, but was at
once elected honorary vice-president, which office she still
holds.

In all these years she has given liberal financial support to
mission work, and has kept in close touch with our mission-

aries on the field, and has cheered them with letters and gifts. A lifelong member of Ebenezer Church, Columbia, she has been active in every good work within the congregation as well as a generous supporter of all the causes of the Church at large.

ALLWORDEN, Mrs. W. G.—A daughter of Capt. and Mrs. John C. Seegers, of blessed memory. For many years she has been a quiet but active mission worker in her home church and in the synod. She was elected treasurer of the Woman's Synodical Society in 1898, and filled this office with marked ability and faithfulness up to November, 1919, when she resigned, having most carefully looked after the financial work of the Society for 21 years continuously. Immediately upon her resignation she was elected honorary treasurer of the Society, and this honorable title will remain hers throughout her faithful and useful life.

SEEGERS, Mrs. F. W.—One of the outstanding missionary workers in this synod. She was a charter member of the Woman's Missionary Society of Ebenezer congregation, and organized the first children's missionary society of the South Carolina Synod, and of the United Synod in the South. She has been the leader of such societies,—now called "The Light Brigade" —ever since organized, 36 years ago; and is now the treasurer of the Woman's Missionary Society of this synod. In addition to all these activities, she is Superintendent of the Primary Department of Ebenezer Sunday School, and holds membership on the Executive Board of the Woman's Missionary Society of the United Lutheran Church in America.

Honorarius

Finding it impossible within the limits set for this history, to give detailed accounts of all the deserving persons who have at sundry times rendered valuable service in the synod's life, we find it necessary to group a number of these in condensed form:

Dr. Patrick Todd was treasurer of the Synodical Widow's Fund, 1845-1858. *Joseph Wingard* was treasurer of the Seminary Fund, 1849-1858, when he died; he had also been treasurer of the Foreign Mission Fund, 1838-1849. *John J. Dreher* was treasurer of the Mission Fund, 1850-1867. *John P. Aull* was prominent as contributor, trustee, and a liberal helper in the building of Newberry

CAPT. GEO. S. HACKER

College, 1857-1878, and he was treasurer of the Widows' Fund, 1867-1871. *Maj. J. P. Kinard* was treasurer of the Widows' Fund, 1858-1869, and had materially aided in the building of Newberry College when it was first located in the town of Newberry, and made very important concessions when the College was again located in Newberry—as did also *Wallace A. Cline*, one of the builders of the first college. *Simeon Corley* was treasurer of the synod, 1856-1862, and was succeeded by W. W. Houseal, noted elsewhere in Biographies. *F. C. Blum*, of Charleston, S. C., was the treasurer of the Disabled Ministers' Fund, 1858-1867. *Col. West Caughman* was elected treasurer of the synod in 1835 and served to 1847, being succeeded by John Rauch, and in 1855 S. Corley became the treasurer, as stated above. *Col. Thomas W. Holloway* was treasurer of the Widows' Fund for many years, and was a trustee of Newberry College, and one of its warmest supporters through a long series of years.

Capt. Geo. S. Hacker, treasurer of Bachman Endowment Fund one term, 1885. *Maj. Godfrey Leaphart*, twelve years treasurer of Bachman Endowment Fund (1891-1903). *Henry C. Holloway, Esq.*, treasurer of General Endowment Fund from its foundation in 1916 to present time. *James B. Hunter, Esq.*, treasurer of Semi-Centennial Endowment Fund (1919), following Dr. O. B. Mayer, to present time. *U. B. Whites*, last treasurer of Foreign Missionary Society (1871), when the funds went into care of synodical treasurer. *Robert F. Bowe* did efficient work as statistical secretary (1915-16) in compiling synodical budget, etc.

We find also the name of *G. W. Dingle*, of St. John's Church, Charleston, S. C., who was treasurer of the Seminary Fund, 1881-1886, and otherwise active in the work of this synod. *Otto Tiedeman, Jr.*, filled this office 1886-1891; and last, but not least, we note that *Dr. George Y. Hunter* has filled this position with great acceptability from 1907, and continues to serve.

We thank God for the life and service of all these brethren and for all who have been thus faithful to the trusts committed to them.

Chapter XI

RETROSPECTIVE AND PROSPECTIVE

A personal knowledge of many of the ministers and laymen who have been prominent in the life of this synod justifies the statement that few, if any synods could ever boast of stronger men, of men more loyal to God and to the Confessions of the Church On its roll have been men of broad scholarship, deep learning and of undoubted piety; many of her preachers were men of power; and their influence abides.

A noteworthy fact is that of the provision made by our sainted fathers for the spiritual welfare of the slaves in the Old South. Their infants were baptized, the young people instructed and confirmed, and seating capacity was provided in most of the churches that they might attend the services and hear the word of God. In some cases leading colored men on the plantations were encouraged to preach the Gospel to their fellow-slaves.

The heroism and the self-sacrificing spirit of the early founders of this synod would put to the blush many who are today easily discouraged by what they term their "arduous labors". Many, without stated salaries, served four and five congregations, and rode from twenty-five to two hundred miles on horseback to carry the Gospel to the widely-scattered Lutherans. A case in point was that of Rev. Michael Rauch, who rode two hundred miles from his South Carolina home to preach to the Salzburgers in Georgia. On reaching the Savannah River he found that it was overflowing its banks, but he pleaded with the ferryman to put him across the river. At the risk of life they crossed, landing two miles below the ferry on the other side; but the Salzburgers heard the Gospel at the appointed hour!

These men, like St. Paul, toiled with their own hands that they might "make the Gospel without charge"; and we have entered into their labors.

The progress of this synod along constructive lines is one of the remarkable features of its historic life. From simple log houses it has moved steadily onward until today churchly structures greet the eye of the observer, and in almost every house of God will be found modern equipment of the most approved pattern. Its Sunday Schools have progressed from the most primitive style of instruction, until the courses of study have reached a high stage of efficiency. The number of Sunday Schools has increased step by step with the growing number of congregations, and there has been a corresponding increase in the membership of both. A more recent development has been the "Summer School for Church Workers".

Sunday School Normals were held in some of the conferences as early as 1909. For several years these Normals were authorized and conducted by the district conferences. In 1911 synod adopted a report authorizing a synodical Sunday School Normal and appointed a committee to conduct it, the Sunday Schools to bear the expenses. The churches of the Tennessee Synod on this territory were invited to co-operate, and they complied. Now the Normal began to broaden in its operations. Hitherto Sunday School work had occupied its only efforts. Other needs of the Church claimed attention, and the Sunday School Normal changed its name and broadened its program. The Summer School for Church Workers is now the official name, with a program for every department of church work.

For several years the Summer School for Church Workers was held in Newberry College; during recent years in Summerland College. From the beginning of the Normal the attendance and the interest have been inspiring and promising. Watching closely the needs of the Church and enlisting a competent faculty, the School has grown to the point where dormitory and class-room space is at a premium. The length of the school term has grown from two to nine days. While the plan has greatly broadened, the emphasis is where it was at the beginning—training leaders for the Sunday School.

From a partially trained ministry the synod now points with pride to a thoroughly educated clergy, the equal of any denomination in this land. Time was when the president could only give spare moments to the official business of the synod. But we have now passed the experimental stage of a salaried president. This office was created by the synod at its convention in 1919 and Rev. H. J. Black was elected president, to serve for a term of four years. At its convention in 1923 the synod reelected President Black and recorded its appreciation of his diligence and devotion in the great task committed to him.

REV. H. J. BLACK, D.D.

Not the least noteworthy in the progress of the synod is the pleasing fact that the laymen and women of the synod now stand in the front rank of efficiency, liberality, and progressive leadership, and all this is telling in better and greater work for God and His Kingdom.

The prospect promises greater things to come, and the next centennial year, we have every reason to believe, will "exceed in glory".

APPENDIX

Ministers Connected With the South Carolina Synod from January, 1824, to November, 1924

NOTE.—Many of the pastors named in this list accepted calls into other synods, but in many cases they returned. To trace all these moves would be very difficult. It was therefore thought best to give the date on which they first entered this synod, and the latest date of their connection with the synod.

Names.	First admitted.	Connection to date.
John P. Franklow	1824	1829
John Y. Metze	1824	1833
Godfrey Dreher	1824	1837
Michael Rauch	1824	1869
Jacob Moser	1824	1865
Samuel Herscher	1824	1825
John Bachman	1824	1874
C. F. Bergman	1824	1832
Jno. C. A. Schoenberg	1824	1826
Stephen A. Mealy	1824	1840
Jacob Wingard	1826	1831
C. B. Wessell	1826	1827
J. D. Scheck	1827	1841
J. C. Hope	1827	1853
J. C. Schwartz	1827	1831
Wm. D. Strobel	1829	1831
Geo. Haltiwanger, Sr.	1833	1849
Herman Aull	1833	1852
Robert Cloy	1833	1853
E. L. Hazelius	1833	1853
F. F. Harris	1834	1839
S. Bouknight	1834	1876
David Hungerpeler	1836	1840
Jacob Kleckley	1836	1860
E. A. Bolles	1836	1893
J. P. Ring	1836	1852
Elijah Hawkins	1836	1837
P. A. Strobel	1836	1855
Wm. Berly	1836	1873
David Bernhardt	1836	1843
Levi Bedenbaugh	1836	1860
W. G. Harter	1837	1841
Jacob Crim	1837	1839
S. R. Shepherd	1838	1855

Names.	First admitted.	Connection to date.
W. H. Smith	1839	1843
J. P. Margart	1840	1870
Geo. Haltiwanger, Jr.	1840	1862
C. B. Thuemmel	1841	1843
N. Aldrich	1841	1866
F. Becker	1841	1841
P. A. Strobel	1841	1855
J. F. W. Leppard	1841	1852
P. Kistler	1841	1856
F. W. Humsoth	1842	1847
C. F. Bansemer	1842	1889
E. B. Hort	1842	1863
G. H. Brown	1842	1855
H. Stoudenmire	1842	1863
P. W. Hawkins	1843	1851
G. H. Haigler	1844	1860
Levi Daily	1844	1855
E. Keiffer	1844	1851
Elijah Elmore	1844	1860
David Shealy	1844	1879
A. W. Lindler	1844	1913
J. H. Bailey	1845	1892
J. D. Stingley	1846	1855
S. Bailey	1848	1855
E. Dufford	1848	1879
B. N. Hopkins	1848	1853
J. B. Lowman	1848	1875
L. Mueller	1848	1898
A. J. Karn	1849	1862
J. B. Anthony	1849	1858
R. Godfrey	1849	1858
G. D. Bernheim	1849	1858
G. Guelner	1849	1855
M. Posey	1849	1852
S. W. Bedenbaugh	1849	1860
Emanuel Caughman	1849	1881
Jacob Austin	1849	1920
W. H. Fink	1850	1851
C. M. Shepperson	1851	1853
T. S. Boinest	1851	1871
Lewis Eichelberger	1852	1859
J. H. W. Wertz	1852	1883
D. I. Dreher	1853	1855
W. A. Houck	1853	1874
R. J. Hungerpeler	1853	1856

Names.	First admitted.	Connection to date.
W. Epping	1854	1861
B. F. Berry	1854	1889
C. H. Bernheim	1855	1866
C. D. Austin	1855	—
Jacob Hawkins	1855	1895
M. Whittle	1858	1861
J. N. Derrick	1858	1871
Paul Derrick	1858	1877
W. S. Bowman	1859	1880
Theophilus Stork	1859	1860
J. A. Brown	1859	1862
J. F. Wilken	1860	1865
D. M. Blackwelder	1860	1866
J. L. Smithdeal	1860	1866
J. M. Schreckhise	1860	1866
Festus Hickerson	1862	1864
J. P. Smeltzer	1862	1887
W. Eichelberger	1862	1867
A. R. Rude	1863	1883
B. Kreps	1862	1887
A. Angerer	1861	1865
A. D. L. Moser	1863	1883
J. A. Sligh	1863	1917
J. H. Cupp	1865	1866
J. H. Honour	1866	1885
D. P. Camman	1867	1881
D. Kyser	1867	1895
Carl Weber	1867	1869
S. T. Hallman	1868	In synod 1924
W. W. Hicks	1869	1871
H. S. Wingard	1870	1883
J. D. Shirey	1870	1882
C. P. Boozer	1871	1921
Geo. A. Hough	1871	1880
T. W. Dosh	1872	1876
J. H. C. Shierenbach	1872	1875
H. W. Kuhns	1873	1878
Geo. W. Holland	1874	1895
Z. W. Bedenbaugh	1874	1921
J. D. Bowles	1874	1914
J. F. Probst	1874	1890
S. S. Rahn	1874	1889
E. A. Wingard	1875	1900
J. B. Haskell	1875	1884
S. P. Hughes	1876	1882

Names.	First admitted.		Connection to date.
Edward T. Horn	1876		1897
J. Heckel	1878		1890
J. F. Kiser	1879		1895
L. E. Busby	1878		1896
Wm. Stoudenmire	1878		1880
J. H. Wilson	1880		1919
Peter Miller	1880		1884
L. K. Probst	1881		1903
I. P. Hawkins	1881		1884
J. Q. Wertz	1881		1889
J. Steck	1882		1906
J. E. Bushnell	1884		1917
M. O. J. Kreps	1884	In synod	1924
A. J. Bowers	1884	In synod	1924
J. W. S. Sheppard	1884		1884
J. S. Moser	1884		1885
Holmes Dysinger	1884		1888
J. C. Brodfuehrer	1885		1889
A. B. McMackin	1885		1887
A. G. Voigt	1885		1898
C. A. Marks	1886		1890
J. B. Fox	1886		1899
E. E. Barclay	1886		1888
J. E. Berly	1886		1890
M. M. Kinard	1887		1903
W. A. Julian	1888		1893
R. C. Holland	1888		1898
M. J. Epting	1888		1895
W. C. Schaeffer	1888		1892
H. F. Schede	1888		1889
J. G. Graichen	1889		1906
Henry P. Counts	1889		1891
P. H. E. Derrick	1889		1920
J. H. Wyse	1890		1898
Karl Bolt	1891		1903
W. A. Deaton	1891		1897
J. D. Shealy	1891	In synod	1924
J. A. B. Scherer	1891		1903
S. C. Zettner	1891		1896
T. O. Keister	1891		1895
S. L. Keller	1891		1893
J. W. Butler	1892		1894
W. K. Sligh	1892		1924
R. E. Livingston	1892		1918
S. P. Shumpert	1892		1915

Names.	First admitted.		Connection to date.
W. A. C. Mueller	1892		1924
G. J. Martz	1893		1898
O. B. Shearouse	1893	In synod	1924
A. Freyschmidt	1893		1897
B. W. Cronk	1894		1911
C. E. Weltner	1894		1914
S. C. Ballentine	1894		1918
N. D. Bodie	1894		1893
C. M. Fox	1894		1897
Geo. S. Bearden	1895		1922
Jas. D. Kinard	1895		1924
H. A. McCullough	1895	In synod	1924
S. L. Nease	1895		1906
J. G. Schaid	1896		1908
J. W. Horine	1897	In synod	1924
J. C. Trauger	1897		1897
T. W. Shealy	1897		1900
H. J. Mathias	1898		1903
I. J. Long	1898	In synod	1924
Y. von A. Riser	1898		1916
M. G. G. Scherer	1899	In synod	1924
W. W. Ritchie	1899		1899
A. R. Taylor	1899		1922
P. D. Risinger	1899		1922
W. H. Hiller	1899		1914
Chas. H. Armstrong	1900		1903
W. H. Greever	1901	In synod	1924
H. C. Grossman	1901		1908
W. A. Lutz	1902		1905
J. K. Efird	1901		1905
W. L. Seabrook	1902		1907
P. E. Monroe	1902		1924
S. P. Koon	1902	In synod	1924
Chas. Koerner	1903		1912
C. A. Freed	1903	In synod	1924
L. P. Boland	1903	In synod	1924
D. B. Groseclose	1903	In synod	1924
J. P. Miller	1903		1906
J. L. Buck	1904		1906
W. B. Aull	1904	In synod	1924
J. B. Haigler	1905	In synod	1924
T. B. Epting	1904		1910
J. W. Nease	1905		1908
V. C. Ridenhour	1905		1906
J. C. Wessinger	1905	In synod	1924

Names.	First admitted.	Connection to date.
Wm. J. Finck	1906	1906
J. C. Dietz	1906	1909
J. B. Derrick	1906	1916
C. J. Sox	1906	1907
J. B. Harman	1906 In synod	1924
W. P. Cline	1907 In synod	1924
D. A. Sox	1907	1922
C. Armand Miller	1908	1912
J. I. Miller	1908	1908
J. H. Harms	1908	1918
Edw. Fulenwider	1908	1920
J. L. Yonce	1907	1922
A. G. Voigt	1908	1912
R. B. Tarrant	1908	1921
O. C. Petersen	1908 In synod	1924
T. S. Brown	1909 In synod	1924
E. H. Kohn	1909	1911
C. W. Hoppe	1909	1910
J. D. Mauney	1909	1911
J. W. Oxner	1910 In synod	1924
H. J. Black	1910 In synod	1924
I. E. Long	1910 In synod	1924
J. B. Umberger	1911	1915
E. C. Witt	1911	1916
W. E. Pugh	1911	1913
E. W. Leslie	1911	1921
J. A. Linn	1912	1914
W. A. Dutton	1912 In synod	1924
Geo. J. Gongaware	1913 In synod	1924
C. L. Miller	1913	1922
P. E. Shealy	1910	1921
V. L. Fulmer	1913	1915
H. R. Karstens	1913 No record after ordination	1913
H. M. Brown	1913 Died	1913
Bernard Repass	1913	1916
M. L. Kester	1913	1918
H. E. Beatty	1914	1922
H. C. Bell	1914	1918
M. D. Huddle	1914	1919
M. C. Riser	1914 In synod	1924
W. J. Roof	1914	1915
E. F. K. Roof	1914	1917
J. C. Seegers	1914	1918
J. L. Smith	1913 In synod	1924

Names.	First admitted.		Connection to date.
L. A. Thomas	1914		1917
R. H. Anderson	1914		1915
H. S. Petrea	1915	In synod	1924
V. Y. Boozer	1916		1923
C. J. Shealy	1915	In synod	1924
W. H. Riser	1917		1924
E. C. Cronk	1917		1921
A. M. Huffman	1917		1919
W. A. Riser	1917		1921
W. H. Roof	1917		1922
Enoch Hite	1918		1920
Geo. S. Bowden	1919		1922
Wm. K. Gotwald	1919		1923
R. R. Sowers	1919		1923
J. Howard Worth	1919	In synod	1924
Thomas F. Suber	1919	In synod	1924
C. K. Rhodes	1920		1922
S. L. Blomgren	1920		1923
A. B. Obenschain	1920	In synod	1924
H. A. Kistler	1920	In synod	1924
J. A. Shealy	1921	In synod	1924
R. A. Goodman	1921	In synod	1924
Geo. W. Nelson	1921	In synod	1924
P. D. Brown	1921	In synod	1924
A. W. Ballentine	1922	In synod	1924
R. M. Carpenter	1922		1923
J. L. Cromer	1922	In synod	1924
S. W. Hahn	1922	In synod	1924
E. H. Seckinger	1922	In synod	1924
I. M. Senter	1922	In synod	1924
W. D. Wise	1922	In synod	1924
L. L. Lohr	1922		1923
J. W. Mangum	1923	In synod	1924
H. B. Schaeffer	1923	In synod	1924
P. C. Sigmon	1923	In synod	1924
Henry A. Schroder	1923	In synod	1924
M. R. Wingard	1923	In synod	1924
T. C. Parker	1924	In synod	1924
D. L. Miller	1924	In synod	1924
F. K. Roof	1924	In synod	1924
E. K. Bodie	1924	In synod	1924
F. G. Morgan	1924	In synod	1924

APPENDIX

Chronological Record

Time of convention.	Place.	Important action.
1824	January 14-15	St. Michael's, Lexington	Organization; Qualifications for membership.
1824	November 18-21	St. John's, Lexington	Require lectures to young people.
1825	November 21-27	St. Matthew's, Orangeburg	Provide certificates of ordination.
1826	November 21-27	St. Michael's, Lexington	Appoint first home missionary.
1827	November 23-26	Ebenezer, Georgia	Report license of two ministers.
1828	November 20-24	St. John's, Charleston	Sound keynote Theological Training School.
1829	November 20-23	Lutheran Church, Savannah, Ga.	Movement for establishing Theological Seminary.
1830	November 19-22	St. Paul's, Newberry	Establish Theological Seminary; Rev. J. G. Schwartz, first professor.
1831	December 9-13	Sandy Run, Lexington	Offers for Seminary received.
1832	November 17-21	St. Matthew's, Orangeburg	Lexington selected permanent location of Seminary.
1833	November 16-21	St. Stephen's, Lexington	Report nine Seminary students enrolled.
1834	November 15-20	Ebenezer, Georgia	First report of Seminary directors.
1835	November 14-19	St. Nicholas', Barnwell	Establish three conferential districts.
1836	November 12-16	St. John's, Calk's Road	Ordination of first (three) graduates of Seminary.
1837	November 11-16	St. John's, Charleston	Organize Foreign Missionary Society.
1838	November 10-14	St. John's, Broad River	Report ($124.31) first anniversary Missionary Society.
1839	November 9-13	Sandy Run, Lexington	Pledge support state law on intemperance.
1840	November 14-18	St. Paul's, Newberry	Adopt plan to establish classical school.
1841	Nov. 27-Dec. 1	Jerusalem, Georgia	Pledge support of India Missionary.

Year	Date	Place	Action
1842	November 12-16	St. Mark's, Edgefield	Rearrange conferential districts.
1843	November 11-16	St. Matthew's, Orangeburg	Establish Disabled Ministers' Fund.
1844	November 2-6	St. Stephen's, Lexington	Adopt plan for congregational missionary societies.
1845	November 8-12	Savannah, Georgia	Establish Ministers' Widows' Fund.
1846	November 14-18	St. John's, Charleston	Urge religious instruction of slave population.
1847	November 20-24	Mt. Pilgrim, Coweta Co., Ga.	Authorize special Conference in Georgia.
1848	November 18-24	Sandy Run, Lexington	Movement to endow second Seminary professorship).
1849	November 10-14	St. Andrew's, Lexington	Propose Southern Church Convention.
1850	November 8-13	Beth Eden, Newberry	Adopt memorial tribute to Henry Muller.
1851	November 7-11	Ebenezer, Georgia	Substantial aid for Mississippi mission field.
1852	November 12-17	St. Mark's, Edgefield	Organize society for Relief of Disabled Ministers.
1853	November 11-16	St. Matthew's, Orangeburg	Authorize annual reports on state of religion.
1854	November 10-14	Mt. Pilgrim, Coweta, Georgia	Seminary directors authorized to secure charter for college.
1855	November 8-14	Bethlehem, Pomaria	Decide removal of Seminary to Newberry.
1856	November 6-11	Mt. Calvary, Edgefield	Authorize erection of college building at Newberry.
1857	Oct. 29-Nov. 3	St. Michael's, Lexington	Trustees report contract awarded for college building.
1858	Oct. 28-Nov. 1	Pine Grove, Orangeburg	Enforcement of church discipline urged upon pastors.
1859	Oct. 27-Nov. 1	Beth Eden, Newberry	Installation of College president and Seminary professor.
1860	October 25-30	Luther Chapel. Newberry	Members in Georgia to form synod in that State.
1862	*January 16-20	St. Paul's, Pomaria	Delegates elected to Salisbury Convention.
1862	Oct. 22-Nov. 4	Mt. Lebanon, Orangeburg	Publication committee for Southern Lutheran.
1863	October 16-20	Bethlehem, Newberry	First report of Southern General Synod delegates.
1861	October 13-17	Beth Eden, Newberry	Spiritual welfare of soldiers provided.

*Postponed Convention of 1861.

Chronological Record—Continued

	Time of convention.	Place.	Important action.
1865	October 12-15	St. Matthew's, Orangeburg	Authorize reopening of Newberry College.
1866	October 13-22	St. Mark's, Edgefield	Encouraging reports from congregations.
1867	†September 24-25	Luther Chapel, Newberry	Authorize adjustment of Newberry College debt.
1867	November 14-19	Wentworth St., Charleston	Plan for General Theological Seminary.
1868	November 15-21	St. Paul's, Newberry	Decide removal of Newberry College to Walhalla.
1869	October 14-18	St. John's, Walhalla	Congregations formed into pastorates.
1870	November 17-21	St. John's, Charleston	Authorize annual election of officers.
1871	October 12-16	Newville, Prosperity	Adopt plan to endow Newberry College.
1872	October 10-14	St. John's, Calk's Road	Removal of Theological Seminary to Salem, Va.
1873	†July 23-25	Luther Chapel, Newberry	Consider relocation of Newberry College.
1873	October 16-21	Mt. Pleasant, Barnwell	Decide to continue College at Walhalla.
1874	October 15-20	Mt. Lebanon, Orangeburg	Congregations report celebration of synod's 50th anniversary.
1875	October 14-19	St. Luke's, Newberry	Work of synodical missionary reported.
1876	October 10-15	St. Stephen's, Lexington	Consider permanent location of Newberry College.
1877	†April 3-5	Luther Chapel. Newberry	Relocate Newberry College at Newberry.
1877	October 16-21	St. Matthew's, Orangeburg	Report $12,000 for Bachman Endowment Fund.
1878	November 13-18	Mt. Pleasant, Barnwell	Trustees report completion of new college building.
1879	October 21-26	Grace, Prosperity	Urge adequate support of beneficiary education.
1880	October 14-19	Luther Chapel, Leesville	Children's Missionary Society organized.
1881	October 4-9	Orangeburg Church	First bequest ($400) Newberry College.
1882	November 9-13	St. Matthew's, Charleston	Lack of ministers stressed.
1883	November 8-13	Bethlehem, Pomaria	Celebrate 400th anniversary birth of Luther.

†Extra Convention.

Year	Date	Place	Action
1884	May 27-28	Ebenezer, Columbia	Provide support of Theological Seminary.
1884	November 6-10	Pine Grove, Orangeburg	Reopening of Seminary at Newberry College.
1885	October 22-26	St. Stephen's, Lexington	Report of Salisbury Diet.
1886	October 13-17	St. John's, Walhalla	Delegates report formation of United Synod.
1887	November 3- 7	Grace, Prosperity	United Synod urged to establish Theological Seminary.
1888	October 24-29	Ebenezer, Columbia	Introduction of Common Service.
1889	October 16-20	Mt. Lebanon, Orangeburg	Disabled Ministers' Fund authorized.
1890	October 21-26	Luther Chapel, Newberry	Disapprove ministers as candidates for political office.
1891	October 21-25	Holy Trinity, Augusta, Georgia	Elect Rev. A. G. Voigt Seminary professor.
1892	October 19-23	Mt. Tabor, Newberry	Cooperate in establishment of Orphan Home.
1893	October 18-24	St. John's, Calk's Road	Authorize certain days for special offerings.
1894	October 24-28	Mt. Pleasant, Barnwell	Adopt protest against nation aiding sectarian schools.
1895	October 23-27	St. Michael's, Lexington	Office of synodical superintendent proposed.
1896	October 21-25	Bethlehem, Pomaria	Enlarge scope of Children's Missionary Societies.
1897	October 20-24	Macedonia, Lexington	Disapprove of indulgence in alcoholic beverages.
1898	November 2-7	St. Andrew's, Charleston	Holland Memorial Fund established.
1899	October 18-22	St. Luke's, Prosperity	Lay delegates make first report on state of religion.
1900	October 24-28	Ebenezer, Columbia	Provide for more accurate statistics.
1901	October 23-27	Luther Chapel, Leesville	Report transfer Theological Seminary to United Synod.
1902	October 22-26	Holy Trinity, Little Mountain	Movement for new building for Newberry College.
1903	November 11-15	St. Paul's, Columbia	Contract for $20,000 reported for college building.
1901	November 9-13	Orangeburg Church	Indications of merger with Tennessee Synod congregations.
1905	November 8-12	St. Paul's, Pomaria	Commend work of United Synod Publishing Company.

Chronological Record—Continued

Time of convention	Place	Important action.
1906 November 7-11	St. Matthew's, Augusta, Georgia	Begin Semi-Centennial Fund of Newberry College.
1907 November 6-10	Woman's Memorial, Spartanburg	Report college endowment fund ($150,000) raised.
1908 November 4-3	Grace, Prosperity	Commend Deaconess work of Pastor Wellner.
1909 November 10-14	St. Stephen's, Lexington	Effort for Home Mission fund of $5,000.
1910 November 9-13	St. Andrew's, Charleston	Payment of synodical debt makes gratifying progress.
1911 November 7-10	Pine Grove, Orangeburg	Lowman Home established by gift of Mrs. Malissa Lowman; begin movement for woman's college.
1912 *May 28	Summerland Inn	Tentative acceptance of Summerland property for Woman's College.
1912 October 22-25	Church of Redeemer, Newberry	Report of first Sunday School Normal.
1913 *May 8	St. Paul's, Columbia	Formal acceptance of Summerland property.
1913 October 21-24	Church of Ascension, Columbia	Report first session Summerland College (62 students).
1914 October 20-23	First Church, Greenville	Urge cooperation with Laymen's Missionary Movement.
1915 November 9-12	Newberry College	Provide missionary training in Sunday Schools.
1916 Oct. 30-Nov. 2	St. John's, Walhalla	Finance Committee's first ($20,000) budget.
1917 November 13-16	Pomaria Church	Adopt constitution United Lutheran Church in America.
1918 December 10-12	Holy Trinity, Elloree	Propose salaried president; authorize educational campaign.
1919 November 13-16	Holy Trinity, Little Mountain	Success of educational campaign for $300,000.
1920 November 9-10	Churches of Charleston	First convention with salaried president.
1921 Oct. 30-Nov. 4	Wittenberg, Leesville	Adopt constitution proposed in 1920.
1922 November 22-24	Grace, Prosperity	Merger with congregations of Tennessee Synod.
1923 November 12-15	Zion, Lexington	First report publication of Lutheran Messenger.

*Extra Convention.

Officers of Synod

Term	President.	Secretary.	Treasurer.
1824	Godfrey Dreher	Samuel Herscher	Samuel Herscher
1825	John Bachman	Samuel Herscher	Godfrey Dreher
1826	John Bachman	C. F. Bergman	Godfrey Dreher
1827	John Bachman	C. F. Bergman	Godfrey Dreher
1828	John Bachman	C. F. Bergman	Godfrey Dreher
1829	John Bachman	C. F. Bergman	Godfrey Dreher
1830	John Bachman	C. F. Bergman	Godfrey Dreher
1831	John Bachman	S. A. Mealy	Godfrey Dreher
1832	John Bachman	S. A. Mealy	Godfrey Dreher
1833	John Bachman	S. A. Mealy	Godfrey Dreher
1834	S. A. Mealy	John C. Hope	Godfrey Dreher
1835	S. A. Mealy	John C. Hope	West Caughman
1836	S. A. Mealy	John C. Hope	West Caughman
1837	S. A. Mealy	John C. Hope	West Caughman
1838	E. L. Hazelius	John C. Hope	West Caughman
1839	John Bachman	John C. Hope	West Caughman
1840	John Bachman	John C. Hope	West Caughman
1841	John C. Hope	William Berly	West Caughman
1842	John C. Hope	William Berly	West Caughman
1843	John C. Hope	William Berly	West Caughman
1844	John Bachman	William Berly	West Caughman
1845	John C. Hope	William Berly	West Caughman
1846	John C. Hope	William Berly	West Caughman

Officers of Synod—Continued

Term	President.	Secretary.	Treasurer.
1847	John C. Hope	G. Haltiwanger, Jr.	John Rauch
1848	John C. Hope	G. Haltiwanger, Jr.	John Rauch
1849	William Berly	J. F. W. Leppard	John Rauch
1850	William Berly	J. F. W. Leppard	John Rauch
1851	J. F. W. Leppard	J. B. Anthony	John Rauch
1852	C. Haltiwanger, Jr.	J. B. Anthony	John Rauch
1853	C. Haltiwanger, Jr.	J. B. Anthony	John Rauch
1854	C. Haltiwanger, Jr.	J. B. Anthony	John Rauch
1855	J. B. Anthony	J. P. Margart	Simeon Corley
1856	J. B. Anthony	J. P. Margart	Simeon Corley
1857	J. B. Anthony	J. P. Margart	Simeon Corley
1858	Samuel Bouknight	J. P. Margart	Simeon Corley
1859	E. B. Hort	Jacob Hawkins	Simeon Corley
1860	E. B. Hort	Jacob Hawkins	Simeon Corley
1862	E. B. Hort	Jacob Hawkins	W. W. Houseal
1862	J. P. Margart	T. S. Boinest	W. W. Houseal
1863	William Berly	T. S. Boinest	W. W. Houseal
1864	William Berly	T. S. Boinest	W. W. Houseal
1865	T. S. Boinest	Paul Derrick	P. E. Wise
1866	T. S. Boinest	Paul Derrick	P. E. Wise
1867	Samuel Bouknight	Jacob Hawkins	P. E. Wise
1867	T. S. Boinest	Paul Derrick	P. E. Wise
1868	T. S. Boinest	Paul Derrick	P. E. Wise

1369	A. R. Rude	Jacob Hawkins	P. E. Wise
1870	Jacob Hawkins	J. A. Sligh	P. E. Wise
1871	W. S. Bowman	I. H. Honour	P. E. Wise
1872	I. P. Smeltzer	I. D. Shirey	P. E. Wise
1873	I. P. Smeltzer	G. A. Hough	P. E. Wise
1873	Paul Derrick	H. S. Wingard	P. E. Wise
1874	H. S. Wingard	G. A. Hough	P. E. Wise
1875	J. A. Sligh	S. T. Hallman	P. E. Wise
1876	E. A. Bolles	C. P. Boozer	P. E. Wise
1877	E. A. Bolles	C. P. Boozer	P. E. Wise
1877	J. H. Honour	I. D. Shirey	P. E. Wise
1878	J. D. Shirey	E. T. Horn	P. E. Wise
1879	J. F. Probst	E. T. Horn	P. E. Wise
1880	G. W. Holland	S. P. Hughes	P. E. Wise
1881	Jacob Hawkins	L. E. Busoy	P. E. Wise
1882	E. T. Horn	L. K. Proost	P. E. Wise
1883	E. T. Horn	L. K. Probst	P. E. Wise
1884	E. T. Horn	L. K. Probst	P. E. Wise
1884	Jacob Steck	S. T. Hallman	P. E. Wise
1885	E. A. Wingard	S. T. Hallman	P. E. Wise
1886	S. T. Hallman	A. B. McMackin	P. E. Wise
1887	S. T. Hallman	J. E. Bery	P. E. Wise
1883	S. T. Hallman	J. E. Bery	P. E. Wise
1889	J. H. Wilson	I. E. Bery	P. E. Wise
1890	I. H. Wilson	M. J. Epting	P. E. Wise
1891	W. C. Schaeffer	M. J. Epting	P. E. Wise
1892	L. E. Busby	M. J. Epting	P. E. Wise

Officers of Synod—Continued

Term	President.	Secretary.	Treasurer.
1893	L. E. Busby	S. T. Hallman	P. E. Wise
1894	R. C. Holland	S. T. Hallman	P. E. Wise
1895	R. C. Holland	S. T. Hallman	A. H. Kohn
1896	M. M. Kinard	S. T. Hallman	A. H. Kohn
1897	M. M. Kinard	S. T. Hallman	A. H. Kohn
1898	J. H. Wilson	S. C. Ballentine	A. H. Kohn
1899	E. A. Wingard	S. C. Ballentine	A. H. Kohn
1900	C. P. Boozer	S. C. Ballentine	A. H. Kohn
1901	C. P. Boozer	S. C. Ballentine	A. H. Kohn
1902	Z. W. Bedenbaugh	S. C. Ballentine	A. H. Kohn
1903	Z. W. Bedenbaugh	S. C. Ballentine	A. H. Kohn
1904	M. O. J. Kreps	S. C. Ballentine	A. H. Kohn
1905	M. O. J. Kreps	J. D. Kinard	A. H. Kohn
1906	M. G. G. Scherer	J. D. Kinard	A. H. Kohn
1907	M. G. G. Scherer	J. D. Kinard	A. H. Kohn
1908	C. A. Freed	S. P. Koon	A. H. Kohn
1909	C. A. Freed	S. P. Koon	A. H. Kohn
1910	J. D. Kinard	S. P. Koon	A. H. Kohn
1911	J. D. Kinard	P. E. Monroe	A. H. Kohn
1912	W. H. Greever	W. B. Aull	A. H. Kohn
1912	W. H. Greever	W. B. Aull	A. H. Kohn
1913	W. H. Greever	W. B. Aull	A. H. Kohn
1913	W. H. Greever	W. B. Aull	A. H. Kohn

1911	P. E. Monroe	W. B. Aull	A. H. Kohn
1915	P. E. Monroe	W. B. Aull	A. H. Kohn
1916	Edw. Fulenwider	W. B. Aull	W. A. Counts
1917	Edw. Fulenwider	W. B. Aull	W. A. Counts
1918	H. J. Black	W. B. Aull	W. A. Counts
1919	H. J. Black	C. J. Shealy	W. A. Counts
1920	H. J. Black	C. J. Shealy	W. A. Counts
1921	H. J. Black	C. J. Shealy	W. A. Counts
1922	H. J. Black	C. J. Shealy	W. A. Counts
1923	H. J. Black	C. J. Shealy	D. F. Efird

CORRESPONDING SECRETARY AND VICE-PRESIDENT

NOTE.—These offices are given here in the order of their institution by the provisions of the Constitution. The office of Corresponding Secretary was instituted in 1842 and abolished in 1880; Vice-President instituted in 1814 and abolished in 1920.

Corresponding Secretary

1842	C. B. Thummel	1857	L. Eichelberger
1843	E. L. Hazelius	1858	L. Eichelberger
1844	E. L. Hazelius	1859	L. Eichelberger
1845	J. R. W. Leppard	1860	J. P. Smeltzer
1847	J. R. W. Leppard	1861	J. P. Smeltzer
1848	J. R. W. Leppard	1862	J. P. Smeltzer
1849	E. B. Hort	1863	J. P. Smeltzer
1850	E. B. Hort	1864	J. P. Smeltzer
1851	E. B. Hort	1864	J. P. Smeltzer
1852	E. B. Hort	1864	T. P. Smeltzer
1853	L. Eichelberger	1865	J. P. Smeltzer
1854	L. Eichelberger	1866	J. P. Smeltzer
1855	L. Eichelberger	1867	J P Smeltzer
1856	L. Eichelberger		

1868	J. P. Smeltzer
1869	J. P. Smeltzer
1870	J. P. Smeltzer
1871	A. R. Rude
1872	J. H. Honour
1873	A. R. Rude
1874	H. W. Kuhns
1875	H. W. Kuhns
1876	H. W. Kuhns
1877	J. A. Sligh
1878	A. R. Rude
1879	J. Hawkins
1880	J. Hawkins

Officers of Synod—Continued

Vice-President

Year	Name	Year	Name	Year	Name
1871	E. A. Bolles	1890	W. A. Julian	1906	J. W. Horine
1875	J. H. Honour	1891	W. A. Julian	1907	C. A. Freed
1876	W. S. Bowman	1892	C. P. Boozer	1908	J. D. Kinard
1877	J. D. Shirey	1893	C. P. Boozer	1909	J. D. Kinard
1878	J. F. Probst	1894	M. M. Kinard	1910	S. P. Koon
1879	L. Muller	1895	M. M. Kinard	1911	S. P. Koon
1880	A. R. Rude	1896	J. H. Honour	1912	P. E. Monroe
1881	C. P. Boozer	1897	W. A. C. Mueller	1913	P. E. Monroe
1882	J. P. Smeltzer	1898	W. A. C. Mueller	1914	Edw. Fulenwider
1883	J. A. Sligh	1899	C. P. Boozer	1915	Edw. Fulenwider
1884	E. A. Wingard	1900	Z. W. Bedenbaugh	1916	H. J. Black
1885	J. A. Sligh	1901	Z. W. Bedenbaugh	1917	H. J. Black
1886	J. H. Wilson	1902	M. O. J. Kreps	1918	H. J. Black
1887	S. S. Rahn	1903	M. O. J. Kreps	1919	H. A. McCullough
1888	S. S. Rahn	1904	W. I. Seabrook	1920	H. A. McCullough
1889	W. A. Julian	1905	W. I. Seabrook		

Treasurers of Various Funds

Theological Seminary Fund

Year	Name	Year	Name
1831	Henry Muller	1839	Henry Muller
1832	Henry Muller	1840	Henry Muller
1833	Henry Muller	1841	Henry Muller
1834	Henry Muller	1842	Henry Muller
1835	Henry Muller		
1836	Henry Muller		
1837	Henry Muller		
1838	Henry Muller		

Year	Name	Year	Name	Year	Name
1843	Henry Muller	1871	Jacob F. Schirmer	1898	Otto Tiedeman, Jr.
1844	Henry Muller	1872	Jacob F. Schirmer	1899	Otto Tiedeman, Jr.
1845	Henry Muller	1873	Jacob F. Schirmer	1900	Otto Tiedeman, Jr.
1846	Henry Muller	1874	Jacob F. Schirmer	1901	Otto Tiedeman, Jr.
1848	Henry Muller	1875	Jacob F. Schirmer	1902	Otto Tiedeman, Jr.
1849	Henry Muller	1876	Jacob F. Schirmer	1903	Otto Tiedeman, Jr.
1850	Joseph Wingard	1877	Jacob F. Schirmer	1904	Otto Tiedeman, Jr.
1851	Joseph Wingard	1878	Jacob F. Schirmer	1905	Otto Tiedeman, Jr.
1852	Joseph Wingard	1879	Jacob F. Schirmer	1906	Otto Tiedeman. Jr.
1853	Joseph Wingard	1880	Jacob F. Schirmer	1907	W. P. Roof
1854	Joseph Wingard	1881	G. W. Dingle	1908	W. P. Roof
1855	Joseph Wingard	1882	G. W. Dingle	1909	W. P. Roof
1856	Joseph Wingard	1883	G. W. Dingle	1910	W. P. Roof
1857	Joseph Wingard	1884	G. W. Dingle	1911	W. P. Roof
1858	Jacob F. Schirmer	1885	G. W. Dingle	1912	Geo. Y. Hunter
1859	Jacob F. Schirmer	1886	J. D. Cappelmann	1913	Geo. Y. Hunter
1860	Jacob F. Schirmer	1887	J. D. Cappelmann	1914	Geo. Y. Hunter
1861	Jacob F. Schirmer	1888	J. D. Cappelmann	1915	Geo. Y. Hunter
1862	Jacob F. Schirmer	1889	J. D. Cappelmann	1916	Geo. Y. Hunter
1863	Jacob F. Schirmer	1890	J. D. Cappelmann	1917	Geo. Y. Hunter
1864	Jacob F. Schirmer	1891	Otto Tiedeman, Jr.	1918	Geo. Y. Hunter
1865	Jacob F. Schirmer	1892	Otto Tiedeman, Jr.	1919	Geo. Y. Hunter
1866	Jacob F. Schirmer	1893	Otto Tiedeman, Jr.	1920	Geo. Y. Hunter
1867	Jacob F. Schirmer	1894	Otto Tiedeman. Jr.	1921	Geo. Y. Hunter
1868	Jacob F. Schirmer	1895	Otto Tiedeman, Jr.	1922	Geo. Y. Hunter
1869	Jacob F. Schirmer	1896	Otto Tiedeman, Jr.	1923	Geo. Y. Hunter
1870	Jacob F. Schirmer	1897	Otto Tiedeman, Jr.		

Officers of Synod—*Continued*

BACHMAN ENDOWMENT FUND

Year	Name	Year	Name	Year	Name
1873	Geo. S. Hacker	1885	Godfrey Leaphart	1897	C. P. Boozer
1874	O. L. Schumpert	1886	Godfrey Leaphart	1898	C. P. Boozer
1875	O. L. Schumpert	1887	Godfrey Leaphart	1899	C. P. Boozer
1876	O. L. Schumpert	1888	Godfrey Leaphart	1900	C. P. Boozer
1877	O. L. Schumpert	1889	Godfrey Leaphart	1901	C. P. Boozer
1878	Conrad Ehrhardt	1890	Godfrey Leaphart	1902	C. P. Boozer
1879	Godfrey Leaphart	1891	Godfrey Leaphart	1903	C. P. Boozer
1880	Godfrey Leaphart	1892	C. P. Boozer	1904	C. P. Boozer
1881	Godfrey Leaphart	1893	C. P. Boozer	1905	C. P. Boozer
1882	Godfrey Leaphart	1894	C. P. Boozer	1906	C. P. Boozer
1883	Godfrey Leaphart	1895	C. P. Boozer	1907	C. P. Boozer
1884	Godfrey Leaphart	1896	C. P. Boozer	1908	C. P. Boozer
1909	C. P. Boozer	1914	C. P. Boozer	1919	C. P. Boozer
1910	C. P. Boozer	1915	C. P. Boozer	1920	J. S. Wheeler
1911	C. P. Boozer	1916	C. P. Boozer	1921	J. S. Wheeler
1912	C. P. Boozer	1917	C. P. Boozer	1922	J. S. Wheeler
1913	C. P. Boozer	1918	C. P. Boozer	1923	J. S. Wheeler

SEMI-CENTENNIAL ENDOWMENT FUND

Year	Name	Year	Name	Year	Name
1907	O. B. Mayer	1913	J. B. Hunter	1919	J. B. Hunter
1908	O. B. Mayer	1914	J. B. Hunter	1920	J. B. Hunter
1909	O. B. Mayer	1915	J. B. Hunter	1921	J. B. Hunter
1910	O. B. Mayer	1916	J. B. Hunter	1922	J. B. Hunter
1911	O. B. Mayer	1917	J. B. Hunter	1923	J. B. Hunter
1912	O. B. Mayer	1918	J. B. Hunter		

General Endowment Fund

Year	Treasurer	Year	Treasurer	Year	Treasurer
1912	H. C. Holloway	1916	H. C. Holloway	1920	H. C. Holloway
1913	H. C. Holloway	1917	H. C. Holloway	1921	H. C. Holloway
1914	H. C. Holloway	1918	H. C. Holloway	1922	H. C. Holloway
1915	H. C. Holloway	1919	H. C. Holloway	1923	H. C. Holloway

Educational Fund

Year	Treasurer	Year	Treasurer
1919	A. H. Kohn	1921	R. C. Counts
1920	R. C. Counts	1922	R. C. Counts
		1923	R. C. Counts

Foreign Missionary Society

Year	Treasurer	Year	Treasurer	Year	Treasurer
1838	Joseph Wingard	1850	John J. Dreher	1862	John J. Dreher
1839	Joseph Wingard	1851	John J. Dreher	1863	John J. Dreher
1840	Joseph Wingard	1852	John J. Dreher	1864	John J. Dreher
1841	Joseph Wingard	1853	John J. Dreher	1865	John J. Dreher
1842	Joseph Wingard	1854	John J. Dreher	1866	John J. Dreher
1843	Joseph Wingard	1855	John J. Dreher	1867	John P. Aull
1844	Joseph Wingard	1856	John J. Dreher	1868	John P. Aull
1845	Joseph Wingard	1857	John J. Dreher	1869	John P. Aull
1846	Joseph Wingard	1858	John J. Dreher	1870	John P. Aull
1847	Joseph Wingard	1859	John J. Dreher	1871	U. B. Whites*
1848	Joseph Wingard	1860	John J. Dreher		
1849	Joseph Wingard	1861	John J. Dreher		

*Funds transferred to custody of synodical treasurer after this year.

Officers of Synod—Continued

Widows' Fund

Year	Treasurer	Year	Treasurer	Year	Treasurer
1845	Patrick Todd	1854	Patrick Todd	1863	T. W. Holloway
1846	Patrick Todd	1855	Patrick Todd	1864	T. W. Holloway
1847	Patrick Todd	1856	Patrick Todd	1865	T. W. Holloway
1848	Patrick Todd	1857	Patrick Todd	1866	T. W. Holloway
1849	Patrick Todd	1858	John P. Kinard	1867	T. W. Holloway
1850	Patrick Todd	1859	John P. Kinard	1868	T. W. Holloway
1851	Patrick Todd	1860	John P. Kinard	1869	T. W. Holloway
1852	Patrick Todd	1861	John P. Kinard		
1853	Patrick Todd	1862	T. W. Holloway		

The society ceased operations at the close of the term of the treasurer last named.

Children's Missionary Society

Year	Officer	Year	Officer	Year	Officer
1880	A. R. Rude	1889	L. K. Probst	1898	M. M. Kinard
1881	A. R. Rude	1890	L. K. Probst	1899	M. M. Kinard
1882	A. R. Rude	1891	T. O. Keister	1900	M. M. Kinard
1883	L. K. Probst	1892	T. O. Keister	1901	M. M. Kinard
1884	L. K. Probst	1893	T. O. Keister	1902	M. M. Kinard
1885	L. K. Probst	1894	T. O. Keister	1903	C. A. Freed
1886	L. K. Probst	1895	M. M. Kinard	1904	C. A. Freed
1887	L. K. Probst	1896	M. M. Kinard		
1888	L. K. Probst	1897	M. M. Kinard		

Archivist

S. T. Hallman 1907-23   W. P. Houseal 1920-23

Necrologist

Statistical Secretary

1915	C. L. Miller		1917	C. L. Miller
1915	R. F. Bowe		1917	E. C. Cronk
1916	C. L. Miller		1918	C. J. Shealy
1916	R. F. Bowe		1919	W. H. Riser

1920	H. S. Petrea
1921	H. S. Petrea
1922	H. S. Petrea
1923	H. S. Petrea

INDEX

General

INDEX

INDEX

INDEX

Theis, Christian, 21.
Theological Seminary, establishment of, 59-60.
  Directors of, election of, 62.
  Opening of, 63.
  Cooperation of North Carolina Synod in support of, 64.
  Gift of Henry Muller to, 66.
  Location at Newberry, 69.
  Located at Columbia, 78.
  Removal to Salem, Va., 78.
  Discontinuance of, 78.
  Transference to control of United Synod, 80.
  Location of, at Mt. Pleasant, Charleston, 81.
  Location of, at Columbia, 82.
Theological students, first ordination of, 64.
Tiedemann, Otto, Jr., 282.
Thummel, C. B., special commendation of, 66.
Training School, missionary, 51.
Treasury, synodical, first receipts of, 107.
Tidings, Sunday School and missionary paper, publication of, 102.
Todd, Patrick, 71, 281.
Trinity, Elloree, 42.
Trustees, Board of, first election of, for Newberry College, 70.
  First election of, for Summerland College, 89.

United Synod, organization of, 80.
United Synod Publishing Company, organization of, 98.

Valuation, synodical and college property, of, 111.
Voigt, A. G., 78, 80, 82, 98, 117, 168, 183, 200, 209.

Wallburg, F. A., 22.
Wallern, Frederick Joseph, pioneer pastor, 131, (and Mrs. Wallern), graves of, 133.
Wessinger, B. D., 87, 198.
Wessinger, E. L., 198.
Wessinger, J. C., 198.
Welner, C. E., 38, 51.
Wesley, John, commendation of Salzburgers, by, 22.
Whittle, M., 71-72.
Whites, U. B., 282.
Wilson, J. H., 11.
Winesett, W. J., 103.
Wingard, H. S., 77.
Wingard, Samuel, 25.
Wingard, Joseph, 34, 225.
Wiggers, Christopher, 23, 155.
Woman's Memorial Church, aided by Woman's Missionary Society, 48.
Woman's Missionary Society, synodical, organization of, 43.
  Presidents of, 55.
Wulbern, Alice, 36.
Wyse, Mrs. J. H., 45, 55.
Wyse, Lottie, 36.

Yonce, J. L., 204, 223.
Young People, Federation of, 52.
Young People's Federation, foundation of, 117.
  Achievements of, 119.
  Members of, in foreign work, 120.

Zettner, S. C., 186.
Zion Church, 24.

Pastoral and Official

Aldrich, Nicholas, 192.
Angerer, A., 186.
Anderson, R. H., 156, 158, 215.
Anthony, J. B., 132, 141, 156, 165, 168, 172, 187.
Armstrong, C. H., 172, 174, 213, 214.
Aull, Herman, 133, 155, 158, 162, 168, 171.
Aull, W. B., 171, 187, 211, 217, 223.
Austin, 170, 171, 179, 194, 213.

Bachman, John, 169, 181, 194, 195.
Bailey, J. H., 141, 152, 154, 160, 168, 170, 177, 194, 197.
Ballentine, A. W., 120, 149, 175, 187, 219.
Ballentine, S. C., 120, 133, 139, 147, 156, 158, 170, 184, 198, 207, 211, 215.
Bamberg, Isaac, 130, 141, 215.
Bamberg, J. G., 145, 146, 153.
Bansemer, C. F., 149, 186.
Bearden, George S., 148, 152, 159, 162, 170, 171, 196, 205, 215, 219.
Beatty, H. E., 189, 213.
Beck, A. R., 139, 148.
Becker, F., 171, 175, 179, 187, 219.
Bell, H. C., 192, 194, 220.
Bedenbaugh, Levi, 158, 159, 161, 163, 165.
Bedenbaugh, Samuel, 158, 159, 184.
Bedenbaugh, Z. W., 163, 168, 171, 172, 191.
Bergman, C. F., 14.
Bernheim, G. D., 194.
Berly, J. E., 133, 147, 154, 187.
Berly, William, 132, 133, 141, 156, 158, 159, 160, 165, 168, 172, 174, 175, 181, 189, 190.
Bickley, J. J., 209.
Black, H. J., 158, 194, 197, 210, 212, 224.
Blackwelder, D. M., 132, 139, 154, 162.
Blomgren, S. L., 167.
Bocie, E. K., 177.
Bodie, N. D., 162, 168, 174, 189, 215.
Bohn, J. G., 186.
Boinest, T. S., 124, 156, 158, 159, 174, 180, 181, 195.
Boland, L. P., 161, 168, 172, 177, 178, 194, 209, 211.
Boozer, C. P., 127, 130, 147, 158, 162, 165, 171, 175, 176, 193, 199, 203, 206, 216.
Boozer, V. Y., 147, 170, 179, 192, 198, 207.
Bouknight, Samuel, 158, 152, 167, 175, 178, 179, 197.
Bowden, G. S., 218, 224.
Bowers, A. J., 163, 168, 174, 176, 192, 202, 206, 214, 218, 222, 225.
Bowles, J. D., 139, 156, 158, 162, 171, 172, 174, 175, 176, 177, 206.
Bowman, W. S., 183, 194.
Brodfuhrer, J. C., 186.
Brown, G. H., 168, 171.
Brown, J. A., 182.
Brown, P. D., 163.
Brown, T. S., 139, 161, 213.
Buck, J. L., 158, 162, 171, 215.
Bulow, Joachim, 130.
Busby, L. E., 150, 161, 170, 197, 215.
Bushnell, J. E., 192.
Butler, J. W., 193.

Carpenter, R. M., 144, 198.
Caughman, Emanuel, 158, 161, 165, 167, 170, 171, 179, 193, 195.

(314)

INDEX

INDEX

INDEX

Wingard, E. A., 130, 149, 203.
Wingard, Jacob, 125, 132, 141, 153, 163.
Wingard, H. S., 156, 174, 189, 191, 201.
Wingard, M. R., 218.
Winkhouse, M., 135, 153, 148.
Wise, W. D., 147, 170, 180, 187, 197.
Witt, E. C., 149, 213, 214, 222.
Wordman, H. G. B., 122.
Worth, J. Howard, 194.
Wyse, J. H., 156, 158, 171, 176, 202, 211.

Yonce, J. L., 125, 212.

Zettner, S. C., 186.

ADDENDA

Brown, H. M., pastor of St. Michael's
and St. Andrew's (pp. 155 and 165),
January 1, 1913, until his death,
July 22, 1913. (Name inadvertently
omitted in list of pastors.)

Biographical

Allworden, Mrs. W. G., 280.
Aull, W. B., 229.

Bachman, John, 247.
Bachman, W. K., 263.
Baker, Kenneth, 277.
Ballentine, A. W., 229.
Berly, J. E., 255.
Berly, William, 250.
Black, H. J., 229, 250.
Blomgren, S. L., 229.
Bodie, E. K., 230.
Boinest, T. S., 248.
Boland, L. P., 230.
Boozer, C. P., 253.
Boozer, D. L., 265.
Bowers, A. J., 230.
Brown, P. D., 230.
Brown, T. S., 231.

Cappelmann, J. D., 271.
Chisolm, R. G., 264.
Cline, W. P., 231.
Cromer, J. A., 231.
Cromer, J. L., 232.
Cromer, George B., 275.

Derrick, S. J., 276.
Dreher, Godfrey, 247.
Dutton, W. A., 232.
Dutton, W. H., 233.

Efird, C. M., 273.
Eargle, Mrs. Kate, 279.
Epting, Jacob, 266.

Ficken, John F., 270.
Freed, C. A., 233.

Greever, W. H., 234.
Gongaware, G. J., 233.
Goodman, R. A., 233.
Groseclose, D. B., 234.

Habenicht, Mrs. M. S., 279.
Haltiwanger, A. D., 269.
Hahn, S. W., 234.
Haigler, J. B., 234.
Hallman, S. T., 234.
Harman, J. B., 236.
Hawkins, Jacob, 250.
Hazelius, E. L., 248.

Holland, G. W., 252.
Houseal, W. P., 274.
Houseal, W. W., 259.
Horine, J. W., 236.
Horn, Edward T., 253.

Jenny, J. W., 271.

Kohn, A. H., 272.
Kinard, J. D., 237.
Kistler, H. A., 237.
Koon, S. P., 237.
Kreps, M. O. J., 238.
Kreps, Mrs. M. O. J., 278.

Long, I. E., 238.
Long, J. J., 239.

Mangum, J. W., 239.
Mayer, O. B., Sr., 262.
McCullough, H. A., 239.
Miller, D. L., 239.
Monroe, P. E., 239.
Morgan, F. G., 240.
Muller, Henry, 257.

Nelson, G. W., 240.

Obenschain, A. B., 240.
Oxner, J. W., 240.

Parker, T. C., 241.
Petrea, H. S., 241.
Petersen, O. C., 241.

Rast, George D., 269.
Rawl, Mrs. M. C., 278.
Riser, M. C., 241.
Roof, F. K., 242.
Roof, W. J., 242.
Rude, A. R., 249.

Schirmer, Jacob F., 260.
Seegers, Mrs. F. W., 280.
Seegers, John C., Sr., 261.
Schaeffer, H. B., 242.
Scherer, M. G. G., 242.
Schroder, H. A., 243.
Seckinger, E. H., 243.
Senter, J. M., 243.
Shealy, J. D., 243.
Shearouse, O. B., 243.
Smeltzer, J. P., 244.
Smith, J. L., 244.
Sox, C. J., 245.
Summer, Henry, 257.

Wessinger, J. C., 245.
Wilson, J. H., 256.
Wingard, E. A., 245.
Wingard, M. R., 279.
Wise, Mrs J. L., 279.
Wise, P. E., 261.
Wise, W. D., 248.
Worth, J. Howard, 248.

Congregational

Bachman Chapel, 205.
Bethany, Edmund, 196.
Beth Eden, 171.
Bethel (High Hill), 134.
Bethlehem, Lexington, 169.
Bethlehem, Pomaria, 155.

Cedar Grove, 179.
Church of the Ascension, 224.

INDEX

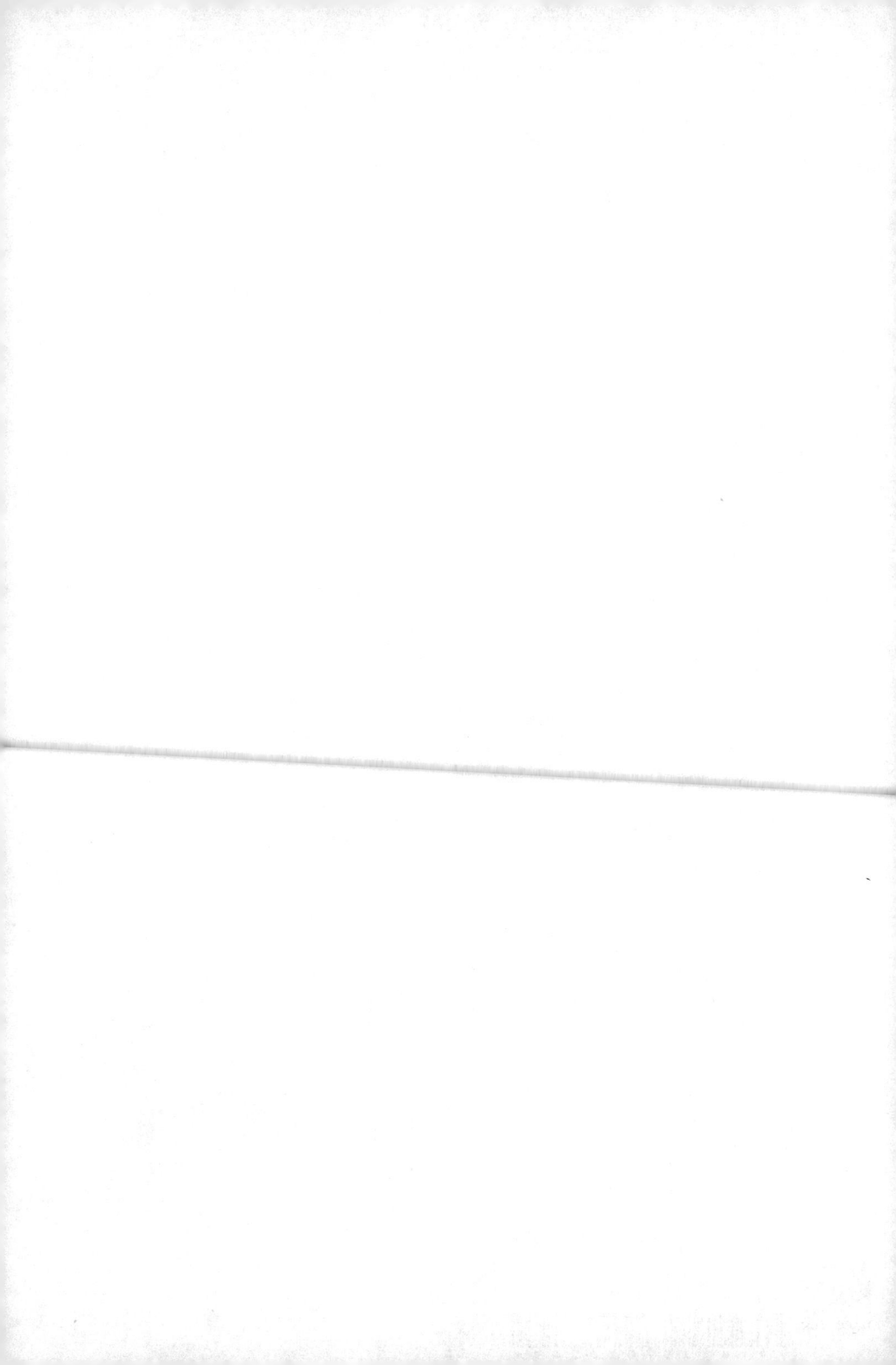

www.ingramcontent.com/pod-product-compliance
Lightning Source LLC
Chambersburg PA
CBHW031358270326
41929CB00010BA/1227